BE SAFE

EVERYTHING <u>YOU</u> NEED TO KNOW TO BE SAFE AND SECURE

ED MORAWSKI

BE SAFE

COPYRIGHT 2008

ED MORAWSKI

INTRODUCTION

Whether you are a business owner or a home owner, a student or a manager, a man or a woman- you need to know how to be safe in the 21st century. Some people think this is the scariest of times- what with terrorists, identify theft, children in danger, and the perception of rising crime. While I would argue that there is just more media emphasis on the threats which face us all, it does pay to be prepared and that's what this guide is about.

Safety and security go hand in hand; it is difficult to have one without the other. Security is the foundation of safety. Security comes in many, many forms but for the purposes of this guide we will break it down into three forms: ELECTRONIC SECURITY, PHYSICAL SECURITY, and perhaps most important- KNOWLEDGE (SECURITY).

Electronic Security is the form many people are commonly familiar with: burglar alarms, fire alarms, surveillance cameras, card access systems, etc. - anything that uses electronics or technology to provide security.

Physical Security is also a form most people see every day: guards, barriers, window bars, etc. Physical security and Electronic security go hand in hand.

Knowledge Security is more virtual. I like to think of it as two distinct aspects: Information security of being informed about security. In this regard we will cover some topics not normally found in a practical guide but which we believe are vital to making choices: Security and Civil Liberty, Loss Preventive –a practical approach, Risk Assessments, and finally a complete glossary of terms.

So in this guide we will cover every aspect of these three main types of security. We will explain them, we will instruct how to best utilize them, and we will demonstrate their strengths and weaknesses so you can make intelligent decisions. We will even dispel many common myths about various forms of security.

But most of all, the purpose of this guide is to inform. Even if you never specify, purchase or arrange for any electronic or physical security, your personal security knowledge is critically important for the wellbeing of yourself and your loved ones.

This guide is free flowing and you may skip around to the sections that interest or pertain to your situation. The first part handles practical application, the second examines the hardware in detail, and the third investigates the strengths & weaknesses of various security systems.

CONTENTS

Security versus Civil Liberties

If you're reading this book then you probably already have an opinion regarding the intrusion of security into everyday life. Some of the concern is legitimate, some is overblown. While it is wise to be concerned and cautious, it is better to use security to your benefit.

As security is increased throughout the United States and the world, does it automatically follow that a loss of personal civil liberties is inevitable? Consider that perhaps the safest man is the one in an isolation cell in a maximum security prison. He is completely alone and immune from bomb threats, terrorists, robbery, and kidnapping. While this is an extreme example, it is certainly evident that personal freedoms have been curtailed in recent years.

But we would counter that security has no more effect on the loss of civil liberties than many politically correct causes. Smokers have lost virtually all right to indulge in their habit. Women cannot wear a fur coat. It is difficult or impossible to build in some areas due to environmentalists. Animals can no longer be used in potentially life saving experiments. Driving large vehicles is discouraged in many areas. Political correctness itself has resulted in the loss of free speech about many subjects. Databases are constantly stuffed with all sorts of personal information about every one of us.

For good or bad, security is here to stay. Is it really any worse to be viewed on surveillance cameras as to be prevented from smoking on a public beach? No, it is simply a matter of perception and life style choices. It is also interesting to note that the same people who would prevent you from smoking on the beach are often the exact same people who rail against the use of surveillance cameras. While one segment is driving us full speed toward a 'nanny' society, this same group cries we are losing our civil liberties through government oversight (read police surveillance). Yes, we truly live in a 'reverse universe'.

A recent development further highlights the polar opposites in the area of civil liberties. RFID tags (Radio Frequency Identification) are devices which can transmit a unique ID number from up to a hundred feet. These devices show promise in such diverse areas as fully automatic checkout at grocery stores, and completely unobtrusive access control; you would simply walk up to a door and the RFID would send your ID to the access control system without you having to do anything. But there are groups vigorously fighting the whole RFID concept due to privacy concerns.

New developments in facial recognition, object video analysis, and more and more powerful computer processors –combined with the omnipresent video surveillance will certainly mean systems that can track a person anywhere. Companies have already demonstrated systems that can capture a face image of an unknown person and search through network connected digital video recorders anywhere in the world for that same person. Imagine someone passes a bad check, they are recorded doing so, their image is loaded into the system, and then an alarm is generated when that person walks into another store.

Between cell phone GPS and widespread video surveillance and facial recognition, someone will know your whereabouts at all times! For all practical purposes, civil liberties have already been lost. If you're a frequent flyer and want to bypass security checkpoints, the government already has all your personal information- and your retinal pattern!

Where will it end? It would appear 1984 is finally upon us and whether it's in the name of security from terrorists- or just good old fashioned marketing, we are living in a virtual electronic police state; an exaggeration perhaps, but only to prove a point.

Security is here to stay and until or if the pendulum swings back, we all need to get used to it- and take advantage of it.

The Loss Prevention Approach

Depending on your unique needs, situation, and location you may need one or all of the available electronic solutions to your security issues. This is why we take the Loss Prevention Approach to providing security solutions. All the suggestions in this guide are based on the philosophy of preventing all types of loss through the best case means.

Too often alarm companies and security contractors take the "get in and get out" attitude when selling security. The customer calls up an alarm company because they "need" a burglar or fire alarm and the alarm company gives them exactly that without asking what or why. They want to make a quick sale and get on to the next one.

These days, forward thinking security vendors will take the *Loss Prevention Approach* to providing a complete *security solution*. A complete security solution will address present and future threats to your business and help achieve *loss prevention* in all areas of your operations.

A burglar alarm by itself will rarely deter, protect or solve anything. The author has witnessed many a burglary where the thief actually broke in through a window that had an alarm company's sign right on it! Talk about deterrent- it was worthless! Many thieves are very aware of slow police response to burglar alarms in most big cities. They know that tripping the alarm means nothing if the police take twenty minutes to arrive or don't even bother to respond at all.

A complete security solution and loss prevention plan would dictate window bars to slow the burglars long enough for police to arrive. It would ensure there are no false alarms to lull police into non-response. But the loss prevention approach also means helping the business owner or managers get a handle on all losses.

We know that more losses are caused by employees than by burglars. Did you know that 87% of losses come from employees while only 5% of shrinkage is from shoplifting? Further, 46% of employee theft occurs right at your checkout! Internal inventory shrinkage, shoplifting, slip & fall lawsuits, employee inefficiency, employee violence, embezzlement, improper accounting, fraudulent returns, waste, and low productivity are responsible for more business loss than burglaries. If you want to be more profitable than you need to look inward as well as outward.

Does that mean you can go without alarms, of course not? But consider the effect of just one item of your retail inventory. For example, let's say an employee helps himself to a hot new DVD player. You, the owner must now replace that item, so already you have to pay double- the original and the replacement. While the replacement DVD player is on order a customer comes in and wants one, since you don't have it you've lost a sale and perhaps a loyal customer. Maybe your salesman that would have sold that player becomes disheartened at losing the sale and works less hard on the next sale or even decides to make up the shortfall in another way.

So the cost of just one missing item can be magnified many times. Although this example applies to retail, commercial and industrial face similar problems. We were once asked to apply these principles to a dairy. This location was actually a bottling plant which accepted the raw milk from dairy farmers and then processed, bottled and distributed it to local supermarkets.

Upon a careful look at their operations we discovered some interesting and startling facts. The dairy farmers delivered their milk 24 hours a day- completely unsupervised! No one had considered the possibility that virtually anyone could drive up and have total access to bulk milk tanks. Not only did this open the owners of the plant to threats from terrorists, which could easily poison the milk but also from extortion. A person knowledgeable of these facts could easily call up the owners and say "pay me $10 million dollars and I'll tell you how I tampered with your milk"- whether they actually did it or not. Not only could this result in an expensive recall but an even larger loss of consumer confidence.

The solution to this operation was card access to insure only authorized trucks were able to enter the grounds and deliver milk and an extensive video surveillance system throughout the production facility. The cameras doubled as operations tools since now all facets of the milk processing could be observed from a central location in the control room. As it turned out, the camera system actually contributed more to production efficiency than security but the operators were secure in the knowledge no one could tamper with any part of the process without being observed.

The Loss Prevention Approach to Security Solutions will be a key factor in choosing the right security contractor for your business, facility, or even your residence. A good security expert will be familiar with your specific business- or will take the time to learn. A security solution will require an investment of time both on the part of the security contractor and yourself to understand all the threats and how they relate to your specific operation.

It may take more than one walk through and spending time with key employees to form a complete program. In fact, your employees already probably know all the weaknesses of your security. On such a fact finding tour of a large retailer, we were speaking with one of the dock workers who pointed out the trash compactor. This loyal employee was fed up with her associates who regularly threw out perfectly good merchandise as being "damaged". They then later went back to the compactor after hours and retrieved them to take home.

This store put all their effort into preventing external threats when a large sum of money was simply pouring out the back door. An alarm contact was soon installed on the trash compactor door along with a camera observing it as well as several on the loading dock. Not only did shrinkage drop dramatically but employee productivity increased as well since they now knew they were being constantly observed.

Think it can't happen at your business? We frequently visit "family" owned operations where all the "employees" are trusted family members. In every case we are told, "I don't have a problem with employees, they are all family." In every case we found internal theft- many times of significant amounts due to drug problems and even gang affiliation. In one case, an owner's son regularly allowed his drug dealer gang to loot the business after hours.

Even if your employees are totally honest and loyal you may still suffer the consequences of poor thinking, inefficiency and laziness on their part. Our favorite example was a large retail food market. All the employees were well paid and provided a generous discount so internal theft seemed to be minimum. The store did handle large amounts of cash and this was kept in a locked safe- or so the owner believed.

When we walked through we tried an age old trick which my father taught me. We simply went to the safe and turned the combination dial until we heard it click and opened it! The employees didn't like having to enter the complete combination every time they had to put cash inside so they always left it on the second to last number. Trouble was anyone wandering through the store and aware of this could have simply opened the safe unobserved and taken the day's receipts. The solution? A drop chute into the safe so it didn't have to be opened every time cash needed to be deposited and cameras to keep an eye on things.

So the Loss Prevention Approach is designed to both provide <u>solutions</u> and keep your losses to a <u>minimum</u>! The Loss Prevention Approach not only must take into account past and present threats but also anticipate future ones.

THREATS

Individuals and businesses face many kinds of threats. If traditional threats weren't enough, in the first part of the 21st century, we now have to add terrorists. In designing an effective security system, we need to understand each threat, its effect on the business, and what measures to take to counter those threats.

External Threats

Business Open

Holdups

Takeover Robberies

Forgery, fraud

Office Theft

Warehouse theft

Executive threats and personal safety

Workplace violence

Vandalism to company property

Vandalism of company vehicles

Vandalism of employee vehicles

Terrorist

Fire

Earthquakes and natural disasters

Business Closed

Burglary

Fire

Earthquakes and natural disasters

Vandalism to company property

Vandalism of company vehicles

Terrorist

Internal Threats

Employee theft of goods and inventory

Forgery, fraud, embezzlement

Employee theft of company assets and tools

Employee theft of proprietary information or customer data

Time card fraud

Increased premiums for worker's compensation insurance

Decreased productivity

Critical functions or processes not operating correctly

We would advise that you copy this list of threats and keep it handy. Use it as a checklist to assess your security and business operations to see if you are vulnerable in any area. While some may not seem to be candidates for an electronic security solution, almost every one can be impacted in one way or another by the right system design.

Fraud, forgery, and embezzlement for example, can be addressed in several ways. With a secure facility or financial area, there is less chance an employee will gain access to checkbooks or cash without your knowledge- or if they do you will certainly be made aware of the fact. Cameras in strategic places can help deter fraud and forgery. Thieves do not like to be recorded or photographed, it inhibits their actions!

Some of these threats are obvious- such as hold ups and burglary or fire. Many are less likely to be taken into account when designing a security system. The Loss Prevention Approach delves deeper and looks at those less obvious threats.

Each of these threats represents not only real cost to the business but also hidden or undocumented expense, which in some cases can be even more significant than the obvious cost. Vandalism to a company vehicle may seem a minor cost and inconvenience; but if the temporary loss of the use of that vehicle means an important delivery can not be made, it could mean the loss of a valuable customer and significant future revenue.

Theft of tools or test equipment, while expensive to replace, also can mean loss of production, and loss or delay of orders. These days, customers will quickly go elsewhere to obtain the service they want. The loss of a $3000 tool could ultimately cost you $30,000 or more in lost future orders.

Even vandalism or theft to employee's property can have real effect on company profitability. The employee becomes distracted, perhaps disheartened, and frustrated by financial loss. They may sue the company or at the very least be less productive, perhaps making critical mistakes. Or they could decide to recoup their loss by stealing from the company. It is very easy for an honest employee to rationalize getting even if they perceive the company was at fault for their loss. Employee moral is a critical aspect of a good Loss Prevention program.

Threats to the safety of executives can have even more devastating effects. Having your chief financial officer or IT manager distracted when they should be making critical business decisions can impact your profitability for many years.

So when budgeting for security, it is vital to consider all factors in your decision. Consider all potential losses to the business or facility and take all these into consideration.

Let's discuss each threat and possible system solutions so you get an idea of how the Loss Prevention Approach works and what each type of security system can provide.

External Threats (Non-employees)

Business Open

<u>Security Threats</u>

Holdups

Takeover Robberies

Forgery, fraud

Office Theft

Warehouse theft

Executive threats and personal safety

Workplace violence

Vandalism to company property

Vandalism of company vehicles

Vandalism of employee vehicles

Terrorist

<u>Non-Security Threats</u>

Fire

Earthquakes and natural disasters

All the security threats while the business is open can be addressed to a large degree by securing the facility or place of business. While this would seem obvious, it is a fact many businesses do not take such threats seriously and fail to follow even elementary precautions or procedures. Simply locking doors and gates and installing some type of access control can limit the thief's ability to gain entry. Cameras will serve to deter and document many of the above crimes. In fact, their mere presence is often enough to cause a thief to look elsewhere for "softer" targets.

If your particular business caters to the general public and therefore requires complete access by outsiders (such as retail establishments) then obviously the task will be much harder and more complex. If at all possible, consider separating the public and private business areas. For instance, even in very small facilities, the financial office or area, as well as the stockroom or warehouse, can be secured and controlled.

Cameras will also be of major benefit in retail. Cameras can be installed to deter shoplifting, check forgery, loading dock thefts, and theft or vandalism of customer, employee, and company vehicles.

While terrorists probably won't be much of a threat in the retail business, they could well be in commercial and industrial facilities. Again, securing the facility itself will also serve to "harden" it as a target. Don't forget vulnerable areas such as air intakes for HVAC systems which are accessible from outside. These can be covered by cameras with motion detection software.

Non-security threats such as earthquakes and natural disasters benefit greatly from simple pre-planning and emergency procedures. Once you have an adequate fire monitoring system in place; you should have written emergency procedures.

Emergency procedures should cover evacuation paths and plans, muster areas (where to gather after the evacuation), emergency phone numbers for local authorities and especially contact numbers for all your employees and personnel.

Internal Threats

> Employee theft of goods and inventory
>
> Forgery, fraud, embezzlement
>
> Employee theft of company assets and tools
>
> Employee theft of proprietary information or customer data
>
> Time card fraud
>
> Increased premiums for worker's compensation insurance
>
> Decreased productivity
>
> Critical functions or processes not operating correctly

Internal threats are those perpetrated by employees (or partners). Luckily, most of the same systems and solutions for external threats apply to internal but in most cases they need to be redirected. For example, some cameras may need to be aimed looking inward instead of outward.

Time card fraud is a special case- and a potentially large loss item depending on the number of employees. Even in small shops however, time card fraud over a period of time can result in startlingly large sums of lost money. One of the best solutions for this problem is "biometric" (see the biometric section or glossary for more information) type readers which insure only that specific employee can clock in or out. If you don't want to go to that expense, just one camera viewing the time clock can be an effective deterrent- if you review the recording and take action. Once the employees know you're watching, they will refuse to clock each other in and out.

Workman's compensation claims arise from workplace accidents and on the job injuries – some of which are false. Cameras can be very effective in reducing such claims- either false or actual- by deterring horse play and unsafe practices such as forklift racing (yes it happens!), overloading, poor loading, failure to use safety procedures and safety harnesses, and other bad habits. But again, the manager or owner has to review the recordings and take immediate action when such behavior is observed.

A bonus of camera and access control systems is that they will also go a long way towards improving productivity and even observing critical processes and functions. All threats can be negated or at least reduced by well designed and thought out electronic security and fire systems.

ELECTRONIC SECURITY

"Electronic" security can be defined as systems designed to detect, deter, and/or control unauthorized persons from interfering with your business or residence. Although much of this guide is directed towards business users, we will also cover residential applications.

Most purchasers of security systems are not experts in security. Often, the facilities manager, IT manager, or even a human resources manager is given the task of physical security. If you find yourself in this position, this guide was written especially for you!

Whether you're a building manager for a 20 story high rise or a two unit apartment, a small business owner or run a chain of retail stores you will find valuable information in this guide. We have included sections pertaining to large plants as well as single family homeowners.

It is not the intention of this guide to make you an expert but to assist you in navigating the sometimes bizarre paths to an effective security solution at a reasonable cost. Like any other arena, the security industry has its share of buzz words, insider jargon, and charlatans.

The adage "you get what you pay for" is just as true when dealing with your security as anything else in life. The big difference is however, your life could easily hinge on the effectiveness of your security system. While you don't have to spend exorbitant amounts of money to get good security, you do have to spend something! One of the key purposes of this guide is to help you make sure you are not spending too much – or too little.

The electronic security industry changes rapidly from year to year. New products and technologies are introduced continually so this guide is intended to keep you up to date. If you take the time to register, you will be included on our email list and receive updates as they become available.

Electronic security systems are somewhat unique in that unlike almost anything else you buy for your property they require labor intensive installation and fairly complex equipment. The actual installation will likely be disruptive and can take from a few days to many months! This guide will help you ensure that disruption will be held to the absolute minimum.

Although this guide will cover all aspects of electronic security, from fire alarms and burglar alarms to sophisticated closed circuit video surveillance (CCTV) and card access systems; it is important to understand electronics can not solve all problems. In many cases physical barriers and human security, in the form of guards, will be required.

It is interesting to note that public police departments are discovering what private security experts have known for many years- that electronic security acts as a "force multiplier". For example, one man watching several cameras has the effect of many since he can observe multiple locations. This is evidenced by the increasing installation of CCTV cameras on public streets.

Let's begin by outlining different strategies for various types of businesses.

RETAIL

Perhaps of all the types of facilities and business' covered in this guide, retail presents some of the highest risks and the toughest problems to solve. If the product you're selling is highly desirable- for example, small consumer electronics; then the problems are multiplied many times.

For the sake of clarity, let's divide our retail business into segments by the types of merchandise we carry- small electronics must be treated quite differently then large consumer items like refrigerators. Let's begin with the easiest and work our way up to the really difficult high risk situations.

TIP: One aspect of any type of retail business which must be of concern to all managers and owners is *record keeping*. Always keep a copy of your business and financial records at home or another safe location other than your business!

Before we go into the specific retail classes let's look at intrusion and fire alarms:

Burglar Alarms

The intrusion market is very competitive so there is no need to spend a lot of money to get a good system. Beware of being talked into buying too much protection however. Typically, the alarm company will lease the system to you and roll the **equipment cost** into the **monitoring** fee. They will usually require you pay the installation fee up front and then the monitoring fee annually. Full service during business hours should be included in this cost. The fee should cover all maintenance including labor and equipment replacement.

The only exception to this would be emergency after hours service calls and damage to equipment caused by negligence or unforeseen circumstances like lightning or water leaks. Always get it in writing however, and make sure you're clear on what is covered and what isn't.

Alarm contracts generally are for FIVE years so make sure you understand what you're signing. The long contract length is required so that the alarm company can recover their equipment investment. You can try to negotiate a shorter length but expect the price to go up considerably. An alternative is to pay the entire cost of installation labor and equipment cost up front and then simply contract for the monitoring only which should be considerably less- often as little as $10 per month.

So what should you get in a simple intrusion system? A typical system consists of a **control panel**, a **keypad** for **arming** and disarming and detection devices. The system communicates to the central monitoring station by phone lines. Most of the time you can use a phone line you already have but many alarm companies prefer you install a **dedicated phone line** just for the alarm. This is not bad advice. Although it increases your total monthly cost, a dedicated line reduces the chance the alarm control won't be able to get through to the central station. Obviously, if the intrusion system can't dial out and deliver the alarm message, the central station won't be aware you have an alarm condition.

Newer systems (and more advanced monitoring companies) now offer "internet" monitoring. Instead of the traditional phone line they use broadband internet access such as DSL or cable. Some systems continuously monitor the condition of the line and can warn if the connection is lost. These are highly recommended because of their speed and security. The cost is usually very much in line with dedicated voice phone lines. Plus if you already have internet access, the alarm transmission is essentially free.

The alarm company will probably throw some technical jargon at you so let's cover a few of those right here:

SPD- single pedestrian door

DPD- double pedestrian door

PIR – passive infrared (motion detector)

PEC – photoelectric cell (another form of motion detector)

HUB – hold up button

Fire Alarms

Fire sprinkler systems are designed to put out a fire by dousing it with water. These systems are controlled at a central location on the property and alarms are transmitted to a **central station,** which in turn notifies the fire department. You as the business owner will probably never be notified of a sprinkler activation since the property management company or landlord/ owner is generally the only one on the **call list**.

While fire sprinkler systems are extremely effective at extinguishing fire, they also come with a huge set of problems for the individual small business owner. The biggest of which is the very water that extinguishes the fire! Often the water damage that ensues is more than the fire itself. At this point, the owner of the business and the owner of the building are somewhat at cross purposes. The building owner is determined to protect the structure, while the small business owner as tenant is mainly concerned with their valuable inventory.

Once a sprinkler head begins discharging water there is nothing to stop it until the water is shut off at the riser! This is usually done by the fire department when they arrive at the scene. Please understand however, the fire department is in no hurry to do this, they are concerned with putting out the fire. The more water that dumps on the fire, the better; as far as the fire department is concerned. The fire department generally won't turn off the water until they are absolutely certain the fire is extinguished. In the meantime it may continue to saturate your inventory.

The best way to protect your investment is to maintain a healthy insurance policy on your inventory. If you are not located in a multi-tenant environment with a sprinkler system or you're renting in a free standing building then you may want to look into installing your own fire alarm system.

Notice we stated Fire Alarm – not fire suppression. Let's take a minute to discuss these terms: a **fire suppression** (or extinguishing) system is one that actually puts out the fire. Examples are sprinklers and halon (hood) systems. While halon and other fire suppression gases are great at not damaging inventory (unlike water), they are quite costly to install and maintain.

A fire alarm system detects or notifies of a fire situation. In fact, most jurisdictions differentiate between fire alarms and fire monitoring. **Fire Alarms** usually mean a notification such as pull boxes, horns and strobes to notify occupants that a fire is breaking out. **Fire Monitoring** systems notify a central station that a fire may be breaking out by using detection devices such as smoke detectors.

Smoke detectors can be very effective at providing an early warning that a fire is imminent. Just a few smoke detectors would be required in a small property and we highly recommend adding these to an intrusion system. One issue may be the local jurisdiction (fire department). Often, local codes require specific design criteria for any type of fire device and many localities prohibit combining intrusion (burglar alarms) and fire detection on the same system.

After that brief interruption, let's get back to classifying retail businesses.

Class C

This type can be defined as large consumer products which cannot easily be transported or shoplifted. Into this category we can also place retail stores selling less "street desirable" items such as furniture, paper goods, fabrics and business supplies or other low cost, bulky items.

Our number one concern should be fire protection. If you are located in a strip center or other multi-tenant location, chances are there is a fire sprinkler system. Check with your landlord and determine what type if any is installed. You should also investigate their liability in case of fire and water damage and take the necessary precautions in adding or maintaining sufficient insurance.

If you are interested in exploring fire monitoring then please read that section.

Other security recommendations for Class C type businesses would be physical barriers such as bars over the windows, roll down barriers for large storefronts, and burglar resistant covers for locks on rear doors.

A simple intrusion alarm system would be prudent, if for no other reason than to make sure your store doesn't get emptied out some night by bold thieves with a large truck or even ex-employees. If you have sufficient physical barriers then simply having the alarm company install **contacts** on the doors (including any roll-up ones) should be adequate. Contacts are magnetic switches which trip the alarm if the door is opened.

This is one case where the alarm company salesman will likely try to talk you into more "protection" such as motion detectors. The only reason to install such detectors is if you run the risk of burglars breaking through walls or the roof. This would be very rare for large merchandise since they would have to remove it through the doors anyway. Resist the temptation or sales pitch to add extra cost you don't need. Your money would be better spent on a fire alarm or smoke detectors.

Class B

These would be retail businesses which have medium risk. Examples would be food stores (not liquor) or other merchandise which is somewhat attractive to thieves- and employees, and can be fairly easy to transport and/or shoplift.

In these types a simple **intrusion** system is essential, along with limited electronic video surveillance- hereafter referred to as **CCTV** (closed circuit television). The video system would help you to deter and detect shoplifting by covering blind areas of your store.

We can't emphasize the deterrent effect of video enough. If thieves know they are being watched they are inclined to go elsewhere. But they have to be aware they are being watched. Some owners tend to want to hide the video cameras in the belief the thieves will be more likely to be caught.

This is only true if the manager or clerk is very proactive in watching the video system. If you expect to make an identification from a video recording- think again. Consider that the person viewing the recording has to know the person! Recordings are generally only useful to compare suspects who have already been apprehended from past robberies or thefts.

A better solution is to install cameras in smoked domes. The domes themselves are visible but the actual position of where the camera is viewing is concealed. We highly recommend placing a video camera and monitor in plain view at the main entrance to your store. When people enter they can view themselves on TV and become highly aware the store has a surveillance system.

A simple CCTV system consisting of just 2 cameras- one at the door and one in a rear aisle can be very effective at deterring shoplifters. The only thing you need to complete it would be two video monitors (TV screens) one at the door again and one at the register or another manned location.

A recorder of some kind would be highly recommended so you can play back the video if need be. This could be vital if you plan on prosecuting shoplifters. The recorder will probably be the most expensive part of the video system so choose wisely. These days most security companies will offer a **DVR** (digital video recorder) which are vastly superior to the old VHS tape machines. A DVR will record the video onto a hard drive for instant retrieval. You can simply go directly to the time you're interested in rather than rewinding and fast forwarding.

DVRs were more expensive than VHS recorders but the prices have come down dramatically and now are comparable or even cheaper. Most of the security equipment manufacturers no longer even produce VHS recorders!

By the way, can you purchase a CCTV system yourself at Costco or Home Depot? Sure, but the quality tends to be low and the installation isn't easy. You have to run special coaxial cable to each camera and terminate it correctly. Professional installers have specialized tools and knowledge. Our recommendation is to leave it to the professionals.

Auto Dealers require special attention since they entail a variety of needs: Showrooms, lot, service area, parts storage and vehicle storage. While auto dealers will benefit most from video surveillance, we rarely see such system actually installed. The general management of auto dealers is highly focused on sales and as such needs a clear understanding of the benefits of video. Movable dome type cameras, called **PTZ** (Pan/Tilt/Zoom) employed on all corners of the lot with controls and video monitors for the sales, service and general managers would allow them to keep an eye on each area of responsibility.

Sales managers could use the system to observe potential customers and dispatch sales people to assist them instead of having the sales team hover around like vultures waiting to pounce. Service managers can keep an eye on the yard, vehicles in the storage lot, and mechanics at work. General managers would have an overall view of all aspects of the business. Finally, the cameras will act as a deterrent to vandalism and theft after hours. If the dealership has several locations it will become cost effective to place a security guard at one of them and link all the locations so that this one person can view the video at all the locations. This would allow the security guard to notify the police immediately if suspicious activity or vandalism was observed at any of the dealerships.

As for the intrusion system, Class B businesses will require a bit more than Class C. This will be especially true if you stock any liquor and / or cigarettes. If you fit into this category then a **motion detector** or two will be required. The motion detector is necessary to detect burglars trying to break in through windows, walls, or the roof (which is very common). These act as a back up to the door contacts- in case the burglars never open a door.

You should have one motion detector covering your storeroom at a minimum and/or one covering the main store or an aisle a potential burglar would have to traverse. Keep the motion detectors to a minimum however as they are very prone to false alarms. There is nothing worse than continually getting woken in the middle of the night after a long hard day, for constant false alarms.

If the area your store is located in dictates, then adding a hold up button is mandatory. These are very inexpensive so have one or two installed behind the counters, under – and in – the cash register. You can even get a "**money clip**" which fits in the $20 bill slot. You place one $20 bill in the clip and then the rest on top. If all the twenties are removed during a robbery then a hold alarm is automatically generated.

Be sure to also have hold up buttons installed in the storeroom, walk in freezers, and restroom. You never know where you or your clerks may be if your store gets held up. If you do opt for the hold up buttons then by all means get an extra camera for the register area. This camera should be in plain view and cover any person in front of the register.

At this point, the DVR should be moved to a secure location. The video evidence contained on it will be critical in the event of a holdup. Often robbers will attempt to remove or destroy video recorders. If this is a concern in your neighborhood then you can circumvent this:

Have the real DVR placed inside a locked cabinet in the rear or even inside your safe if possible. Place an old VHS recorder (with a tape in it) in plain view. If the robber is intent on destroying evidence he'll take the VHS tape but you'll still have the digital recording.

Class A

Liquor stores, gun stores, jewelry stores, small consumer electronics, check cashing, etc.

These stores will require the highest possible levels of security, fire detection and video surveillance. You should review and follow the guidelines for both Class C and Class B but you will also then require a more elaborate system.

In your case, physical barriers should be more substantial and act as the first line of defense. The goal will be to slow down burglars while upping the detection capability to actually detect them before they break in.

Physical barriers:

Avoid windows altogether if possible. If this is not possible or too un-appealing then bars should be placed over them and anchored strongly. Have the alarm company "contact" each set of bars with magnetic pull cords or contacts. These will trip the alarm if the bars are removed.

Metal doors should be used throughout. If glass is a necessity and you have a storefront, consider a roll down metal cover. These are common in Asia and on the east coast because they are very effective. These also need to be contacted to trip the alarm if raised or removed forcibly.

If you can't or won't avoid having glass then by all means have the alarm company install **glass break detectors**. As the name implies, these detect glass breakage. Unfortunately, glass breaks also have major issues. Most are just sensitive microphones that actually listen for the sound of breaking glass. The problem is they can also pick up all types of other sounds and cause false alarms. If they are adjusted sensitive enough to detect breaking glass, they can also alarm on other noises. If their sensitivity is turned down too much, they won't alarm when the glass is actually broken.

The most effective ones- and the least prone to false alarms are the type that actually mount to the glass or the frame and detect vibration. If you don't mind the aesthetic issue then these are the only way to go.

Take special care with your roof. If it's accessible from another building or with a ladder then any skylights should also be covered with bars and those alarmed as well. If your store presents an especially desirable target then you should also take steps to detect intrusion through the roof. This is commonly done through motion detectors (PIR). These can be mounted high up- just inside under the roof to detect someone dropping through. Most alarm companies will insist on mounting the PIRs down on the walls for service reasons but be advised this will allow burglars more time.

It is possible to install vibration detectors on roof beams to detect someone actually trying to saw or cut through the roof. While this is highly recommended it is rarely done except in areas of very high crime or repeated burglaries.

Beams (PEC) can also be mounted on the roof around the perimeter to immediately detect when someone even gets on the roof. These are very prone to false alarms from birds, blowing paper and even dense fog.

If you own a jewelry store or other very high value business you'll want to be familiar with Underwriter's Laboratories (**UL**). Yes the same organization that labels electric cords also maintains standards for burglar alarm system for the insurance industry.

A UL listed system has extremely stiff requirements. The alarm company must be UL listed, the monitoring company must be UL listed (often one and the same), and the equipment used in the burglar alarm system must be UL listed. Then the system must be installed to UL standards and serviced and monitored to UL standards!

Whether your insurance company requires a UL listing or not, it's still a great indication of a particular alarm company's capabilities. It's very tough to get a UL listing and keep it so if the alarm company you're talking to has a UL listing you can be assured of top quality equipment, service and monitoring.

In any case, let's continue with the recommendations for your high risk retail business. Once the intrusion and fire alarms are in place, you are advised to take a long look at a video surveillance system. The Class A store will usually require more cameras than other types. Starting with the main entrance camera and monitor, also known as **Public View**, which is critically important to deter shoplifting and holdups; you'll also want every cash register and counter covered with cameras. You'll want to view the storeroom and loading dock if you have one.

If your business is very high risk, think about placing cameras *outside* to monitor the parking lot, loading dock, and blind areas which can provide early warning of potential threats such as hold ups.

Gun shops and jewelry stores often place a camera immediately outside the main entrance for the same reasons and many even use **mantraps**. This entails installing a second inner door at the main entrance which remains locked at all times. Customers will enter through the outer unlocked door and then are viewed on camera. Once you're satisfied with their purpose, you can buzz then into the shop. The outer door should be programmed to lock when the inner door is opened to prevent a gang from rushing into the store.

Whether you need to go to this extent is strictly a matter of your comfort level but at this point your video system will still be rather complex. How do you view that many cameras? The new DVRs (digital video recorders) also have a built in multiplexer. This allows multiple cameras views (4, 9, or even 16) to display on one video monitor. Software in the DVR allows you to "call up" or display any specific camera view full screen.

A recent development in DVRs even allows for **remote viewing**. If you have a broadband internet connection, you can hook up your DVR to it and this allows you to view your cameras from anywhere you have an internet connection: from home, from another office, or even at the airport or on vacation from your laptop.

Don't purchase a DVR without this capability. Even if you think you'll never use it now, believe me you will at sometime in the near future. Once you hire clerks or help in the store, you'll be able to keep an eye on things no matter where you are: at a conference, or convention, or even laid up with an illness.

One important point to always remember when deciding on your security: employees are the greatest source of loss to business, surpassing burglary and fire loss by far.

Safes & Vaults

If you happen to have a safe of vault, there is very specialized protection available. A typical safe protection package consists of balanced safe contacts (which sense if foreign magnets are introduced near them), shock sensor, vibration detectors, audio listening devices (which alarm on the sound of drills), and heat detectors (to sense attempt to burn through the safe or vault).

In previous times, there was also a proximity detector which could sense someone just touching the safe. While these were very effective (when they worked) they were also prone to mis-adjustment and false alarms.

We recommend vibration and heat detectors and balanced contacts backed by PIR motion detectors covering the safe or vault area. A minimum of two PIRs should be used so they can back each other up. This would provide a very superior, almost foolproof intrusion system.

Chain Retail (Multiple locations)

All the points and suggestions previously made for single location Class C, B & A stores apply to chain locations but multiple location businesses have their own unique set of requirements. Chances are if you own a chain, you have many more employees so you need to take special precautions.

Video surveillance will be critical. Each store should have it's own system including DVR. In the case of chains though, the DVR should absolutely be kept locked away and under the control of a trusted manager. Remote viewing capability is more important than ever. The owner should be able to view the cameras at any location at will from any other location.

Owners should also check recorded video at various times during the night to ensure nothing unusual is occurring. Luckily DVRs also contain **video motion detection** programs. Instruct your security provider to program the DVRs so they only record on motion. This will effectively increase the storage to several times the hard drive sizes while also making it much easier to locate events. When you access the DVR you will get a list of event times displayed. You can then go directly to the specific event time and play back the video from that period. Obviously if your store is closed at 1:00am yet the DVR has recorded motion at that time, something is wrong.

You can and should also direct the alarm company to provide you with weekly or monthly reports of when the intrusion system is armed and disarmed. Some companies offer these reports via their web sites as well. These reports serve as a great tool to check on your managers and employees.

If you see a pattern of the alarm system being armed late then you know someone is staying after hours for some reason. Conversely, if the alarm system is being disarmed late then you know your employees are arriving late for work, possibly causing you lost business.

If employee turnover is a problem with your business then we have a solution for the symptoms at least. **Card Access** systems replace keys and control physical access using card readers and electric locks.

Such systems provide some extremely attractive results to the chain owner:

1. Limit after hours access to the building. You program what time periods the cards can unlock the door. For example, specific cards can only unlock the door for a short time before business hours. This prevents employees from going back after hours or on the weekends.
2. No more expensive re-keying of locks. If the employee leaves or is terminated you only need to inactivate their card. You don't even need the card to do this- just the number.
3. Extensive reporting capability. The system will provide reports on each employee's activity. It can even tell you if an employee attempted to use the card on a door they are not permitted to unlock (storerooms) or they tried to use it after hours.

Card access systems are not only great for security but also provide valuable management tools. The possibilities and return on investment are limitless and a good security vender can demonstrate many uses for both video and card access systems.

A good way to think about the various security systems and how they interact is this:

Fire and burglar alarms tend to <u>detect</u> problems after the fact.

CCTV video surveillance systems tend to <u>document</u> problems, but can also deter threats.

Card access systems are good at <u>preventing</u> threats and problems while also documenting attempts.

Each of the systems has its place in a good overall security plan but when designed and installed together by a knowledgeable **security integrator**, combine into very powerful security solutions for the business owner.

Other Retail Loss Prevention Solutions

As we stated, retail presents many challenges and not all of them are what you might consider security related but electronic security can provide solutions.

EAS (Electronic Article Surveillance)

This is a system of electronic tags or labels affixed to products to deter and detect shoplifting. All products are then scanned by sensors at the store exits. If the person goes through a register or checkout and pays for the item, it is either manually or automatically deactivated and nothing happens when the person goes through the sensors upon leaving. If the item is not deactivated then the sensors detect this and sound a local alarm.

Frankly EAS has not been the savior everyone originally expected. Although effective in stopping amateur and impulse shoplifting, EAS has not effectively stopped professionals. Even worse, the nuisance of false alarms due to employees failing to deactivate tags has not only irritated customers but caused many employees to ignore EAS alarms when they do sound.

Professional shoplifters have discovered many ways around EAS including wrapping items in metal foil and using special bags constructed of metallic fibers to block the sensors from detecting tags. They have also simply obtained the removal tools used by stores and take the tags off clothing and walk out.

RFID tags are coming in the future and as miniaturization progresses further and further, tags may be come so tiny and intelligent that EAS will find a new lease on life. For now, we're not sure they're worth the money or hassle.

Liability

Retail establishments are often targets of legal actions for damages resulting from real or false incidents. Among some of the most common are damage to customer's vehicles from shopping carts, slip & fall- where the customer slips on some wet or messy surface and suffers a fall, and even assaults while on your premises.

Cameras, both inside and outside the store, are the answer to these situations. First, a video system with recording will help you identify whether a claim is true or false. Secondly, cameras will help you determine what actually happened. There have been cases where customers fell but from the video it was apparent it was completely their fault since no water or other debris was present.

Cameras may also deter false claims. When perpetrators discover video systems they will go elsewhere since they know a false claim will likely be disproved.

Cameras outside the store can be a two edged sword since they may indeed record activity that shows the store owner at fault. If you lease space and are not responsible for the parking lot, then let your judgment be your guide in this regard.

Employee Theft and "Sweet hearting"

We previously mentioned that more losses are caused by employees than by burglars and that 87% of losses come from employees and 46% of employee theft occurs right at your checkout.

Besides just outright stealing cash from the register, employees often steal with

accomplices- friends and relatives. Sweet hearting is the act of ringing up less than the actual price of an item when an accomplice is shopping. A friend comes in and brings say $25 worth of product to the register but only $5 is actually rung up. Often the employee will use "No Sale" or "Void" to do this but smarter ones will use a known UPC (Universal Product Code – a barcode) they keep somewhere on their person (or near the register) for this purpose.

This type of employee theft can be detected and documented using POS interface to security video systems. Such systems interface into your POS data stream and capture information on each transaction and then either overlay it or match it up with the video recording. A camera is important to document the transaction, establish the wrong product was rung up and identify the accomplice.

Not all employees are dishonest- some are hired that way! Professional thieves often take jobs at retailers desperate for good help, just to steal. Once on checkout duty, their accomplices will come in and the theft begins. One brazen method is to have the accomplice come to the register with a basket of goods. The employee / thief then dutifully rings up every item and bags it- except they ring them as *returns*! Anyone observing the transaction would think nothing is amiss- unless they saw the POS data along with the video.

These systems can be very simple or very specialized depending on the size of your business and your needs. A one cash register system is very inexpensive but will only document limited exceptions (voids, no sales, cigarettes, etc.) and will require more effort on your part to manage.

Larger systems can gather data from multiple registers and use computer software to analyze the data. These can be very powerful and allow exception reports to be generated on virtually any register transaction- for example, cigarettes less than $1.00. When combined with video you will have a complete picture of day to day operations. Most of these systems can also be used to manage multiple stores from one central location.

In all cases, a video camera directed at each register will provide many benefits including possible detection of employee stealing cash, employee efficiency and productivity (how many people are in line), and even customer interaction.

Exception Reporting

This is special software designed to analyze your POS data and produce reports on suspicious transactions. Good exception reporting applications can be used to discover all kinds of shrink. For example too many items less than $1, which may indicate the checkout person is using a special UPC to reduce sales prices for an accomplice.

Exception reporting can even be configured to send you real time alerts so you can take immediate action. Like many of the electronics systems we discussed, Exception Reporting systems are only of value if you do take action. We once consulted with a large chain where the Loss Prevention department didn't get around to checking exception reports for an average of two weeks! The crooked employees could steal thousands and thousands and disappear long before anyone got around to them.

Whatever systems you utilize, the employees will test it so be prepared to follow through. We observed a situation after the fact where an employee decided to test a newly installed camera system. Reasoning that someone would be watching for a while, he held off. After a few weeks or so, he began holding up a twenty dollar bill in front of the camera every night when he closed up.

After a week of not being questioned, he then put the $20 in his pocket in full view of the camera. When he still wasn't questioned, he just added a $20 to his wallet every night. This went on for three months until the employee quit. It wasn't discovered until a new loss prevention manager came on board and actually reviewed the video recordings.

Commercial Property

Commercial property, whether a small 2 story office or a high rise with hundreds of tenants, especially benefit from card access systems. We'll cover that in a minute after we talk a little about fire alarms. If your building is of any size, it probably has a **fire sprinkler** system and it likely has more than 100 **sprinkler heads**. In most jurisdictions that size will require a fire monitoring system. As the building increases in height, more requirements are added.

In some jurisdictions, more than three floors or 25 feet of elevator travel will also require an **elevator recall** system. This consists of smoke detectors in each elevator lobby which may or may not be part of the sprinkler and fire monitoring system although 90% of the time, these are combined into one system.

If your building is seven floors and above it is usually considered a high rise and a full fire evacuation system will be required. If your building falls into these categories you should already have these systems so we'll just cover some items of which you may not be aware. The most important of which being periodic testing.

Many localities require special sprinkler system tests every five years. These are completed by a sprinkler company, not the alarm company. The fire alarm monitoring company is required to test the monitoring portion of the sprinkler system at least twice a year. The elevator recall smoke detectors should also be tested at the same time. The evacuation system is required to be tested at least once a year.

All these tests will cause some disruption of your tenants- especially the evacuation system. Consequently there is enormous pressure to put it off or do a partial test. Don't fall into that trap. The liability of not performing life safety inspections and tests is mind boggling.

The experts will tell you that fire drills are essential in getting people out of buildings safely. Research has shown over and over that practicing makes people less afraid and gives them more confidence in an emergency. During the 9/11 attack on the twin towers in New York, those people who had previously participated in fire drills or had experience in evacuating buildings or been in actual fires, got out safely and led many others down as well.

Fear paralyzes people. The best way to overcome fear is to learn about what to do and the best way to learn is practice. The larger the building the less you'll want to conduct fire drills because there is so much disruption. To keep this disruption to a minimum, combine the annual fire tests and fire drills.

Schedule the evacuation system test and a fire drill together. When your tenants hear the fire alarm sounding they can be advised that a fire drill is underway. This way you'll also have as close to an actual simulation as possible; and meet all the requirements.

TIP: *Make sure you and your fire alarm contractor document these tests for future reference.*

Of course, this requires some preparation. Meet with your security or fire contractor and develop a plan for the test. Each tenant manager should be provided with clear written instructions listing the date and time of the test. That document should contain clear instructions of what to expect, where to go, how to go, (the elevator will not be usable since they will automatically go to the ground floor and remain there); and a map of where to gather once they are out of the building. For example, have the 1st through the 4th floors people meet in the front. Have the 5th through the 8th meet in the rear, and so on.

You should assign each floor tenant areas to meet so your security people or assistants can insure everyone got out. Each tenant manager should be responsible for checking off their employees and they should in turn provide their check off list to you. You will in turn have a list of all tenants to check off.

A very important note to add to your notice of the fire drill is a liability release. Such a release should accomplish two vital terms: 1. it should release the building manager and owner of any damages resulting from the fire drill and 2. it should release the building owner and manager of any liability resulting in the future from NOT participating in the fire drill. This way you are covered in any event.

A special cover to deter false alarms by Stopper
This is installed over the normal manual pull station and has a horn
Which sounds when the cover is raised.

Fire Drills

Here's your checklist for conducting fire drills:

#1. Meet with your alarm company to plan the fire drill and system test.

#2. Develop a plan using your site map of where each floor's people should meet.

#3. Draft a letter to the tenants including the map and the liability waivers.

#4. Check off each letter you receive from the tenants and follow up with no replies.

#5. Document each tenant who fails or refuses to participate and file these.

#6. The <u>day before</u> the drill:
    A. Walk all the stairwells to make sure they are clear.
    B. Notify the fire department of your intended drill. (They may offer to participate).

#7. Have the alarm company technicians arrive at least one hour early the day of the drill.

#8. During the drill:
    A. Have each tenant manager check off their employees as they arrive at the meeting spot.
    B. Have your security or your assistant collect the check off forms from each tenant.

#9. File the documents as a record you conducted the fire drill.

Bomb Threats

Conducting annual fire drills will also prepare for other emergencies such as bomb threats. Bomb threats can be one of the most frustrating issues property managers face. We have seen situations where bomb threats were phoned in daily at almost the exact same time every day to the same building. Bomb threats have almost completely replaced false fire alarms- where people used to pull fire alarm boxes.

Bomb threats are almost always the work of employees, ex-employees, or more rarely- dissatisfied customers. Employees in tedious, low to mid range paying jobs want a break. You will rarely get a bomb threat in bad weather- unless it's an ex-employee! So the circumstances surrounding the bomb threats are a very good indicator of where they are originating.

So what do you do about bomb threats? If this is the first one you ever received and you are not entirely confident of your security, then it is probably prudent to go ahead and evacuate the building. The police should be notified and they will probably in turn notify the fire department.

Plan on being outside several hours while a thorough search is conducted. The person phoning in the threat is counting on this and wants to go home so many bomb threats will occur in the afternoon. You will probably only want to evacuate your building once since it is so disruptive. Here are some guidelines for what to do if you experience multiple or repeated threats.

What to do about Bomb Threats and how to reduce their nuisance value.

Document- instruct your receptionist – and all tenant receptionists to write down any bomb threats! The log should include the exact time the call was received, male or female caller, any specific details such as: was a certain tenant mentioned? How did they refer to your building (name or address)?

Video Cameras and recorder- it is vital to place cameras at the entrances to your building. This accomplishes two important things:

> One, you'll always know or be able to review who actually came and went. This will be invaluable if a bomb is actually ever found. You will also have a high level of confidence that no one actually planted a bomb if you never see anyone suspicious.

> Two, you'll be able to identify specific persons leaving or re-entering before and after repeated bomb threats. Most pranksters will know better than to use an internal phone so they will likely go out to a pay phone if they're going to do this over and over. By cross checking the time of the bomb threat with who came and went right before and after you should be able to pinpoint suspects.

Restrooms – it's always a good idea to keep these locked at all times- as well as storerooms, janitor closets, phone rooms, electrical rooms, etc. If unmanned areas are not accessible it's much more difficult to actually plant a bomb.

Meetings – meet with your tenant managers and discuss how they feel about bomb threats. Explain the facts and invite participation. Chances are one of them will be invaluable at discovering the source of the bomb threats (since it's almost certainly one of their employees or someone they let go.)

Patterns – If the bomb threats occur in the afternoon, during good weather, it's almost certainly a present employee. They want a break or want to go home. If the threat occurs during bad weather and/or at odd times, it's very likely it's an ex-employee who wants to make it miserable for their ex-employer!

Resolution – unfortunately, the perpetrator will almost never be caught. Generally they grow tired or bored and stop on their own. If you have video and observe someone you think it doing it and someone asks them about it, that's usually enough to scare them into stopping. That's why video systems can be so valuable in cutting short repeated threats.

Unless you catch a suspect in the act of making the call it's very difficult to prosecute- although most police department take bomb threats very seriously these days. If the culprit is not too bright and makes some mistake they could get into a great deal of trouble with the police. The best thing for the building management is to take every step to assist them in making a mistake and hope for the best.

Commercial Security Systems

Multi-tenant commercial properties also represent unique situations in that unlike retail and industrial, a typical office building is made up of "permanent outsiders", almost like a small city. In fact the same principals can be applied to campuses, colleges, and shopping malls. The main characteristics of these facilities are the large numbers of visitors and tenants.

Tenants have slightly less "stake" in the property than the owner/ manager. Visitors generally have none. Human nature being what it is, we need to take these facts into consideration when designing our overall security solution.

Commercial office buildings of any size are much easier to control than large campus type environments so we'll look at those first. Although such buildings can vary from a single story to a hundred, the same principles apply and mostly vary only in quantity.

Assuming you have the fire alarm monitoring / life safety under control (see the previous chapter); we can delve into intrusion. Larger buildings typically don't even have intrusion alarms, mostly due to the problems with constant visitor and tenant traffic. There are easier ways to secure the building which we'll cover next in the card access section.

Many tenants do have intrusion alarms however, for their suites. As the property manager / owner you can chose to be involved or not. Many commercial property managers advise tenants to use a preferred security vendor for example. Intrusion alarms and tenant security can also be a source of *revenue* for the building!

Did that get your attention? Modern intrusion systems can easily handle many multiple "**areas**". An area is a group of individual "**zones**" . A zone is usually one detection device- i.e. a door, a window, or a motion detector. These groups can be individually and independently controlled. So, an enterprising building owner / manager can have a large security intrusion system installed in the building and then each tenant who desires can have their own little area consisting of just the detection they need and a **keypad** which is all managed by the main **intrusion control panel**.

This setup shares the cost of the intrusion control panel and phone line or internet connection (for monitoring) among many tenants so the individual cost is quite low. The building owner / manager can charge back the tenants either in the lease or as an added monthly charge. Since the overall cost divided by the number of tenants is so low, the property manager can easily make a profit on this while still providing their tenants with a *lower cost of security than they could get for themselves*.

This is the classic win-win situation. To give you an idea of the economics, modern alarm control panels can handle over 500 zones, so even if each tenant used 3 devices (which is rare) one panel could be used for over 150 tenant spaces. Assuming a panel cost of $1000 installed, that's about $6 one time cost! At each tenant a keypad and detection devices will have to be added, still a minimal cost.

One caveat, be sure to negotiate with the alarm company on the total monthly monitoring rather than a cost per tenant. You should be able to get the cost down to between $5-$10 per tenant, plus the monthly cost of a business grade DSL $100 (again divided by the total number of tenants) for communication with the monitoring central station.

Also, make sure you have any liability issues covered in your lease agreement. Many courts have upheld the traditional alarm company limit of liability of $250. Also, generally, if you offer security services and the tenant does not take advantage of them, they don't have much of a case. Most times, property managers get into trouble when they offer *no* security.

Video surveillance systems are an absolute must for commercial properties. Because office buildings are so wide open, it is critical to know who is coming and going- as we talked about in the bomb threats section.

As a minimum, cameras should be placed at each main entrance observing persons entering. Cameras should also be located at the loading dock and any parking entrances if these are *under or within the building*. If your budget allows, it is also advisable to add cameras at each exit observing persons *leaving*. There tends to be different views on placing cameras so they observe people entering or leaving. If you document persons coming in then you'll always know who was there. Viewing people leaving is usually done to cut down on internal theft.

Cameras placed *inside* elevator cabs can very useful at tracking people to see where they go and also if they are taking anything when they leave; as well as deterring vandalism, especially in freight elevators.

If your building has parking, it is very advisable to install **public view monitors** at each entrance. Briefly, these are cameras aimed at the driver, connected to a video monitor arranged so that same driver can see themselves on TV! This has a large deterrent effect both on potential car thieves, petty burglaries who break into cars, vandals, and even potential terrorists. The cameras also need to be connected to the main video system and recorded, of course.

We recommend only digital video recorders (**DVRs**) these days. All the cameras must be recorded. The DVR itself should go in the property management office or an air conditioned, secure location- preferably in the basement. The building engineer's office is often a good choice. The DVR should have good "survivability" in case of some worst case scenario.

If you currently have human security or guards and they are stationed at a lobby console, always provide a multi-screen display there for them- *but never the recorder itself!* Security personnel should never have access to the recorder because if the recording shows nothing, it will be assumed it was tampered with- but if the security staff is not able to access the recorder it can never be suggested they erased something.

It is highly recommended that a camera also be placed viewing the console. This will provide invaluable reference if someone complains about the security people and just as important, to help you keep an eye on their activity (or lack thereof).

After video, the next most valuable security system for commercial properties is **card access**. Also known as electronic "key cards", "card key" or just access systems, these are invaluable in controlling who, when, and even what gets into your building.

Unfortunately, they are by far the most expensive security systems to install, maintain, and manage. Add to the basic system the cost of the electric locking hardware (which typically equals the cost of the access system itself) and it can be quite a large sum. If you add elevator access control then expect a large bill from the elevator company as well. There are some steps you can take to alleviate the cost, as well as some new concepts in card access. But first let's discuss the typical card access system and how they relate to commercial, multi-tenant properties.

Card readers replace keys- and can not only save the building owners a fortune in re-keying; but also perform other valuable functions. They can both limit the time people can enter plus they document who and when they entered. Visitors and the general public can be denied access to the building after business hours and on holidays since they won't have the necessary card to enter. Obviously, tenants are permitted 24 hour access under their lease but that actually only applies to the tenant *management*. The tenant's employees can and should be limited.

Card readers no longer require any insertion or "swipe", all current products use "proximity" so that the user only has to bring the card within 2 to 4 inches of the reader. This means cards can be left in your purse of briefcase and be read right through them.

Since card access systems utilize electric locks, they can be programmed to *automatically* lock and unlock the building's doors on a schedule. This will forever relieve you and your staff from manually performing that function. Access systems can adjust the unlocking schedule for holidays or even keep the building locked down completely when desired.

Besides the main lobby doors, elevators are also a prime card access candidate. They not only prevent the general public from accessing all or specific floors but also can prevent tenants from wandering around on other floors. This can keep office theft to a minimum.

Parking is another area where card access is commonly used for monthly parkers. Parking gates can be set up so that visitors are required to pull a ticket but tenants who paid for parking can simply use their access card to bypass the ticket machine and cause the gate to open.

Here's a step by step guide to access control in a commercial office building:

Commercial Card Access

<u>Readers & electric locks at each entrance</u>. The door unlock / lock time can be completely different than the person's (**cardholder**) authorized access time period. For example, the building doors can be programmed to automatically unlock at 7:00am and relock at 5:00pm, while individuals can be assigned any other specific time period- i.e. tenant A's employees can only access from 8:00am to 6:00pm Monday – Friday, while Tenant A's management can access the building 24 hours/ 7 days a week. Tenant B can be a completely different time period and so on.

<u>Readers at elevator call buttons</u>. If you don't want to expense of adding card access to elevators, you can still gain some benefit by having one reader installed at the ground floor elevator lobby. At a certain time, all the elevator cabs come to the ground floor and close. The only way an elevator

can be activated (called) is by reading a card. This will prevent unauthorized people from getting up in the building but will not prevent tenants wandering on different floor.

<u>Readers in the elevator cabs</u>. This presents a very flexible variety of options. All floors can be free access during business hours or certain floors can be locked off and require a card. All floors can be locked off after business hours and require a card. Cardholders are assigned specific floors and specific times they are permitted access. Systems can be set up (as an option) to record exactly which floor button was pressed and limit card holders to only pressing one button at a time (to limit people from letting other people to other floors).

<u>Readers on telephone and electrical rooms</u>. These are aimed at outside vendors such as telephone, data, and electrical contractors. While expensive, adding these readers is very valuable at documenting problems when something goes wrong. The author has investigated numerous incidents of contractors cutting the wrong wires and putting other tenants out of service. By the time someone discovers a problem, it is frequently the next day or days later. Just try to pin the blame or obtain damages without documentation of who was in the telephone or electrical room yesterday. In one case, electricians came into do some tenant improvement work and mistakenly gutted an entire electrical room- putting dozens of tenants out of service for several days. The property manager wasn't even aware they were in their building!

<u>Readers in the parking garage or lot</u>. Most building property managers are aware of card access for parking but here are some valuable tips:

1. Have the readers tied into the safety loops so a vehicle must be present for the card to read. This helps prevent a person from getting out of their car and letting their friends in for free parking.
2. Turn on "**anti-passback**" This prevents a card from being read at the same reader more than once without being read at an exit first. This also prevents tenants from giving their whole office free parking by using one card to open the gate multiple times.
3. **Nesting** – readers and gates can be placed within areas of the garage to allow or disallow prime parking spots. Naturally the building owner / manager charges extra for prime parking spots.
4. Unattended lots. You can set aside parking areas with just a gate and a reader so tenants can park there but no visitors or general public. This way a human attendant can handle a large visitor lot but doesn't have to worry about the monthly parkers.
5. General security- if you do have parking attendants, don't forget *their* security. All booths should be equipped with hold up buttons, telephones, and video monitors (if the garage or lot has a video surveillance system).

All the card activity is completely documented. You can obtain history reports on individual cards, an entire tenant. You can get history by reader and by elevator cab. You can select "granted access" or "denied access" (which usually tells who was trying to go places they shouldn't). You can also specify times, days, and ranges of times and days.

Of course, this must be managed and that is a problem we alluded to at the beginning of this section. Card access systems require a fairly enormous amount of work on the part of the property management. Cards must be continuously added, modified, and inactivated due to tenant turnover. Even though the reporting information is very valuable, card access system generate a lot of data.

Typically, the property manager fails to take into consideration the amount of day to day work which the card access will entail when purchasing it. The worse thing you can do is assign the task to an already overworked receptionist.

So what to do? One solution is to hire someone to maintain the card access *and* handle building security on a full time basis. Such a person will be more conscientious. If you already have security personnel, consider having them trained to manage the system. (But always oversee them).

You can also unload much of the work on the tenants themselves. By adding a web option to most current access control systems, the tenants simply use their web browser to add, delete, or modify their own cards. The system is partitioned so each tenant can only see and manage their group of cards while the property manger has complete oversight of all the cards.

A third option is to outsource the card management. In this scenario, the readers and control panels are physically in your building but the software and database reside on a central server at the security company. You them email, fax or telephone in changes and the security outsource company performs them and "downloads" the changes into your panels. This is possible because all current card access system employ "distributed intelligence". Once they are loaded, they can make decisions and continue to operate via their built in firmware. The doors lock and unlock on schedule and the only time the access control panels need to communicate with the central server is when a change is made. The outsource company will provide you with reports on request.

A new variation on the outsource option is the ability to have the outsource company maintain the database but also allow web access for the tenants and property management. This way you can instantly check a card and obtain activity anytime without going through the outsource security vendor.

Up to this point we've looked at commercial security from the property manager's / owner's viewpoint. But what if you're a tenant? If your landlord has the systems we mentioned in place, you can take advantage of them. The video system can be made accessible over the internet so you can view a specific camera- such as the main lobby or parking lot. This is a great option for both the landlord and tenant because now you can control your own area so to speak. As a tenant you can view visitors before letting them up, or check the condition of a parking lot before leaving late at night.

The same applies to the card access system. If it has a web based interface then you as a tenant can check on card status or make simple changes yourself- as well as obtain history reports. The tenants can also take advantage of the infrastructure as previously mentioned for intrusion alarms. The owner installs the base access control system, the tenants can share that equipment because they usually require just one or two readers on their suite. This makes add-ons very economical. It also allows the building and everyone in it to use one type of access card.

If you as the tenant decide you want a completely separate system that you will manage, just be sure to specify the same vender or at least the same type of card the building uses. This will still allow you to only have to carry one card.

Whether you are a commercial owner / manager or a tenant, if you are engaged in healthcare or financial type business, you may fall under the HIPAA or Sarbanes-Oxley acts. Basically both these Federal codes require detailed documentation about who had access to certain records and when.

Card Access systems are a perfect solution since they both limit and document access. You can simply present your auditor or regulator with card history records as proof the guidelines and codes are being met.

The latest feature of card access is "**Logical Access**" or "**Single Sign On**". This is a system where the card or fingerprint also controls logging on to your computers and / or network. Passwords go away and are replaced with a card or fingerprint. (Actually the passwords are hidden but much "stronger" as many as 64 characters!). These systems can be part of or separate from the physical card access but share databases and cards.

Multi-building / multi-properties

The same guidelines apply but when you manage or own multiple properties you can take advantage of remote access. As long as you have a standard and install the same card access system in all your buildings, you only need one central database. The main office can be the system manager by connecting all the buildings via an internet connection, one person can maintain the system in each. This reduces overall costs and makes person managing the card access system more productive.

If this is still more work than you want to take on, the outsource solution is tailor made for multiple buildings since that is their business model. Some of these outsource companies also monitor the intrusion and fire alarms, as well as video. Since the DVRs generally remain at each building, the property manger and tenants can still take advantage of viewing specific cameras while the monitoring company takes care of viewing the video on alarms.

A final word on multi-tenant commercial building: when considering your security budget, always keep in mind tenant retention. If you happen to enjoy a market area where 100% occupancy is the norm, then you may not be as concerned. But if you aren't in such a position, you may want to factor in the cost of acquiring new tenants; should your present ones decide to move due to perceived poor security.

Commercial Campuses, Shopping Malls, and Educational Campuses

In this section we are covering all types of multiple buildings on large lots- essentially small cities. Because they experience problems and threats similar to small cities, large campuses of all types require a different approach. If you manage, or are a tenant on a campus you are certainly familiar with these problems. Petty theft, auto theft, vandalism, graffiti, shoplifting, loitering, and even gang activity are just the least; often much more serious crimes can and will occur, up to and including assault.

No electronic security system by itself can deal with the problems of a large campus, but electronic systems will serve as invaluable tools for a human security force. Just as in a small city where a police department is required, campus security will for all intents and purposes have to act as a police force.

We expect that your human security force will be managed and well trained in the day to day duties required. There is some disagreement regarding the exact makeup of human security forces as to their uniforms and personal equipment. Some owner / managers prefer very low key uniforms such as blazers but we feel that highly visible police type uniforms represent a high deterrent factor while also in most cases give employees, tenants, and the general public a better level of confidence.

Rarely will security officers be armed these days but that should be a direct consideration of the response time of local police. If your particular campus happens to be at the far end of police response or in a high crime area, or has experienced serious issues, then perhaps this needs to be addressed. It may in fact be prudent to have one supervisor on each shift armed or at the very least have firearms available in the command center but stored under lock and key controlled by the supervisor.

We will forgo any further discussion on the security officers and in this section we will concentrate on the interaction of human and electronic security and suggest minimum configurations for the electronic systems.

Command Center

Generally there will be (and should be) a central location for the security staff and this will serve as the command center. The command center should always be a secure, protected location with video surveillance inside and out. While this may seem excessive to some managers, it should be noted that this location is the single most important (and potentially the weakest) point of your entire security system. If the door is always locked and requires a keypad combination to enter, and if video records who enters and what the security staff inside is doing at all times; there will never be a question.

If the command center is situated so that security officers interact with the general public then we suggest a separate area or room directly attached so that the main command center remains secure while the general public is not intimidated by having to deal through glass or windows.

In any case, all video, alarms, and radio and telephone traffic should terminate into the command center. The Digital Video Recorders and camera controls should be located within. The command center should always be equipped with an emergency generator or UPS (Uninterruptible power supply) and at least one spare cell phone.

There will be some disagreement between management and tenants about intrusion and fire alarm monitoring in the command center. First, the mall itself needs some intrusion protection on common area doors and loading docks and these need to be monitored at the command- and off site if desired. It is the tenant spaces that are controversial. In many malls the tenant's rear doors are part of their space and often lead directly outside. Often, the mall management does not want the liability, while many tenants have policies or requirements for outside monitoring of alarms.

In practical terms, however, the mall security force is right on location and can respond much faster than any police entity- if the police even respond at all. A good compromise is to have the tenant's primary monitoring by the central station of their choice while having a secondary monitor at the command center. This needs to be designed and standardized so that the security force is not faced with an overwhelming variety of alarm monitoring bells and whistles.

The simplest solution is an **annunciator** panel- just a light for each tenant space with a piezo type audible. The light is driven by a standard relay or bell output from the tenant's alarm panel. The output *should never be active until the tenant's alarm is armed.* This eliminates false alarms from tenant employee and avoids any complex bypassing or shunts by the mall security force. If you choose to go this route, decide on an annunciator panel, size it for the total number of tenants and make it a published standard. If tenant's want their system monitored than they must comply with the standard.

Also note that most annunciators can be purchased in banks of zones or modules, for example you may want to start with 8 or 16 and add a like number as expansion becomes necessary. Consult your security vender and purchase one made by a manufacturer with a long history and will likely be around for the foreseeable future. There's nothing worse than having a standard and then the equipment be no longer produced when you need to expand. Luckily, annunciators are relatively inexpensive.

Getting back to video, generally malls and campuses will be equipped with movable cameras commonly referred to as PTZs (Pan / Tilt / Zoom). One security officer in the command center will be assigned to manage the video system and control the cameras to observe various parts of the campus such as parking lots, entrances, and loading docks. This officer will then communicate with other officers on mobile or foot patrols to react and go to locations where something is observed that requires investigation.

Your command center or security office will likely have a "holding area" where suspects are placed awaiting questioning or for the local police. It is imperative that video and preferably audio be placed and recorded in this area. Documenting the holding area will greatly alleviate any potential liability claims. We can't stress enough the importance of this, having witnessed the threats of suits being dropped immediately when the claimant is informed that video exists.

In fact, the potential for losses is much greater from claims of liability for false arrest, false imprisonment, civil rights violations and sexual harassment than any crime most suspects are likely to commit. In one case, a suspect was injured while in *police* custody but filed suit against a mall because he felt they had deeper pockets and did not wish to go against the police department. A video recording was proof positive the suspect was in perfect condition when he was placed into police custody.

In another, an intoxicated female student who was detained, later threatened to file suit for sexual harassment until she was informed she had been on video the entire time she was detained. Cameras should be placed to view overall areas so as to gather and document as much information as possible. Do not concentrate on small areas so as to leave open to interpretation what was going on around the suspect.

All Digital Video Recorders have at least one audio input and some have or can be equipped with one per channel. We suggest that as a minimum, one microphone be located in the holding area and recorded. If your facility has multiple holding areas or interview rooms then the appropriate DVR should be purchased and all rooms recorded for audio and video.

Mobile and foot patrols.

As a minimum security officers must be equipped with either radio or cell phone communications.

All current intrusion and video surveillance systems have the capability to transmit alarms – and video to portable devices such as cell phones and PDAs (and laptops in vehicles). While this can be somewhat expensive and complicated to set up and get working, it could prove valuable if your security force needs to cover a wide area or if your location has a great deal of activity.

Should you desire, such systems also have a huge marketing and publicity factor. Imagine a press conference featuring your campus on the local news demonstrating the capability of showing real time video images directly to roaming security officers. This could go a long way to making the local community and potential tenants or students feel very safe in your campus.

Vehicle patrols can also benefit from video recorders and cameras in the vehicles, just as many police department use. While this goes a step beyond, it can go a long way to satisfying complaints from visitors and the general public if you tend to experience a high number of such nuisances.

Schools and Educational facilities

Violence in our schools, although it has existed in one form or another for many years, has captured the media's attention even more recently. An interesting situation is that educators, traditionally one of the most liberal and politically correct groups in society; seem determined to turn our schools into virtual prisons. Fences, bars, and chains; zero tolerance, shake down locker inspections, drug sniffing dogs, guards and metal detectors fill out the picture.

Think of what we are doing to our children in the name of protecting them. We are raising generations of kids that are conditioned to think nothing of having to walk through metal detectors every day! Talk about erosion of rights- these kids will grow up docile members of society ready to exploited by any future fascist government that might possibly come along in the name of protecting our security.

Is there any hope of curtailing violence in schools without turning them into prisons? The threats to schools and school children are pretty much the same as any other sector. The threats can also be divided into internal and external.

Internal threats, such as the kids themselves bringing guns or weapons to school to wreck havoc on their teachers or classmates, fall into exactly the same scenario as employee violence.

External threats are from violence prone individuals –usually but not always ex-classmates- who gain entry to open campuses to take hostages and kill children, often just to gain attention and publicity. This is a more unique situation not seen as much in the private sector.

The open aspect of the school building or campus is probably the best avenue to attack the problem. While guards and metal detectors are somewhat effective, they certainly are not conducive to an ideal learning environment. Securing school doors with chains and padlocks also doesn't fit into 21st century thinking.

We would propose new thinking in the educational sector. Schools and campuses need to be secured from outsiders, ex-students, and even ex-spouses intent on kidnapping their own children. Access control would seem the ideal starting point for a solution.

All school entrances would be equipped with electric locks and card readers. All students would be issued electronic access cards with photo IDs. This would go a long way to securing the school building without the stigma of a prison environment. Ex-students would be removed from the system immediately upon graduation, expulsion, or suspension rendering them powerless to gain entry. Parent and outsiders would be unable to gain entry unless they visit the office first and obtain an escort.

On new campuses in the planning stages, this concept could be extended to the perimeter of the campus itself. The entire campus should be surrounded by high wrought iron fences and all entry (foot and vehicle traffic) would be only through access controlled gates. This would further serve to keep out unwanted persons while maintaining a more relaxed atmosphere. In fact it is no different or more intrusive than many corporate campuses and facilities.

Cameras would serve as eyes for security personnel who could then be stationed at a centralized security command center, ready to respond if needed. Cameras should be installed in every hallway, classroom, and common area to spot potential violence such as fights or gangs congregating.

Not only would a modern, fresh approach to school security protect our children and their teachers from each other and outside intruders but help alleviate the high security prison atmosphere which seems to the prevalent thinking these days.

Industrial Facilities

Manufacturing, Pharmaceutical, and Chemical plants all have their own highly specialized needs. Straight manufacturing plants have little need for elaborate security systems unless they are engaged in making highly desirable consumer goods or use valuable parts or raw materials which have street value. This is not to say however, that such plants cannot benefit from video surveillance systems.

Video systems can do double duty as security and as process control systems. Conveyor belts, furnaces, hazardous locations, and storerooms are all prime candidates for camera locations. We have seen many instances where workers were able to respond quickly to conveyor belt jams because the control center was able to observe them on video monitors.

Loading docks should always be equipped with cameras to observe loading and unloading and can be helpful in cutting shortages and outright theft of raw materials and finished goods. We have even seen a significant drop in fork lift damage and accidents when cameras were installed because once the operators knew they were being observed they were suddenly much more careful drivers.

Of course, should your company be unionized, it will require some finesse before video systems should be installed. Generally if the installation is deemed necessary strictly due to liability and not security it will go down much easier. It is sometimes preferable to start with just a few cameras on the production line to alleviate concern about "big brother" and then when workers are "comfortable" you can slowly install additional ones to cover more critical areas.

Pharmaceutical companies will require more security due to the nature of the product. Intrusion alarms on storerooms and inventory cages will be required by the Drug Enforcement Administration and card access will be a good solution to limiting and documenting access to those areas. Drug and pharmaceutical companies are also often prone to intense industrial espionage and require rigid access control to research areas and labs both for employees and visitors.

Again, cameras will be very beneficial in monitoring sensitive areas and even "clean rooms". Always place cameras at entrances and the main lobby. Sometimes members of general public will become distressed at drug and pharmaceutical companies for all kinds of reasons- from the high cost of medications to the loss of a loved one. Cameras at the lobby and a rigid visitor control system will help to avoid unpleasant situations and document attempts. All doors leading from the entrance should be locked and controlled at all times. This will prevent "visitors" from rushing past receptionists and gaining entry.

If your company happens to engage in any type of animal research then you have another level of problems from activists that must be addressed. Even if you have escaped attention or not had any problems up to now, be prepared. Animal activists can be some of the most daring and violent criminals. Chances are, one of your own employees or a temporary worker will be the one to tip them off.

Animal labs and housing must be highly secured with card access, fire and intrusion alarms and video cameras inside and outside. Systems must be monitored 24 hours either by a full time, on site security force or an outside central monitoring station. Should an intrusion occur, rapid response will be critical in saving perhaps thousands of man hours of research. Always weigh the cost of the electronic security against the potential loss of research, lab time, and future product profit.

Also consider that once video systems are installed, researchers can actually utilize them to keep an eye on their animals during research periods so a major portion of the system cost may be written off in this manner- for convenience and productivity.

Hazardous chemicals and petrochemical plants

All the points made prior also apply to this segment with a significant caveat- all security equipment placed in hazardous environments must be protected itself from damage from that environment and- it generally will be required to be "explosion-proof" – rated to not cause an explosion. Both these requirements may cause the overall system price to increase by up to a factor of ten.

Only a specialized and highly skilled security contractor will be capable of designing and installing such a system so be sure to get and check references from someone you know and trust in the same business as yours. Expect to pay much more for the equipment and the installation, so choose wisely.

Manufacturing Plants can benefit from Card Access systems if one takes a moment to "think outside the box". We have had great success in securing tool cribs and cages with card readers. Not only do such systems secure the valuable tools but automatically provides complete documentation and audit trails on who checked out a tool and when.

Some government contracts require extensive audits because special tools are often paid for as part of the contract. With a card access system in place, most of the work is done automatically. Cards can be combined with bar code scanners so that the scanner cannot be used until a card is read- proving such a complete audit trail.

Warehouse & Distribution

Warehousing presents some of the biggest security challenges because they can present some very attractive targets. In some areas there are vastly more burglaries and theft at warehouses than retail. Think about it- it you were a thief would you rather break into a retail store with a few items or a warehouse with thousands upon thousands of high value goods. All types of goods are potential targets, from electronics to toys and even food.

Small businesses will likely rent space in mini storage facilities which already should have extensive security. Medium sized businesses which generally need larger storage may rent space in free standing buildings or small complexes. These are particularly attractive targets in that they are usually in remote areas where no one is around at night. It is these types of medium sized, remote warehouse locations that will require fairly sophisticated intrusion systems covering all possible entry points including the roof is the location and structure warrants. If you tend to send employees to these warehouses to pick up or drop off inventory, you should consider a camera system with a remote connection so you can keep an eye on things. Card access on the entry door will also limit and document activity at the warehouse for you.

Larger warehouses and all distribution centers also require very specialized fire alarm systems so let's address these first. Other than the normal fire sprinkler system and monitoring, some warehouses will need to comply with other fire codes that come into effect due to the physical size of the building.

Many very large warehouses will require engine driven fire pumps and all the associated monitoring. Some jurisdictions will require manual fire pull stations and be advised that travel paths in excess of 200 feet are not permitted.

Some jurisdictions look at the height of the storage racks. Referred to as "high pile storage" or high rack storage, these codes can require in-rack sprinklers and smoke detectors. **AHJ**s (Authority Having Jurisdiction- usually the fire inspector) have even required hazardous material handling designations for foodstuffs, such as cooking oil. In these situations it may be advisable to hire a good local consultant to go to bat for you with local city and county governments.

Warehouse Security Systems

Some warehouses operate 24 hours but still close once or twice a year dictating an intrusion system. In fact, even 24 hour operations require 24 hour intrusion on certain areas. Some examples are re-packing areas, and especially fire exits.

It is fairly common practice for employees to help themselves to product and then stash it outside remote fire exits so they can return after work and retrieve it. To discourage this, fire exits which are not to be normally used are alarmed 24 hours and monitored in the security guard post or warehouse manager's office.

Be aware however that even these alarms require specialized equipment. Employees have become aware of alarms in recent year and have figured out a simple magnet can defeat alarm door contacts from the inside. The employee brings a powerful magnetic to work, tapes it over the alarm sensor and then can open the door whenever he pleases without tripping the alarm. A recent walkthrough of a very large distribution yielded 9 magnets taped over remote fire exits so obviously this location had a huge problem.

This can be circumvented by specifying special high security "biased" alarm contacts. These alarm contacts only respond to a special magnet, if another magnet is introduced they immediately go into alarm. These types of contacts are about double the cost but in the overall project their total cost is very low.

The security force and manager needs to take immediate action if this occurs and if the warehouse has a good video surveillance system, it will greatly assist in tracking down dishonest employees. A good video system will also serve operations, paying for itself quickly.

As a minimum cameras should be located on the four corners of the building on the roof. Movable cameras will allow you to observe the complete exterior. **PTZ** dome cameras can be programmed to automatically rotate and zoom in on the door where an alarm is occurring.

If possible, we always recommend cameras on poles facing towards the building loading docks. These should also be movable so the entire yard can be observed at night but during normal business hours these cameras can be used to direct trucks to open loading bays.

It is imperative fixed cameras also be installed viewing the gate and the guard shack viewing both incoming and outgoing truck traffic. This will provide a time documented record of every truck entering and leaving the facility. It is advisable to have two guards stationed at the gate during peak hours so one can check the incoming traffic and the other checking outbound. We have seen numerous instances where thieves simply hook up a fully loaded trailer and drive it right out the gate.

There are automatic barriers available that can pop out of the ground in a few seconds to prevent this. Originally designed to prevent incoming threats, they are equally effective at stopping outgoing thefts. This is only recommended for very high risk operations of course. In all circumstances however, no truck should be permitted to leave without the proper paperwork. Cameras at the gate will, at the very least, document all traffic.

Card access systems are not widely used in large warehouses but can provide many benefits. If your drivers are dedicated to your facility, they can be issued cards and enter and leave through automatic unattended gates which would significantly reduce the need for security man hours. Card access can also be installed on doors from the warehouse to office to ensure outside drivers don't wander through sensitive areas.

Residential

Residential security has been both the bread and butter and bane of security alarm companies. Although a large source of revenue, residential is also the largest source of false alarms and service calls. And although there are large numbers of residential alarms, the actual market penetration is almost absurdly tiny. Of all the types of security systems, problems, and solutions; residential certainly presents the most challenges.

Since residences vary so widely by size and type they can employ every type of security system and solution. Because residential security is such a huge subject, we will divide this guide into the different segments and discuss each separately.

Single family 1000- 5000 square feet

Most of the homes in the United States fall into this category. You'll want a basic intrusion system but don't make the mistake of going too cheap. The low end systems will come with fewer features but even worse is the user interface- the keypad.

Cheap keypads use LEDs while more expensive ones have LCD displays which provide more information in English (or other languages such as Spanish). These are much easier to use and long term you will be glad you spent a few more dollars. You'll want at least two keypads- one near the door you use to enter the house and one in the master bedroom.

One of the main reasons residential alarms are so unique is that the user actually lives there and so at night the system is armed with the owner *inside*. This requires specialized programs and setup quite different from a business where no one is going to be inside while it is armed.

The keypad in the bedroom is just for this purpose. While it is possible to setup a system with just one keypad, it is very difficult to use in practice and you'll soon wish you had another. The end result will be you'll stop using the system because it will be so much trouble. So add the keypad in the bedroom then when you're ready for bed, you can easily arm the system. If you want to get up in the middle of the night for a snack, you can just as easily disarm it- and because it's right there, you won't forget it and cause a false alarm!

Modern systems have features like "Home – Sleep – Away". These are different levels of arming such that no devices are active while "Home", then when the system is put into "Sleep" the windows and doors are armed but motion detectors are not until you enter the "Away" mode. Away would indicate no one is home so go ahead and arm every device.

Even more importantly, if something does happen- like a fire or break in, the keypad is right there to alert you; and the LCD display will let you know exactly what and where. Modern alarm systems can and should pinpoint each type of detector installed in your house. Each device should be individually zoned; for example, the basement door, or the kitchen window, or the smoke detector in Billy's room.

The communication portion of the alarm is not quite as important as in a business since the owner is home most of the time. If this is the case in your household, then using your phone for the alarm to transmit to the central monitoring station is perfectly fine. If the house is empty during the day or you travel a lot, then monitoring by internet connection is highly recommended. This can be a DSL or cable modem. Some companies proclaim the use of wireless or radio but that's probably more trouble than it's worth.

So you get a good quality alarm panel and 2 or 3 higher end LCD keypads, what else do you need? This is where you can save some money, by not getting too much! Here are the recommended minimums:

Smoke detectors – if you're going to the expense of installing a central station monitored alarm why would you not have a fire alarm as well? Unfortunately, the smoke detectors that came with your house will probably not work with your new alarm. Typically, such smoke detectors are powered by 120 VAC house power and don't have the correct outputs for the alarm. If you already have these, leave them alone and supplement them with system smoke detectors. One in the hallway on each floor is generally sufficient. Never install them near bathrooms however.

Carbon Monoxide Detector- not widely used (unfortunately) but readily available and a real life saver. There are probably more deaths due to carbon monoxide poisoning (it is completely odorless) than fires. Install it in the basement or near the kitchen.

Door Contacts- all doors leading into the home should be equipped with alarm door sensors. If you have a garage, the roll up or tilt up garage door should also be alarmed. Most people will tell you motorized doors can't be opened from the outside- and they're correct; however a thief can break into the house and open it from the inside and steal your car. For the small amount extra, go ahead and do it and give yourself some extra protection.

If you have small children (up to teenage) then alarm contact on their bedroom doors is not a bad idea. Kids do get kidnapped, it's very rare but it does happen. Again, the little extra money is well worth the peace of mind.

Liquor cabinets, gun cabinets, valuable collections, tool boxes are all areas you may want to add to the alarm system. All can be protected with contacts or other specialized devices.

Windows – we don't recommend going to the expense of doing windows unless there is a very good reason. Windows can be contacted just like doors but the installation is complex and therefore expensive. They are better places to spend your money. If you do decide you need some windows protected then you should only do windows which are completely hidden from public view and accessible from the ground.

Glass Break Detectors – These are slightly more effective in a residential environment so if you have large areas of glass on sides of the house that are not visible from public view, then GBDs might be a good solution. Remember though that most burglars will enter through a door. Even if they break a window next to the door or in the door, they'll still open the door to get in which will trip the alarm anyway.

Panic Buttons – It is usually not necessary to add these since virtually all keypads have a panic feature built in. As long as you're close to one you can send a panic with a special key or combination. This is why we recommend a keypad by the front door and in the bedroom.

Motion Detectors- Passive Infrared motion detectors (PIRs) are usually very effective in residences. You'll want to have them installed where a burglar might enter by opening a door, through a window or 2nd floor balcony or even the basement if it has windows. Place them in the kitchen, hallways or large common areas. If you have a two story which is accessible by climbing then by all means place one in the second floor hallway.

Don't go overboard with PIRs, they make moving around difficult for you at night with the system armed so consider the day to day operation. Just one or two PIRs will be very effective if placed properly.

They are many add-ons to a residential security system that can huge benefits:

> Wireless remote controls (similar to remotes for your car) can be used to arm or disarm the system.

> Telephone interfaces so you can actually call your alarm from anywhere and control it.

> Internet connections that allow you to check on the security system from anywhere while away.

> Outdoor flood lights that come on automatically.

> Strobes on the roof to signal police helicopters that the alarm has been activated.

> Some systems allow card readers to replace PINs to arm and disarm.

> There are systems that can email you if specific events occur- such as an alarm or even if your child is late coming back from school. Most of these features cost very little when the system is installed so be sure to discuss your wants and needs with the alarm company.

Apartments, condos, duplexes and other multi-tenant residential

All the same points apply except the system will usually be smaller than single family. The biggest difference of course, if that you share common walls with strangers. The affects your system in that a fire could be much more likely but chances are the apartment or condo complex will already have a fire alarm system. But always install your own smoke detectors to provide you with an early warning.

Also, security can be affected because of noise and vibration; even pounding on walls can set off motion and glass break detectors and cause false alarms. Although it is extremely rare, burglars could enter your unit through the common wall. This is probably unlikely unless you have some high value items, but if you do, then additional motion detectors may be required.

Estates – More than 5000 square feet on large lots, ranches, vacation cabins

These types of residences require more attention just because they represent more risk. The risk comes from size, location, and isolation. All the same points apply as in single family but the system will require much more protection. Internet monitoring (if possible) is an absolute must especially on vacation homes. On remote residences, also be sure your alarm company installs extra standby batteries in case power is off for extended periods of time.

The typical 7 amp hour battery should last 24 hours or more, adding another in parallel will double that to 48 hours and so on. Batteries are cheap; the protection they afford is not.

On those remote locations, especially in the mountains, you may want to add temperature monitoring to warn you if the temperature drops to the pipe freezing range. Water leak sensors could also be valuable early warning devices of impending disasters.

Continuing with remote locations, consider adding cameras with internet access so you can check on your retreat anytime from the comfort of your primary residence or office. No, it's not that expensive and could save hours of driving –or a big surprise the next time to you decide to get away.

Driveway sensors are available to sense when a vehicle approaches the home. These are only really effective if the home is set back, on a large property, or it's located in a remote location with it's own road or driveway. They are relatively inexpensive and very effective. It's quite simple to connect a driveway sensor and a digital video recorder to "mark" the recording when a vehicle comes down the drive so you can easily go back and view the event.

Estates are pretty much in a class by themselves and as such also require special attention. If you live in a large estate with a long drive then the driveway sensor can alert you with a chime or even by a video when someone approaches. We recommend this even if the estate if fenced. Once you allow someone to drive onto your property, you want to make sure they actually only drive up to the front door and not wander off somewhere else.

If you have a gate, you'll want a camera and a way to speak to someone. The best way to speak to someone at a gate is a hands free telephone or door station. Don't allow an intercom to be installed. An intercom requires a dedicated base station or master which can be very inconvenient. A telephone however, can be programmed to dial your phone system so you can answer it from anywhere in the house. All such systems have a door opening feature so you can just enter a code on any phone to open the gate.

A camera viewing the driver is the minimum, another camera viewing the overall vehicle is helpful. Either way, you can have the video sent into your home entertainment system so you can view it on any television in the house. This is preferred over dedicated video monitors.

The ideal system is one which a visitor drives up and presses the call button. Your phones then ring throughout the house. You can go to the nearest phone and TV and talk to and observe who is at the gate. If you're satisfied you can then enter a code on the phone and the gate will open. You will then get an alert that the vehicle has entered the grounds by the driveway sensor.

You should have additional cameras mounted outside on the roof to view the four corners around your home. You should be able to see the vehicle approach and park and see exactly who gets out and make sure it's who you were expecting and not anyone else – or additional people you weren't expecting.

If you are wealthy – and / or have children, you just can never be too careful. Your children unfortunately are a target and must be protected. Even if you don't believe this is the case, you can tell yourself the camera you install outside can be used to keep an eye on them while they're playing. That alone is worth the peace of mind.

Panic rooms and safe rooms

If you are in the position of thinking you need one, then you probably do. These don't have to be as elaborate as you see in the movies. Usually a secure windowless room with a good quality solid core steel door will be sufficient. What is important is that it be equipped with a video monitor and both a land line phone and a cell phone. The land line phone should not be part of the home's phone system, it should be a separate line and number. The cell phone should have an extra battery and a charger. Check it periodically to make sure it working.

It's really only necessary to have a small supply of water since the room is only intended to protect you and your loved ones until police or private security arrive. We're not really talking about an extended stay here. If you're really concerned then by all means add standby power in the form of a solar backup system or as a last resort, a generator. Some limited food supplies can be added. Military rations MREs can be an excellent choice since they have a very long shelve life and are readily available at surplus and survival stores or on the internet.

Should you own a gun?

Well, we do; but it's strictly a matter of personal choice. You may initially feel uncomfortable but a class in firearms training will almost certainly change your attitude. Women especially, seem to completely change their position once they learn how to use a gun. Even children as young as nine can be excellent candidates for firearms training. Both women and children usually become very proficient and end up being excellent shots once they are trained.

If you do decide to try it, then a gun safe is absolutely mandatory. If you have a safe room, keep it in there, otherwise it should be located somewhere handy- usually your bedroom. After all, if you're going to have weapons you need to have access to them in an emergency.

Perimeter protection

On estates it's best to extend the protection perimeter out as far as possible to provide the earliest possible warning of an intrusion. The best way to accomplish while remaining cost effective is with **beams**- active infrared. These require a transmitter and receiver facing each other in line of sight. You should select portions of your property that intruders must pass through to get to the house.

These devices are unobtrusive and their beams are completely invisible. They should be mounted so that the lower beam is about 2-3 feet from the ground, this way they will be unaffected by small animals. At that height it would be possible to crawl under one but at night it would be unlikely an intruder will even spot it. If your risk is extremely high, then additional beams can be placed at angles closer to the home to increase the detection possibility.

Don't overlook boat docks, landings, and even airstrips if they are on your property. Steep hills and cliffs are not deterrents to determined thieves. Beams should be placed adjacent to all areas from which an intruder could approach. Although it does raise the awareness level, beams can be powered by solar panels and can transmit alarms signals via radio to the house if distances are considerations.

Circle within a circle

This concept should be the basis for your estate security plan. The first circle is at the absolute outer edge of your property. The next circle should be at the middle distance from the home to the edge. The next circle is at the home itself using alarm contacts on all perimeter doors. The inner circle consists of interior motion detectors and finally a safe room if you desire. Video cameras should be placed so that each circle can be observed if an intrusion is detected.

Estates and vacation homes imply wealth and will likely mark you as a potential target. It's just a fact of life you are going to have to worry more about your assets and spend more to protect them. Chances are some thief has already taken an interest in those assets.

A last word on residential security

The number one goal should be ease of use. If the system is too complicated or hard to use or causes too many false alarms, it will never be used. This is worse than not having a system at all. At a very early point in the process you should request a demonstration and an exact set of operating instructions. If you or *any* member of the family does not understand or feel comfortable with it, then demand something else or find another alarm company. Even your children should be able to use the system because chances are likely that they will.

Unless you live in a large estate and have a private security consultant, you will have to rely on this guide and your own research to get the best system for your money. In the low-mid range residential market the competition is fierce but unfortunately the alarm company sales force is not highly trained except to get the order and get out.

Many alarm company sales people will never have heard of many of the items we've mentioned here, some don't even know their companies offer them. Chances are your system will take at least two appointments- one initial contact and another when a more experienced sales rep or technician is brought in because you asked too many difficult questions! Don't hesitate to be demanding.

Fire alarms

Although fire alarms are not strictly speaking 'security' systems, they are such an integral part of personal and business protection we will explain them here.

First, fire systems must be separated into two categories: **Suppression** and **Detection**.

Fire Suppression Systems actually put out fires via some extinguishing agent. Most people are familiar with Sprinkler systems which use water. There are also systems that use inert gases to "smother" the fire. Halon used to be the most common but has been replaced with FC-3-1-10 or trade name PFC-410. These types of systems are generally used in restaurants (Hood systems) and computer rooms.

A fire suppression system by Fenwal

Fire sprinklers are by far the most common and the recent trend is to install them in single family homes as well as businesses. Sprinklers are extremely effective at putting out fires but they do have some negative aspects- the biggest one being the very agent they use- water.

First let's clear up one misconception. Contrary to what you see in the movies, all the sprinklers in the building do not discharge water when there's a fire. Only the head nearest the fire is affected. As long as the fire is contained to one small spot then only one head will ever discharge water.

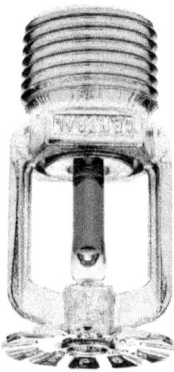

Typical Sprinkler Head

Please note however, that once a sprinkler head is activated the water will *not* stop flowing until it is turned off at the riser or main water line. This means that if a small fire in a trashcan is immediately extinguished the water will continue and possibly flood the building until someone arrives and turns off the main sprinkler system. The fire sprinklers can not be turned back on until the sprinkler head is replaced.

For these reasons, the sprinkler system must be monitored at all times. This is where the fire alarm or fire monitoring system comes in. The fire alarm monitors the **water flow** and **valve tampers.** Since sprinklers are filled with static water (until a head is activated and discharges water), monitoring the flow is the key to determining a sprinkler head has discharged. Once the head bursts and discharges, water begins flowing through the system and the fire alarm detects this and transmits a signal to the **central monitoring station**.

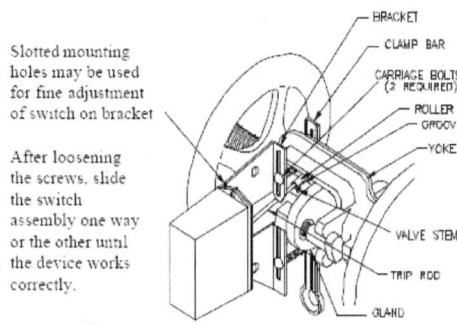

OS&Y Valve tamper

The valves are also monitored to ensure no one turns off water to the building and then starts a fire; or service people forget to turn the water back on after maintenance. There are sometimes many other conditions monitored depending on the exact type of sprinkler system and the area of the country. Colder climates, for instance, require special "dry" systems so that sprinkler pipes don't freeze and burst.

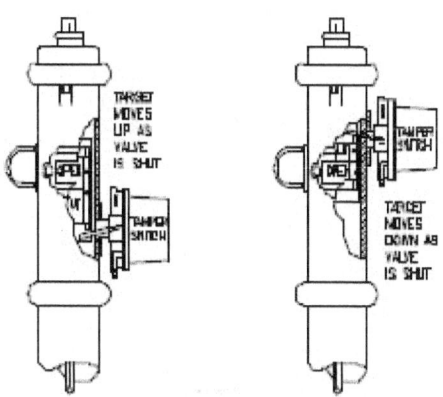

Post Indicator Valve (PIV) Switch

You can see fire monitoring systems are critical not only to reporting fires but also to limiting water damage. Often, more damage can actually occur from water than from the fire itself, especially if prompt action is not taken to turn off the water.

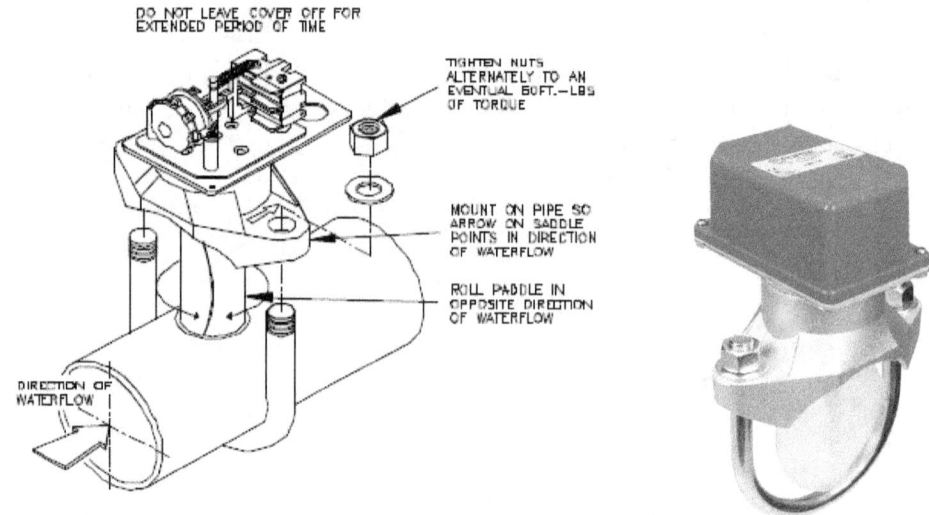

Water Flow Switch

Fire Detection Systems

Let's turn our attention to the electronic fire detection and monitoring systems. As we discussed, a fire monitoring system typically just monitors the condition of a fire sprinkler or suppression system. But fire suppression systems only act *after* a fire has started. Fire detection systems can provide early warning of an impending fire.

The best example of fire detection is the common **smoke detector**. A smoke detector, as the name implies, detects smoke using a tiny photoelectric cell. Smoke passes between the photocell sensor where the detector measures it to prevent false alarms from dust particles. These photocells are so sensitive they can detect smoke before it becomes readily visible to the naked eye.

Smoke Detector

In very hot areas, heat detectors replace smoke detectors. These alarm when a fixed temperature is reached- typically 190 degrees but there are type that also measure the **rate of rise**. If the temperature suddenly increases dramatically, the detector trips and signals an alarm. Heat and smoke detectors are often used in combination in different areas of the building.

Heat Detector (note the Do Not Paint)

Similar to smoke detectors are **smoke beams**. These are exactly like the active infrared beams used in intrusion systems and need a transmitter and receiver. When smoke passes between them, it causes an alarm. These are used in large open areas such as churches, gymnasiums, and atriums.

Smoke Beam (Reflector Type)

All these devices need a control panel or transmitter. There is intelligence required to monitor the devices and transmit the alarm. On smaller systems the fire control panel also transmits the alarm. On larger systems, a fire control panel handles the control portion and a separate transmitter handles the alarm signal.

Fire Keypad / Annunciator

Fire alarm systems consist of a keypad or annunciator that acts as a user interface and the control panel. The control panel not only monitors the fire detection devices but also the wiring, the power, the standby battery, and the phone line.

A phone line is required to transmit the fire alarm to the central station. National fire codes (National Fire Protection Association NFPA 72) requires two forms of communication. This is usually accomplished with two voice grade phone lines but newer systems can use the internet.

Once the control panel detects an alarm it transmits the information to the central station where it is decoded by an alarm receiver and displayed to an operator. The operator will see an exact description of the location and type of alarm signal. Depending on the type of signal, the operator will then notify the fire department.

There are many and varied codes and regulations governing fire alarm systems. Because systems must meet these codes to the letter, they require very specific design and quantities of devices. You may be surprised to learn that in many jurisdictions you can't just install one smoke detector in a specific area. Systems have to be designed and installed to code. Fire codes are designed to offer sufficient level of protection and not lull owners into a false sense of security.

If you feel the fire alarm system being proposed is not justified and is too much, ask to see the relevant portion of the fire code that applies in your area. Don't be surprised however if systems vary between alarm companies, there is a lot of room for interpretation of the fire codes. Always get a guarantee in writing that the fire system will comply.

Fire Horn / Strobe unit used for Evacuation

Fire Bell

Manual Pull Stations – the right one has a glass rod

FIRE ALARMS IN DEPTH

Intended for Property Managers & Building Engineers

How does my fire alarm system work? What should I know about maintenance and testing? How often should a fire alarm system be tested? People have many misconceptions about fire alarms and sprinkler systems, which will be discussed and explained.

If you are a property manager and have faced these questions or would like to know more about electronic fire alarms, this guide was written for you. If you want to teach your service technicians and building engineers on how to inspect fire alarms or just educate them on all aspects of fire alarms then this book will accomplish that.

Typical Fire Sprinkler System

Fire Alarm Basics

Many people tend to confuse the distinction between fire *alarms* and fire *suppression* systems. Fire alarms are meant to warn occupants and or authorities that a fire is imminent or in progress. Fire suppression (also known as extinguishing) is meant to put out the fire.

Fire Suppression

These systems can be divided into several categories:

Fire Sprinkler systems are designed to put out a fire by dousing it with water. These systems are controlled at a central location on the property and alarms are transmitted to a **central station,** which in turn notifies the fire department.

Fire Extinguishers are generally self-contained portable appliances to be manually used to fight a fire. No alarms are generated by their usage.

There are also systems that use inert gases to "smother" the fire. Halon was once common but has been replaced with FC-3-1-10 or trade name PFC-410. These types of systems are generally used in restaurants (Hood systems) and computer rooms. These systems are almost always monitored.

Fire Alarms

Alarms can be divided into categories.

Fire Warning (also known as Evacuation or Life Safety) consist of audible and visual devices such as horns, strobes, bells, and sometimes speakers to warn occupants to evacuate the building. These usually include **Manual Pull** stations and a connection to other fire detection systems such as sprinklers, heat detectors and smoke detectors.

Fire Monitoring systems are used to notify a remote site that either an alarm has occurred or there is trouble with some part of the overall fire system.

The various systems are often combined in many different designs. Fire sprinkler systems are required to be monitored if there are more than 100 sprinkler heads. Fire warning systems do not necessarily have to be monitored since they are intended to warn occupants but most likely they will have a fire alarm transmitter to send an alarm signal to a central monitoring station.

In the past it was often common to send fire alarm signals direct to the fire department but as the population grew this practice was eliminated. All fire alarms are now transmitted to private central monitoring stations. Operators are on duty 24 hours and once an alarm is received they in turn notify the fire department. This system allows exceptions- such as maintenance on the sprinkler system. The service technicians notify the central station or monitoring company in advance so they will not dispatch the fire department.

One of the most important and frequently overlooked basic functions for the property manager or owner to perform is to ensure the central monitoring station has an up to date **call list**. This is simply a list of names and phone numbers for the alarm company monitoring site to call in case of emergency. Because of the nature of fire alarms which do not generate activity like a burglar alarm; these lists are often overlooked and consequently are years out of date. If the alarm company doesn't have an up to date list they can't notify you of a problem or disaster.

All About Fire Sprinkler Systems

The typical fire sprinkler system consists of the following components:

Riser -   The main pipe feeding the building sprinkler system

Shut off valves –   O.S.& Y. (Outside Stem & Yoke) near or on the riser

                                 PIV (Post Indicator Valve) near the city water supply

Sprinkler Heads-   The actual discharge heads located throughout the building

Sprinkler Riser with OS&Y Valve

While fire sprinkler systems are extremely effective at extinguishing fire, they also come with a huge set of problems for the property manager or building owner. The biggest of which is the very water that extinguishes the fire! Often the water damage that ensues is more than the fire itself.

Once a sprinkler head begins discharging water there is nothing to stop it until the water is shut off at the riser! This is usually done by the fire department when they arrive at the scene. The fire department generally won't turn off the water until they are absolutely certain the fire is extinguished.

The same applies if a sprinkler head is accidentally discharged- such as knocking one off with a ladder, an all too common occurrence. The water supply to the fire sprinkler riser is endless since it is directly connected to the city water supply in most areas. The only way to stop the flow of water once a sprinkler head opens is to shut it off at the main valve. This valve is located on or near the sprinkler riser and is usually a large red wheel mounted to a valve called an O.S.&Y or Outside Stem & Yoke. You need to turn this valve several turns clockwise to turn off the water. These valve handles are often chained and locked to prevent vandalism and nuisance alarms but the locks are required to be "breakaway" so they can easily be released.

The water supply can be shut off at either the PIV or the OS&Y. Generally speaking the OS&Y is more conveniently located and quicker to access since the PIV are usually located far from the building.

OS&Y valve is easily identified by the large wheel handle

Turn this wheel clockwise until it stops to turn off the water to this sprinkler riser. OS&Y valves control only the specific riser to which they are attached.

PIV valves have a handle, which must be released, pulled up and then turned, very similar to a fire hydrant. A characteristic of PIVs is a window that displays the words: OPEN or SHUT. On an operating system, the window must always display OPEN.

PIV valve – the display must always show OPEN

Since PIVs are often located in public areas, the handles are usually locked with breakaway padlocks.

In some instances – usually very large warehouses- the PIVs are mounted on the building right outside the riser location.

Building Mounted PIV

Fire sprinklers are by far the most common form of fire suppression and are extremely effective at putting out fires to the point they are being installed in even single-family homes in some areas.

First let's clear up one misconception. Contrary to what you see in the movies, all the sprinklers in the building do not discharge water when there's a fire. The way a sprinkler system works is a sprinkler "head" has a glass vial with a special chemical sealed inside. This vial holds a valve closed or shut so no water is released. When a fire occurs in the vicinity of a sprinkler head, the heat build-up causes the chemical in the vial to expand until the glass bursts. This releases the valve and consequently the water.

Only the head nearest the fire is affected *unless* the fire gets larger. If the fire continues to expand and the heat reaches more heads then those will burst and release more water. If the fire is contained to one small spot then only one head will ever discharge water.

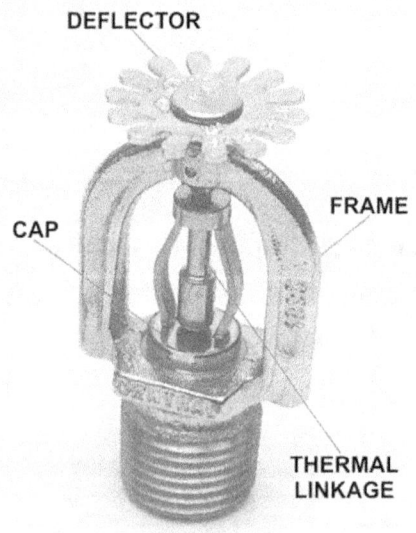

DEFLECTOR

FRAME

CAP

THERMAL
LINKAGE

This type of head uses a mechanical thermal sensor others use glass vials

Remember once a sprinkler head is activated the water will *not* stop flowing until it is turned off at the riser or main water line. This means that if a small fire in a trashcan is immediately extinguished the water will continue and possibly flood the building until someone arrives and turns off the main sprinkler system. The fire sprinklers cannot be turned back on until the sprinkler head is replaced. Sprinkler heads are *one time use only*. Once a sprinkler head discharges it must be replaced.

Most sprinkler system installations include a cabinet with spare heads.

Spare Sprinkler Heads

A Fire Sprinkler Riser

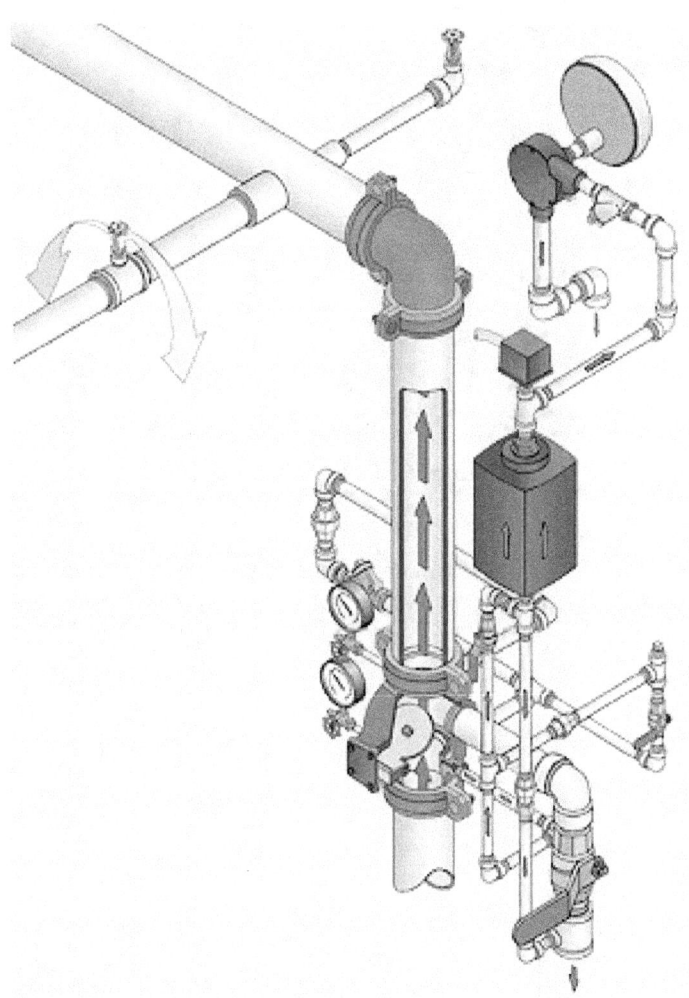

Dry Sprinkler Systems

So far we have only mentioned common "wet" sprinkler systems. Wet systems are defined as sprinklers systems that are filled with water at all times. This is fine in warmer climates but in colder areas unheated buildings must use a different solution to prevent the sprinkler pipes from freezing.

"Dry" fire sprinkler systems solve the freezing problem by filling the pipes with compressed air. The air pressure forces the water to stay below ground (or freezing) level where it won't freeze. If a fire occurs, the sprinkler heat still functions the same but initially it releases air instead of water. Once the head discharges, all the air rushes out of the system and then the water begins to flow through the system.

Dry systems require much more maintenance and have more components and more monitoring. Obviously, the air compressor is a critical piece of equipment because if it fails, the air will eventually leak out and water will flow. If it's freezing at the time, you can imagine the considerable damage that will occur.

The compressor is at bottom left.

In either case there are numerous valves for maintenance and testing on every sprinkler system. The gauges show water pressure and air pressure if it's a dry system. On a dry system the air pressure must exceed the water pressure.

In some areas, the city water supply is not sufficient to provide enough flow or capacity to the sprinkler system so alternatives are provided. Some buildings- especially in the eastern area of the United States have water towers or tanks on the roof. These are gravity fed to the fire sprinkler system. The water level in these tanks must be monitored- this is called water tank level.

In very large distribution centers and warehouses, which have many dozens of risers, a fire pump is used to pressurize the city water. These fire pumps are either electric or engine driven and are located- logically enough- in a pump house. The pump house is often quite a distance from the main building.

This photo shows two fire pumps side by side

Pumps rooms require lots of maintenance and special valves. All functions of the engine, pump, power and all the numerous valves are monitored with special devices.

Sprinkler systems have one more component – a bell. While it used to be common practice to install a mechanical water powered bell – called a water gong; it is now more usual to find an electric bell. The sprinkler company usually supplies the electric bell and often uses 120 VAC –so be careful!

Computer Rooms and Data Centers

Because of the delicate electronics inherent in computers, data centers are often protected by another type of fire suppression that uses chemicals or more commonly – inert gas. As we mentioned previously, the inert gas smothers the fire by depriving it of oxygen. The system works by replacing the oxygen in the room with the gas. While this method does not cause damage to computers & servers, it is decidedly not friendly to humans.

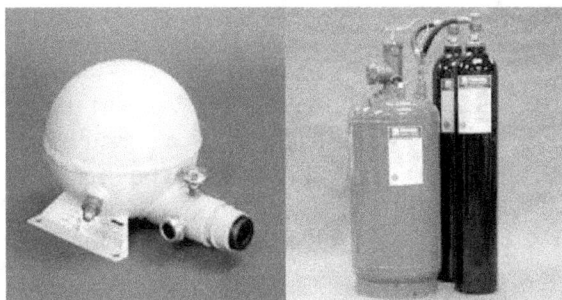

Types of Gas Discharge Containers by Fenwal

Data center fire suppression systems have additional features that further separate them from other fire systems. Typically, more than one smoke detector has to go into alarm before any discharge can take place. This is a safety feature to prevent accidental discharge from a false alarm and is called cross-zoning. Since two smoke detectors must sense smoke before an alarm, it is much less likely to have a false discharge.

Also there is always an **ABORT** switch. This is used by an operator in the room to halt the discharge sequence if they determine there is no fire danger.

Since these systems are usually owned and operated by private companies, the typical property manager will not get involved with them. Such systems are always independent and separate from the building fire system. Computer room systems have a separate fire control panel but are usually monitored by the main building fire control panel which actually summons outside help should a discharge occur.

It is extremely important to note that chemical and gas fire suppression systems are dangerous in enclosed areas because they will quickly remove the oxygen. You do not want to be in the room if they discharge. The author has had the occasion to visit a data center shortly after the gas was discharged accidentally and still found it impossible to breathe.

Monitoring the Fire System

Due to the critical nature of all fire suppression systems and their complexity, they must be monitored at all times. This is where the fire alarm or fire monitoring system comes in. The fire alarm monitors the **water flow** and **valve tampers.**

Since sprinklers are filled with static water or air (until a head is activated and discharges water), monitoring the flow is the key to determining a sprinkler head has discharged. Once the head bursts and discharges, water begins flowing through the system; the fire alarm detects this and transmits a signal to the **central monitoring station**. The monitoring company in turn notifies the fire department.

The valves are also monitored to ensure no one turns off water to the building and then starts a fire; or service people forget to turn the water back on after maintenance. There are sometimes many other conditions monitored depending on the exact type of sprinkler system and the area of the country. As we discussed, colder climates, for instance, require special "dry" systems so that sprinkler pipes don't freeze and burst. These systems require monitoring of Air Pressure, Compressor Power, and often water pressure.

You can see fire-monitoring systems are critical not only to reporting fires but also too limiting water damage. Often, more damage can actually occur from water than from the fire itself, especially if prompt action is not taken to turn off the water.

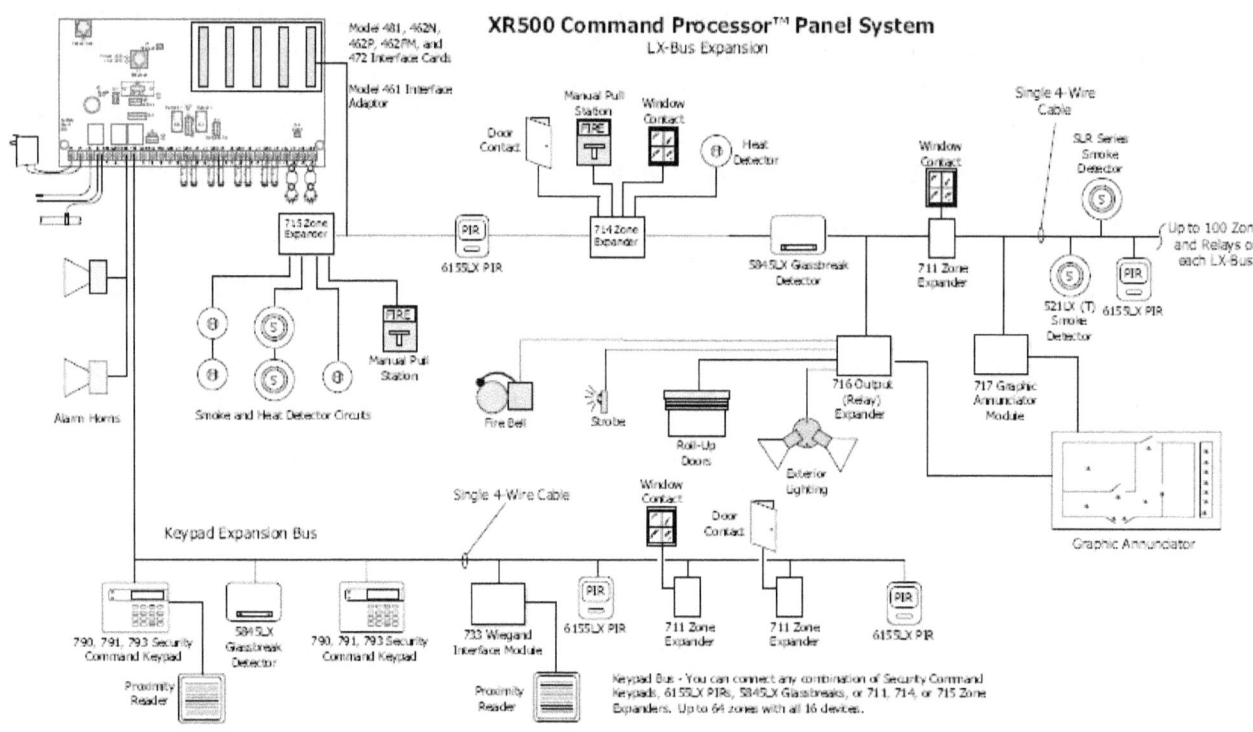

A complete fire monitoring system diagram from DMP

Although this diagram shows security devices combined with fire monitoring, most jurisdictions do not permit combination fire and burglary systems.

Fire monitoring systems are very sophisticated. They have standby batteries which by code must provide a minimum of 24 hours of backup power. They supervise all internal functions themselves, such as AC line power, standby battery condition, phone line or communication path condition and condition of the wiring and circuits connected.

If the fire monitoring panel uses regular dial up phone lines for communication, then a test signal is required to be sent to the monitoring station at least every 24 hours.

Fire Alarms

There are several types of fire alarm systems:

Fire Monitoring – sprinkler or water flow monitoring and fire panel monitoring

Fire Warning – evacuation and life safety systems

Fire Detection – smoke and heat detectors

Since we just explained about fire sprinklers, let's cover fire monitoring systems first.

If your building is of any size, it probably has a fire sprinkler system and it likely has more than 100 sprinkler heads. In most jurisdictions any sprinkler system of more than 100 heads will require a fire monitoring system.

The monitoring system will consist of flow monitoring and valve tamper monitoring at a minimum. Also known as **Valve Supervision,** the valve tamper insures the valves controlling the sprinkler system are open and ready to flow water at all times.

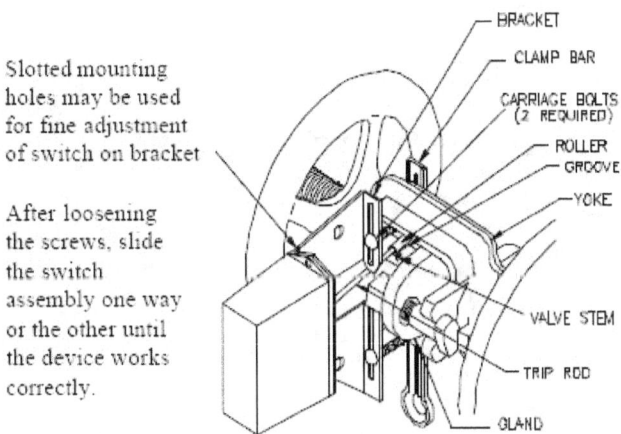

Installation of a valve tamper on an OS&Y

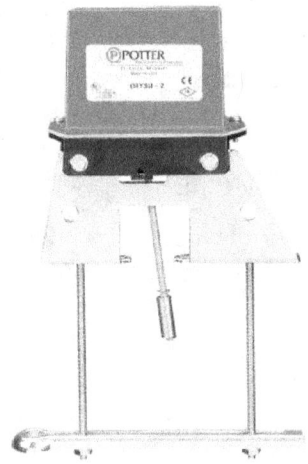

An O.S. & Y. Tamper Switch

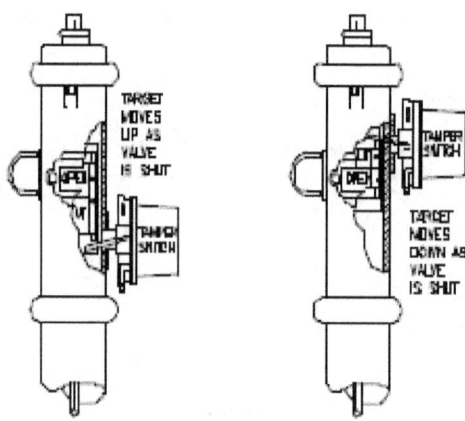

Installation of a PIV Tamper Switch

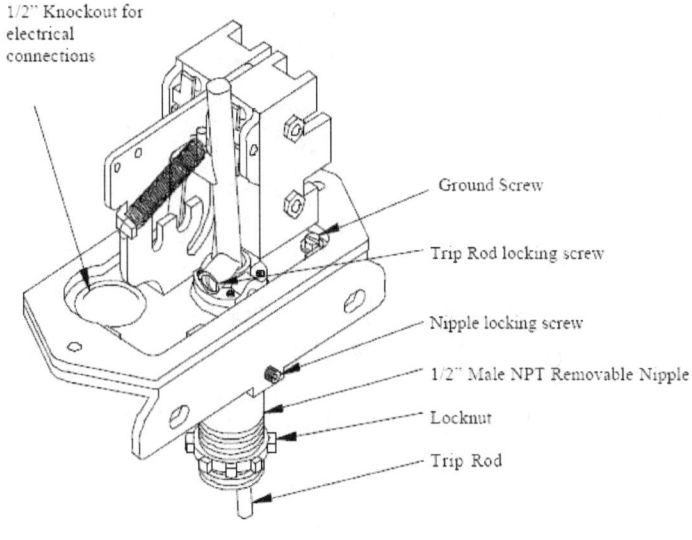

1/2" Knockout for electrical connections

Ground Screw

Trip Rod locking screw

Nipple locking screw

1/2" Male NPT Removable Nipple

Locknut

Trip Rod

An actual PIV tamper switch from Potter Electric

The device that generates the actual fire alarm however, is the water flow switch. This is a deceptively simple device consisting of a plastic paddle and an electric switch.

Water Flow Switch from Potter Electric

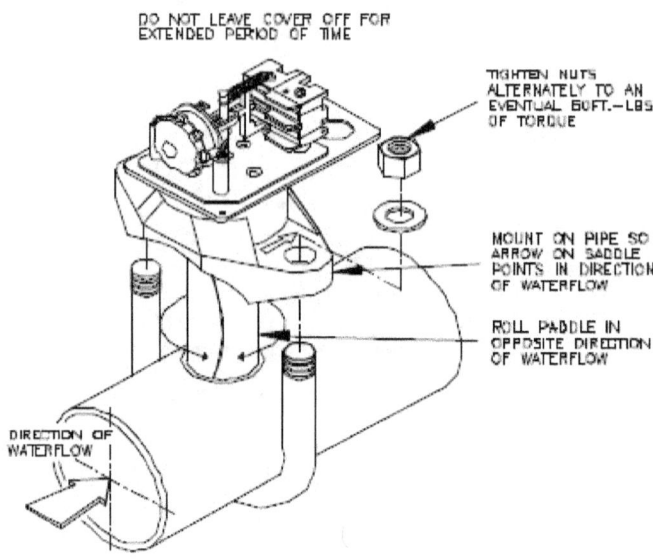

As you can see, a plastic paddle or vane is installed inside the sprinkler riser pipe. Since the water is static in a sprinkler system, the paddle remains stationary and no alarm occurs.

If a sprinkler head discharges, the water in the sprinkler system will begin to flow and that will cause the paddle in the flow switch to move, which in turn closes the switch, which then generates an alarm.

Since city water pressure does fluctuate occasionally, which could cause the paddle to move slightly, fire monitoring systems have a built in "retard". The retard is a time delay of 10-30 seconds. If the paddle should move, it must remain in the changed position past the retard time for the alarm to be generated. If your building is experiencing false water flow alarms (which frequently happens if there is major construction in the vicinity) then the retard time probably needs to be increased. The retard is set either at the water flow switch itself or programmed into the fire control panel.

Fire Control Panel

All these devices need a control panel or transmitter. The control panel contains the intelligence required to monitor the devices and transmit the alarm. On smaller systems the fire control panel also transmits the alarm. On larger systems, a fire control panel handles the control portion and a separate transmitter handles the alarm signal.

Fire alarm systems consist of a keypad or annunciator that acts as a user interface and the control panel. The control panel not only monitors the fire detection devices but also the wiring, the power, the standby battery, and the phone line.

A typical Fire Monitoring panel from Digital Monitoring Products
Showing all the accessories required

Fire Monitoring Panel Keypad / Display / Annunciator

The keypad is the part of the system you usually see since it is required to be mounted in a central location such as the front lobby reception area. The keypad is typically red and displays alarms, trouble conditions, or supervisory messages. It is used to reset or silence the alarm- as well as programming the panel by the installer or service technicians.

Sufficient standby batteries must be installed to provide complete system functions for at least 5 minutes – after 24 hours of power outage. In other words, the system must function flawlessly even if the city power is out for up to 24 hours straight.

Fire codes in effect after 1996 also require a smoke detector to be installed above or in the same room as the fire panel. This is to provide early warning if a fire threatens the fire panel itself.

Although modern fire control panels are fully capable of doing both fire and burglar alarm monitoring, fire departments usually do not allow this. Fire monitoring must be separate from security.

EOL (End of Line) Supervision

Just a word on "supervision"- this is a term used to describe how a fire panel insures that all the wiring in a security system is intact. Supervision makes sure that no wires are cut when the system is disarmed or armed. A resistor of a specific value- usually 3000 ohms- is placed across the circuit at each detection device then the control panel sends a constant voltage through this circuit and measures it. If the voltage drops or the current increases, the panel senses the change as either a short or open and alerts the user or transmits a trouble signal.

Communication

A phone line is required to transmit the fire alarm to the central station. National fire codes (National Fire Protection Association NFPA 72) requires two forms of communication. This is usually accomplished with two voice grade phone lines but newer systems can use the internet.

Once the control panel detects an alarm it transmits the information to the central station where it is decoded by an alarm receiver and displayed to an operator. The operator will see an exact description of the location and type of alarm signal. Depending on the type of signal, the operator will then notify the fire department.

The system communicates to the central monitoring station by phone lines. Residences can use the phone line already there but many alarm companies prefer businesses install a **dedicated phone line** just for the alarm. This is not bad advice. Although it increases your total monthly cost, a dedicated line reduces the chance the alarm control won't be able to get through to the central station. If the intrusion system can't dial out and deliver the alarm message, the central station won't be aware you have an alarm condition.

Newer alarm systems (and more advanced monitoring companies) now offer "internet" monitoring. Instead of the traditional phone line they use broadband Internet access such as DSL or cable. Some systems continuously monitor the condition of the line and can warn if the connection is lost. These are highly recommended because of their speed and security. The cost is usually very much in line with dedicated voice phone lines. Plus if you already have Internet access, the alarm transmission is essentially free.

Whichever type of communication you use, ensure the phone line is protected where it enters the building. This is something to be especially aware of in residential applications. You don't want the phone line exposed where someone can easily cut it- accidentally or on purpose.

Fire monitoring systems installed after about 1996 will have a few additional devices. Besides the keypad / annunciator installed in the lobby, newer national fire codes (NFPA 72) now require a horn / strobe to also be mounted in a manned area near the main entrance to the premises.

The reason for this was the subject of much discussion in the fire industry prior to 1996. Water flow alarms were typically silent and often the fire department would show up at a building because an alarm was generated to the central monitoring station but the occupants were unaware of it. The horn / strobe was mandated to provide some notification to the occupants without the expense of a complete evacuation system.

This same code also requires one manual pull station to be installed "as an alternate means of summoning the fire department". This pull station (if installed) is usually at the fire panel or the same location as the keypad. Some jurisdictions do not require it be installed at all however.

Knox Boxes

Although not strictly a part of the fire system, most jurisdictions require a key safe mounted outside the building for the fire department's use. Commonly called "Knox Boxes" in some areas (because they are made by the Knox Company), these boxes are tiny vaults set into the wall of the building about 8 to 10 feet off the ground (so a ladder is required to access them). These vaults all use the same master key to open them which is in the possession of the fire department trucks. Inside the Knox box will be a key to the building so the fire department does not have to force entry or break down a door.

Knox boxes are typically also monitored so someone will be notified if the box is opened. If the building has an intrusion (burglar alarm) system, then the Knox box is usually monitored by it. In some cases the box is monitored by the fire system.

Typical Knox-Boxes by the Knox Company

Fire Permits

Most localities and jurisdictions require the building owner (or installer) obtain a fire alarm permit before any type of fire alarm system can be installed. In order to obtain such a permit, a complete set of blueprints detailing the fire alarm system is required. The plans must show the location of all fire devices, quantities, wiring, and mathematical calculations proving the finished system will function to code.

These plans are usually provided by the alarm contractor and will cost several hundred dollars due to the complexity of what must be provided. Even a simple water flow monitoring system must indicate the entire building floor plan, the location of all fire sprinkler risers and valves as well as the fire monitoring devices.

Calculations such as standby battery capacity and backup time, voltage drop of audible devices, and conduit sizes must be shown.

Data sheets and approvals of all fire monitoring devices must be submitted and finally the actual methods of wiring the system must be shown.

Fire systems must conform to national and local codes so the plans must essentially prove this compliance before a permit will be issued. After the permit, a fire inspector will be scheduled to come out and test the system.

This protects the property manager by insuring the fire alarm functions correctly.

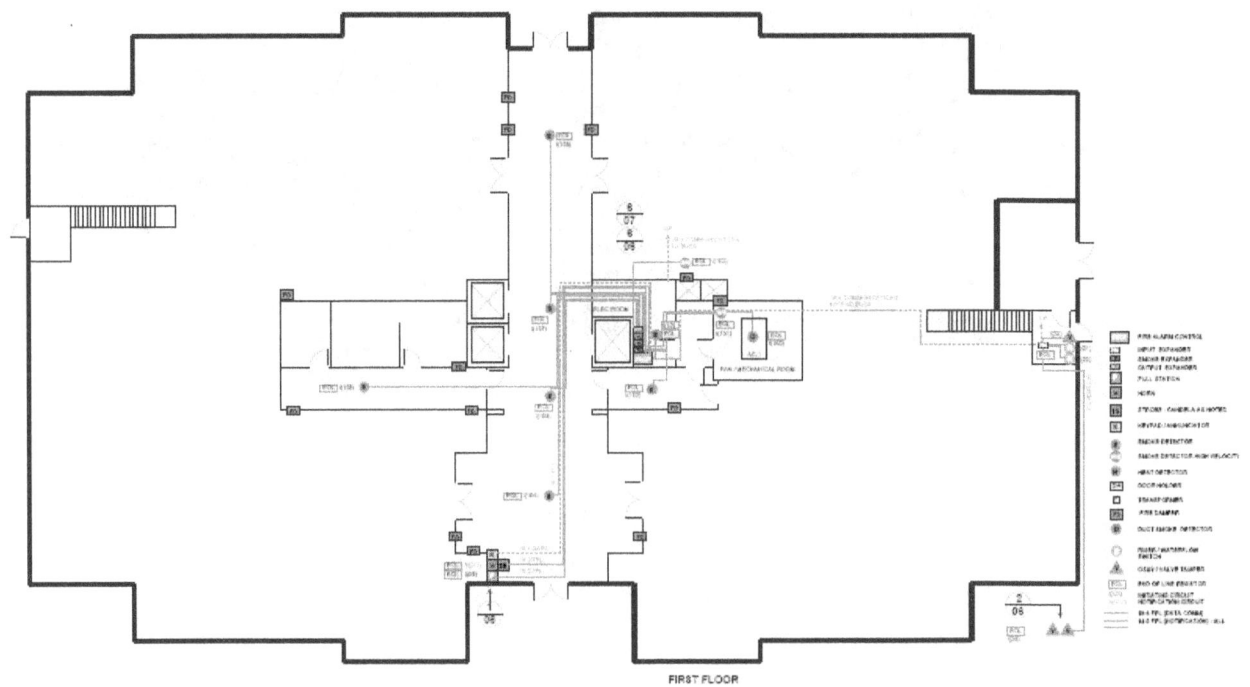

An example of a fire alarm floor plan for submittal

Monitoring

The fire system is usually monitored by some outside party. While you could simply just sound a siren or ring a bell upon an alarm, it is pretty clear this wouldn't accomplish much unless you have neighbors that are present 24 hours a day and willing to call the fire department. The fire department themselves almost never accept alarms directly, so the only alternative is to contract with a central monitoring station. Usually, the alarm company that installs and services your alarm will monitor it. In some cases they may contract it out to a third party.

In any case, the monitoring company is obviously critically important. The safety of your property ultimately depends on their action or inaction. When an alarm is received at the central station, an operator must interpret it and take the appropriate action- such as notifying the fire department. Sounds simple doesn't it? The problems arise when the operator must begin to make judgment calls regarding the signals.

Some things you do want to insist on are "Call Lists" and pass codes. The central station will maintain a list of names and phone numbers to call on alarms or other kinds of trouble or questions. Make sure this list is always up to date. It's not fun coming to work on Monday morning to find your property suffered a fire into and no one was notified because all the phone numbers were bad.

Also make sure the pass words or code words are current and sensible. The central station will issue you, and whoever else you request, a pass code word or number to be used when communicating with them. If you need to speak to someone at the central station because you accidentally set off the alarm, they will ask you to identify yourself by this code.

UL - Underwriter's Laboratories

Yes the same organization that labels electric cords also maintains standards for fire & burglar alarm system for the insurance industry.

A UL listed system has extremely stiff requirements. The alarm company must be UL listed, the monitoring company must be UL listed (often one and the same), and the equipment used in the burglar alarm system must be UL listed. Then the system must be installed to UL standards and serviced and monitored to UL standards!

Whether your insurance company requires a UL listing or not, it's still a great indication of a particular alarm company's capabilities. It's very tough to get a UL listing and keep it so if the alarm company you're talking to has a UL listing you can be assured of top quality equipment, service and monitoring.

Fire Warning Systems

Also referred to as Life Safety or Evacuation systems, these types of fire alarms are designed to warn building occupants to evacuate the premises. These systems consist of manual pull stations, fire horns, and fire strobes at a minimum but are usually combined with other fire suppression and fire detection devices to comprise a complete fire alarm system.

Fire alarm devices are typically separated into two groups – Initiating and Notification. Horns and strobes are Notification devices while manual pulls are examples of Initiating devices.

Fire warning systems are fairly complex and must be designed to strict standards. In order to pull a fire permit (which will always be required for these types of systems) a very detailed set of blueprints will have to be generated.

One of the most complex tasks of the designer will be to insure the system complies with the fire code that deals with the ADA or American's with Disabilities Act. Essentially, this requires visual warning devices called strobes for the hearing impaired. Such strobes come in various intensities and each intensity covers a different size area. As an example, a wall mounted 110 candela (cd) strobe has an effective area of 54 feet by 54 feet. This means multiple strobes would have to be installed to cover a large area.

The NFPA 72 fire code is rather specific about placement of strobes while audible devices (fire horns) only need to be in sufficient quantity to be clearly audible above ambient noise – usually considered to be 15 decibels above ambient noise level. Strobes will need to be placed in common areas such as hallways, restrooms, and conference rooms. Most jurisdictions will also require them in open office areas with cubicles.

A typical Fire Horn / Strobe combination unit by Wheelock

Fire horns and strobes come in many different configurations and designs. There are both wall mount and ceiling mount units available but both have different ratings. Ceiling mount units are usually more effective since they are not blocked as easily as wall units but cover less overall area and require more power to drive them. Strobes are always required in "common areas" such as restrooms, meeting rooms, and conference rooms.

An alternative to horns – and common in high rise buildings- is the fire speaker. The speaker can generate warning tones and voice instructions. Pre-recorded voice messages inform the occupants to evacuate the building.

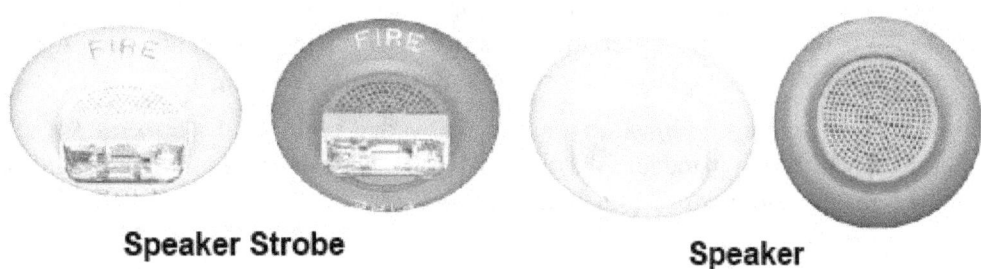

Speaker Strobe   **Speaker**

Speakers come with and without strobes so combinations can be used. Generally speaking, speaker systems are more expensive than horns since special audio amplifiers are required and must be duplicated so there is a backup.

Fire speaker systems are not to be used as public address systems and in most jurisdictions it is illegal to use one except in an emergency. Since the only microphone is in the fire control room it is usually not possible anyway. But many customers and property managers don't understand this restriction. It is really for the concern of occupants since the fire system is critical to life safety.

Such audible voice warning systems are taken over by fire department personnel when they arrive on scene to help direct the evacuation since high rise buildings often contain thousands of occupants.

Manual pull stations

Pull stations must be installed at every exit on every floor and not more than 200 feet apart. There is some "wiggle" room in the placement of manual pull stations depending on the specific building design but at a minimum there should be one near every fire exit.

Pulls station come in many variations. Older models used a glass rod to deter people from pulling the handle. Once the pull station is used, the glass rod breaks so it is evident which station was pulled. The glass rod must be replaced before the station can be used again.

Newer manuals use a key reset. Once the manual is pulled, a key is required to reset it and close the handle. Building owners and managers should insure they have either a supply of glass rods or the proper key on hand to reset manual pull stations.

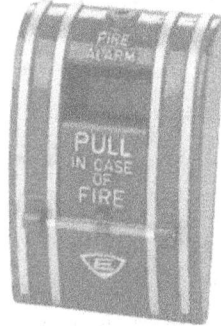

A "break glass" manual pull

by Edwards Signal

A key reset manual pull

by Potter Signal

If you experience false alarms from vandals tampering with manual pulls then a device exists to deter this. A person must lift a cover to access the actual manual. Lifting the cover activates a local horn which will hopefully scare off any vandals but would be ignored by someone who truly needs to report a fire.

Safety Technology Inc "Stopper"

Fire Control Panel

As fire systems get more complex- such as in the case of evacuation systems, a more intelligent fire control panel is needed to run, monitor, and power all the devices. Large and complex fire alarms can consist of hundreds or even thousands of initiating and notification devices. Voice evacuation systems also require large audio amplifiers for all the speakers.

Fire Control panels are always located out of harms way in fire control rooms or electrical or telephone rooms. Because of this, graphic or LCD annunciators are installed in common areas to notify occupants of trouble with the same or specific information about alarms.

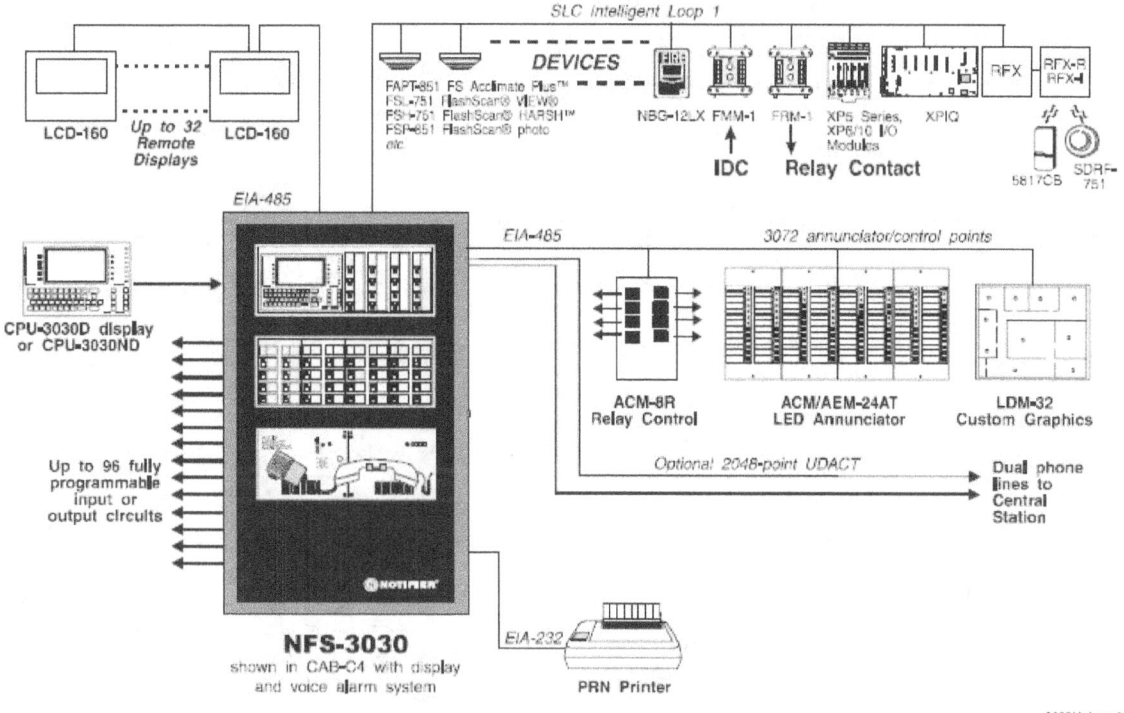

A system diagram by Notifier

This type of fire panel can also have built in audio amplifiers for fire speaker systems as well as many relays for controlling fire dampers and exhaust fans.

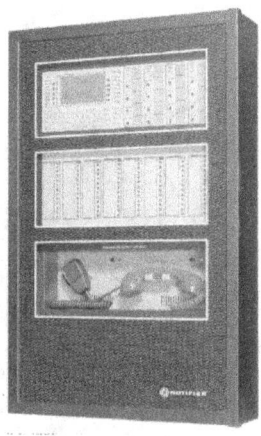

An actual Notifer Fire Control Panel

Fire panels and devices at this level have a significant degree of intelligence. They can determine and adjust the sensitivity of smoke detectors for example, and notify technicians when service is required,- before it becomes an issue.

They have extensive programs which control all the functions of the complete system. For example: if a particular smoke detector trips then energize a specific relay to close a fire damper.

These fire panels can also be networked across many buildings to provide a complete campus wide fire alarm system.

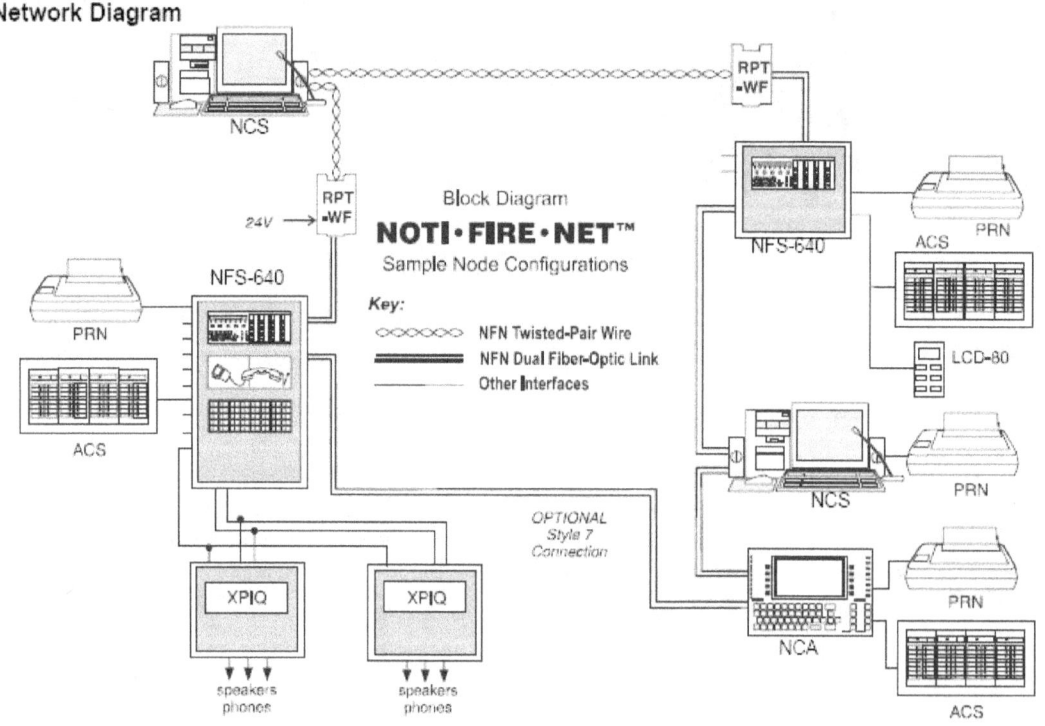

Fire Detection Systems

There are still more types of fire alarm devices and systems. As we discussed, a fire monitoring system typically just monitors the condition of a fire sprinkler or suppression system. But fire suppression systems only act *after* a fire has started. Fire detection systems can provide early warning of an impending fire.

The best example of fire detection is the common *smoke detector*. A smoke detector, as the name implies, detects smoke using a tiny photoelectric cell. Smoke passes between the photocell sensor where the detector measures it to prevent false alarms from dust particles. These photocells are so sensitive they can detect smoke before it becomes readily visible to the naked eye.

A Smoke detector by System Sensor

Smoke detectors have the most varied designs of all fire devices. They come in hundreds of shapes and styles but one characteristic is always present- a series of holes or grills to allow smoke to enter the detector.

Smoke detectors are tested with a magnet:

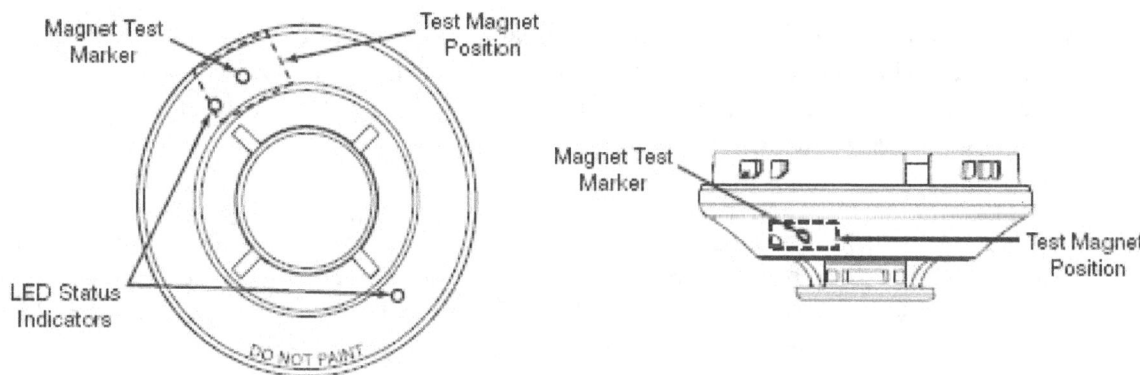

Similar to smoke detectors are **smoke beams**. These are exactly like the active infrared beams used in intrusion systems and need a transmitter and receiver. When smoke passes between them, it causes an alarm. These are used in large open areas such as churches, gymnasiums, and atriums.

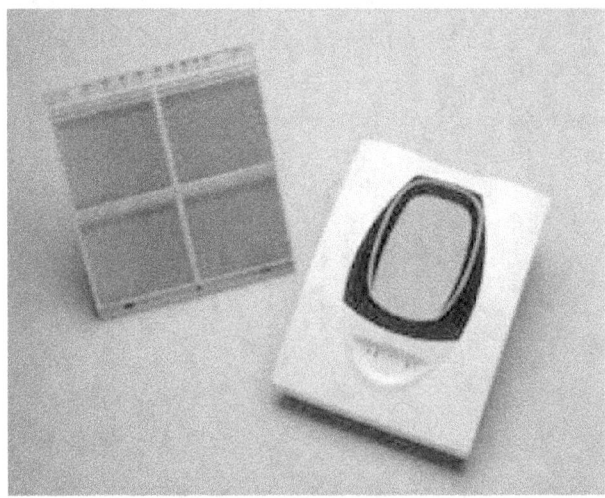

A Smoke Beam by System Sensor.

This particular design uses a reflector to bounce the beam back to the transmitter / receiver. Others use a separate transmitter and receiver.

Elevator Recall

In most jurisdictions, more than 8 feet of elevator travel will also require an **elevator recall** system. This consists of smoke detectors in each elevator lobby which may or may not be part of the sprinkler and fire monitoring system although 90% of the time, these are combined into one system. Activation of any smoke detector must bring all elevator cabs to the first floor – or an alternate floor should the first floor smokes detect smoke.

Recent code changes have dictated additional smoke & heat detectors in elevator shafts and machine rooms. These devices must shut off power to the elevator controllers in case of fire and are typically called "shunts" They are connected so both a heat and a smoke must go into alarm before any action takes place.

HVAC

Air handler units which produce more than 2000 CFM (cubic feet per minute) of air flow will also require Duct Smoke Detectors. These are specialized smoke detectors installed near the air conditioning ducts. A sampling tube is inserted into the actual duct work and carries sample air to the detector. If smoke is sensed, the detectors send a signal either directly to the air handler- or through the fire control panel to shut down. By shutting down the air handler, smoke is prevented from traveling throughout the building.

A typical Duct Detector with the sampling tube on the left rear.

Most fire departments do not consider the duct detector to be a fire warning device but only a fire supervisory device so no alarm is usually generated. Check local codes before making any assumptions however.

Since Duct Smoke Detectors are hidden away inside air conditioning ducts, they usually come with a Remote Test & Reset Station. This is a key operated station from which you can test the detector or reset it if it goes into alarm.

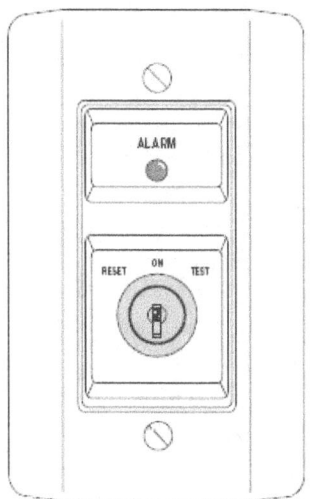

Remote Duct Detector Test Station

Heat Detectors

In very hot areas, heat detectors replace smoke detectors. These alarm when a fixed temperature is reached- typically 190 degrees but there are type that also measure the **rate of rise**. If the temperature suddenly increases dramatically, the detector trips and signals an alarm. Heat and smoke detectors are often used in combination in different areas of the building.

Heat detectors are typically only used in buildings without fire sprinklers and can be mounted above the ceiling, in attics, in garages, or other areas a smoke detector is not appropriate because of the environment.

A typical Heat Detector

An important point about heat detectors- they are usually one time use only. In other words, once a heat detector trips into alarm, it must be replaced. Also, it is very important never to paint a heat detector (nor a smoke detector for that matter) because that will negate its heat sensing abilities.

How do you tell a heat detector from a smoke detector? The smoke detector is usually larger and has holes or grills to allow smoke to enter the detector body. Unfortunately, some heat detectors also have grills so the best way to tell is to look closely at the detector itself, it should be labeled as a heat detector.

Fire System Technology

Most of these fire control panels and devices are **addressable**. This means each device has a unique identity so alarms and problems can be pinpointed to the exact device. This is extremely helpful in determining the location of a fire as well as for maintenance and service. Addressable systems also use less wire since typically a two wire data loop is all that's required to connect hundreds of smoke detectors and manual pull stations.

Fire Codes and system design

There are many and varied codes and regulations governing fire alarm systems. Because systems must meet these codes to the letter, they require very specific design and quantities of devices. You may be surprised to learn that in many jurisdictions you can't just install one smoke detector in a specific area. Systems have to be designed and installed to code. Fire codes are designed to offer sufficient level of protection and not lull owners into a false sense of security.

If your building is seven floors and above it is usually considered a high rise and a full fire evacuation system will be required. If your building falls into these categories you should already have these systems so we'll just cover some items of which you may not be aware. The most important of which being periodic testing.

Many very large warehouses will require engine driven fire pumps and all the associated monitoring. Some jurisdictions will require manual fire pull stations and be advised that travel paths in excess of 200 feet are not permitted.

Some jurisdictions look at the height of the storage racks. Referred to as "high pile storage" or high rack storage, these codes can require in-rack sprinklers and smoke detectors. **AHJs** (Authority Having Jurisdiction- usually the fire inspector) have even required hazardous material handling designations for foodstuffs, such as cooking oil. In these situations it may be advisable to hire a good local consultant to go to bat for you with local city and county governments.

Testing of a New Fire System

Once a fire alarm permit is issued, it will require a test and inspection by a fire department inspector. You should require the fire alarm contractor to perform a pre-test before the fire inspector comes out to make sure everything is in order.

Insist on a thorough point by point test in your presence and offer to help. This is where a detailed equipment list comes in, you can check off each device as you go. You will also learn much about the system in the course of testing it. We have seen so many instances where the customer was too busy on completion day and just signs it off instead of actively participating in the testing.

Test each device for functionality. For example, each water flow, each valve tamper, each smoke detector if installed. Have the installer disconnect one wire from a manual pull and make sure the keypad displays some trouble indication.

While time consuming, testing of all HVAC Duct detectors and fire dampers is critical as well.

Service on the Fire Alarm

Unfortunately, many fire alarm companies fail when it comes to service. It is widely known in the industry that many contractors do not service their customers- they are mainly in it for the initial installation. When you're evaluating bids take this into consideration and always ask references about their service experience after the sale.

Service departments are expensive to run and rarely pay for themselves unless they maintain service contracts with customers. Even when a company does provide service it is not always the best. Most service departments will consist of both newer and more experienced technicians.

Frequently companies will send out the newer techs first because the experienced one is busy doing the difficult calls. Although companies track what is known as "call backs" – having to go back a second or third time to fix a problem- it is still very common. You can fully expect not to have a problem fixed the first time unless it is very simple.

We will give you a tip that in virtually every company there is at least one guru who can fix your system. This person is protected and hard to communicate with- quite naturally because he is busy. He may be a manager, or engineer, or just a senior technician but if you persist and ask for them, you will eventually get to them and have your problem solved.

If you want good service from your fire alarm contractor then you must be selective when first contracting for the system. Let's face it many property managers will choose the lowest cost provider to install the system and then wonder why it is so difficult to get service.

Base your decision on which company provides the best service first.

Periodic Fire Alarm Testing

Routine testing s required by the national fire code NFPA 72. Many localities require special sprinkler system tests every five years. These are completed by a sprinkler company, not the alarm company. The fire alarm monitoring company is required to test the monitoring portion of the sprinkler system at least twice a year. The elevator recall smoke detectors should also be tested at the same time. The evacuation system is required to be tested at least once a year.

Testing Frequencies for Fire Alarm System Devices		
Device Type	Testing Frequency	Notes
Control Panel Devices	Annually	
Engine Driven Generators	Weekly	
Control Unit Trouble Signals	Annually	
Emergency Voice Alarm Equipment	Annually	
Remote Annunciators	Annually	
Duct, heat, and smoke detectors	Annually	Functional test
Magnetic door holders	Annually	
Valve tamper switches	Semiannually	
Water flow devices	Semiannually	
Horns, strobes	Semiannually	
Digital Dialers	Annually	

Building owners and property managers are not only allowed but encouraged to test their own systems. If you do; be sure to keep records of all tests as outlined by NFPA. See the back of this guide for the form.

Testing Procedures

Water Flow Testing

1. NFPA Requires semi-annual testing of water flow monitoring devices.
2. Flow switches are required by UL to trip between 4 to 10 gpm (gallons per minute). Most all flow switches trip at close to 10gpm. Except the VS-G which trips at 3gpm.
3. A proper flow test consists of opening an inspectors test valve which is usually a 1/2" ball valve or a ball valve with a reduced orifice equal to the smallest sprinkler in the premises and flowing water until the device trips.

4. If a device does not pass a flow test:

Remove the cover and move the trip rod by hand, does it move freely? If it does not, remove the device and check for obstructions in the pipe. Check to make sure the device moves freely when it is not installed. If it does not, replace it.

For the screw in flow switches models VSR-SF, VS-SP, VSR-SFG, VSR-SFT, make sure the correct paddle is installed for the size and type of tee the device is installed in. Also make sure that the device is installed in the proper tee and is installed in the correct manner.

Was the paddle trimmed when the device was installed? If yes, replace the device

DO NOT TRIM THE PADDLE.

Does the test valve go directly to a drain? It should **not** go through a hose. Hoses create friction loss. If it must go through a hose, the hose ID should be at least 1/2" and as short and straight as possible.

To determine the flow rate place a 5 gallon bucket under the test valve and open the valve for 30 seconds. If the bucket fills, the flow rate is at least 10 gpm. If it is not 10gpm it may not trip.

Testing Pressure Switches

1. The BVL (Bleeder valve) should be used to test pressure switches that are used to detect a drop in pressure.

2. The BVL is a 1/2" ball valve with a small hole drilled in one end. The valve is normally kept open. When it is closed it will bleed of the pressure from the valve to the pressure switch. This allows the person performing the test to only bleed off the small amount of pressure between the valve and the pressure switch instead of bleeding off the pressure in the entire system. This not only saves time and money, it also prevents accidental tripping of a dry pipe valve by bleeding too much air off the system.

3. The BVL should be connected in line with the pressure switch and a pressure gauge. When the valve is slowly closed, the person performing the test can watch the pressure drop on the gauge to determine that the pressure switch is tripping at the proper pressure.

Testing Smoke Detectors

Use either canned smoke (available from alarm supply houses) or a magnet mounted on a long stick (preferred method). See the detailed illustration in the smoke detector section

Sprinkler System Testing & Maintenance

NFPA Journal®, *July/August 2005*

One cannot overemphasize the importance of maintaining and testing a fire alarm system, the responsibility for which falls squarely on the system's owner. Testing the entire system and its components will verify the correct operation of the system, as well as the correct location of its components as originally designed.

One way to ensure that a fire alarm system is properly maintained and tested is to follow the minimum requirements found in Chapter 10 of NFPA 72®, National Fire Alarm Code®, which cover new and existing fire alarm systems as well as single- and multiple-station smoke and heat alarms and household fire alarm systems. NFPA 72 allows a building owner to maintain and test systems in accordance with requirements that exceed those of the code, such as those imposed by some insurers, but not with those that fail to meet the code's requirements.

Before testing begins, NFPA 72 requires that "all persons and facilities receiving alarm, supervisory, or trouble signals and all building occupants" be notified of the testing to prevent them from responding unnecessarily. Because the very act of testing a fire alarm system impairs its normal operation, leaving occupants without the protection the system normally provides, the service technicians and the occupants should fully understand the procedures to follow should a real alarm occur during the test impairment. Notifying the occupants that testing has concluded and that they should treat any alarm from that point forward as a true alarm is equally important.

NFPA 72 also requires the owner and service technicians to coordinate the testing to prevent interruption of critical building systems equipment and the inadvertent operation of suppression systems connected to the fire alarm system.

Since the initial testing of a fire alarm system sets the base line of operation against which the system's continued performance will be measured, owners must also understand that all "building modifications, occupancy changes, changes in environmental conditions, device location, physical obstructions, device orientation, physical damage, improper installation, degree of cleanliness, or other obvious problems that might not be indicated through electrical supervision" (A-10.3.1) can affect system performance. If a visual inspection of the system discloses any of these conditions, qualified persons should correct the condition immediately. Once the repairs have been made, technicians should perform additional testing to ensure the system will operate properly. NFPA 72 also requires those doing the testing to notify, in writing, the owner or the owner's designated representative of any impairment found and not corrected within 24 hours.

Section 10.4.2.2 of NFPA 72 requires testing all fire alarm systems and all equipment or systems associated or interfaced with fire alarm systems in accordance with the methods outlined in Table 10.4.2.2. Testing frequencies should comply with those outlined in Table 10.4.3.

Whether you own a protected building, operate a service company, or work as an authority having jurisdiction, using the requirements and methods outlined in Chapter 10 of the National Fire Alarm Code will help you ensure the operational reliability of fire alarm systems.

Wayne D. Moore, P.E., FSFPE, is chair of the National Fire Alarm Code Technical Correlating Committee.

Fire Drills

All these tests will cause some disruption of your tenants- especially the evacuation system. Consequently there is enormous pressure to put it off or do a partial test. Don't fall into that trap. The liability of not performing life safety inspections and tests is mind boggling.

The experts will tell you that fire drills are essential in getting people out of buildings safely. Research has shown over and over that practicing makes people less afraid and gives them more confidence in an emergency. During the 9/11 attack on the twin towers in New York, those people who had previously participated in fire drills or had experience in evacuating buildings or been in actual fires, got out safely and led many others down as well.

Fear paralyzes people. The best way to overcome fear is to learn about what to do and the best way to learn is practice. The larger the building the less you'll want to conduct fire drills because there is so much disruption. To keep this disruption to a minimum, combine the annual fire tests and fire drills.

Schedule the evacuation system test and a fire drill together. When your tenants hear the fire alarm sounding they can be advised that a fire drill is underway. This way you'll also have as close to an actual simulation as possible; and meet all the requirements.

Of course, this requires some preparation. Meet with your security or fire contractor and develop a plan for the test. Each tenant manager should be provided with clear written instructions listing the date and time of the test. That document should contain clear instructions of what to expect, where to go, how to go, (the elevator will not be usable since they will automatically go to the ground floor and remain there); and a map of where to gather once they are out of the building. For example, have the 1st through the 4th floors people meet in the front. Have the 5th through the 8th meet in the rear, and so on.

You should assign each floor tenant areas to meet so your security people or assistants can insure everyone got out. Each tenant manager should be responsible for checking off their employees and they should in turn provide their check off list to you. You will in turn have a list of all tenants to check off.

A very important note to add to your notice of the fire drill is a liability release. Such a release should accomplish two vital terms:

 1. it should release the building manager and owner of any damages resulting from the fire drill and

2. it should release the building owner and manager of any liability resulting in the future from NOT participating in the fire drill.

This way you are covered in any event.

FIRE ALARM Liability concerns

Liability can be one of the most complex and Byzantine subjects imaginable. This section is designed to help you avoid liability with simple suggestions; but always consult an attorney with any questions. Legal actions resulting in damages are most likely going to occur when you own or manage a facility where the general public has access; although your own employees are certainly cause for concern. Liability usually results if it can be shown that you did not take sufficient action to prevent physical harm to someone.

Some examples of actual cases may be in order. We were involved with a large software company that was building a new headquarters campus consisting of four buildings. Since the occupancy initially was B (Business) nothing special was required by the fire code except sprinkler monitoring because each building contained more than 100 sprinkler heads.

During the final design stages, it was decided to add a large meeting room sufficient for employees from all four building to attend. This created an occupancy load for that room only above 300 people and made it an A (assembly) occupancy. This in turn mandated a fire life safety evacuation system (horns and strobes) for that area. Typically in most jurisdictions, this would have required the whole building containing the A occupancy to comply and install a full fire evacuation system throughout. The fire department in this case negotiated with the architect and decided that the system only needed to be in that one room.

The fire alarm contractor was asked to provide such a system for the meeting room only but objected due to potential liability on their part. The reasoning was solid- what if a fire broke out in another part of the building and occupants were not warned and someone was injured or killed? It could be argued in court that the company chose to protect some people in the meeting room but not other employees due to cost considerations. What do you think a jury would decide?

The software company requested a legal opinion from their lawyers, who agreed with the security contractor. Install the fire evacuation system in the entire building. This was done and later when all four buildings were occupied, an employee safety committee recommended that the fire evacuation system be extended to all four buildings. Since the situation was now a matter of record, the company agreed and all four buildings have fire evacuation systems that actually exceed fire codes.

This same logic can be applied to all types of fire alarms. Suppose you had horns and strobes installed in an executive headquarters building but not in the other buildings. An employee is then injured during a fire in one of those other buildings. Can you imagine their attorney arguing in court- "The Company installed a life safety system for the executives but was too cheap to do the same for the employees".

The key is to apply all fire systems evenly to all areas.

Applicable Codes and Standards

The main recognized governing authority for fire alarms and sprinkler systems is the National Fire Protection Association (NFPA). Sprinklers are covered under NFPA 10 and fire alarms are regulated under NFPA 72.

There are other standards such as the Uniform Building Code and Uniform Fire Code but most jurisdictions have adopted NFPA 72 in part or all into their local codes. Keep in mind however that editions of the NFPA 72 change from year to year and some jurisdictions require compliance with certain years. As this is written for example, most fire autorities are still on the 1999 version.

Here are some handy references for hard to find sections of the various codes:

NFPA 101 References: (1997)

Manual Pull Minimums	7-6.2.3
Manual Pull Travel	7-6.2.4
Manual Pull Required for Water flow	7-6.2.5

NFPA 72 References: (1999)

24 Hour Standby / 5 Minutes Alarm	1-5.2.6
Smoke Detector by FACP	1-5.6
Manual Pull Locations	2-8.2.2
Within 5 ft of exit opening	
Each exit, each floor	
Manual Pull by FACP	3-8.3.1.2
Air Handlers	3-9.5
Placard	1-6.2.3.2

UFC References (1997)

Sprinkler Monitoring – All valves	1003.3.1
Horn / Strobe for Occupant Notification	1003.3.2

NEC References (1996)

Fire Alarms	760	
Fire Alarms Underground		
(Circuits extending outside building)	800-11	
	800-51	
Underground Circuits	225-4	
Wet Locations required	310-8	TW THW THHW THWN type wire

INSPECTION AND TESTING FORM

DATE: _____

TIME: _____

SERVICE ORGANIZATION

Name: _____

Address: _____

Representative: _____

License No.: _____

Telephone: _____

MONITORING ENTITY

Contact: _____

Telephone: _____

Monitoring Account Ref. No.: _____

TYPE TRANSMISSION
- ❏ McCulloh
- ❏ Multiplex
- ❏ Digital
- ❏ Reverse Priority
- ❏ RF
- ❏ Other (Specify) _____

Control Unit Manufacturer: _____

Circuit Styles: _____

Number of Circuits: _____

Software Rev.: _____

PROPERTY NAME (USER)

Name: _____

Address: _____

Owner Contact: _____

Telephone: _____

APPROVING AGENCY

Contact: _____

Telephone: _____

SERVICE
- ❏ Weekly
- ❏ Monthly
- ❏ Quarterly
- ❏ Semiannually
- ❏ Annually
- ❏ Other (Specify) _____

Model No.: _____

Last Date System Had Any Service Performed: _____

Last Date that Any Software or Configuration Was Revised: _____

ALARM-INITIATING DEVICES AND CIRCUIT INFORMATION

Quantity	Circuit Style	
_____	_____	Manual Fire Alarm Boxes
_____	_____	Ion Detectors
_____	_____	Photo Detectors
_____	_____	Duct Detectors
_____	_____	Heat Detectors
_____	_____	Waterflow Switches
_____	_____	Supervisory Switches
_____	_____	Other (Specify): _____

Alarm verification feature is disabled _____ enabled _____.

(NFPA Inspection and Testing, 1 of 4)

FIGURE 10.6.2.3 Example of an Inspection and Testing Form.

ALARM NOTIFICATION APPLIANCES AND CIRCUIT INFORMATION

Quantity   Circuit Style

_____   _____   Bells
_____   _____   Horns
_____   _____   Chimes
_____   _____   Strobes
_____   _____   Speakers
_____   _____   Other (Specify): _____

No. of alarm notification appliance circuits: _____
Are circuits monitored for integrity? ❑ Yes ❑ No

SUPERVISORY SIGNAL-INITIATING DEVICES AND CIRCUIT INFORMATION

Quantity   Circuit Style

_____   _____   Building Temp.
_____   _____   Site Water Temp.
_____   _____   Site Water Level
_____   _____   Fire Pump Power
_____   _____   Fire Pump Running
_____   _____   Fire Pump Auto Position
_____   _____   Fire Pump or Pump Controller Trouble
_____   _____   Fire Pump Running
_____   _____   Generator In Auto Position
_____   _____   Generator or Controller Trouble
_____   _____   Switch Transfer
_____   _____   Generator Engine Running
_____   _____   Other: _____

SIGNALING LINE CIRCUITS

Quantity and style of signaling line circuits connected to system (see NFPA 72, Table 6.6.1):
Quantity_____ Style(s)_____

SYSTEM POWER SUPPLIES

(a) Primary (Main): Nominal Voltage _____ Amps _____
Overcurrent Protection: Type _____ Amps _____
Location (of Primary Supply Panelboard): _____
Disconnecting Means Location: _____
(b) Secondary (Standby):
_____ Storage Battery: Amp-Hr. Rating _____
Calculated capacity to operate system, in hours: _____ 24 _____ 60
_____ Engine-driven generator dedicated to fire alarm system:
Location of fuel storage: _____

TYPE BATTERY

❑ Dry Cell
❑ Nickel-Cadmium
❑ Sealed Lead-Acid
❑ Lead-Acid
❑ Other (Specify):

(c) Emergency or standby system used as a backup to primary power supply, instead of using a secondary power supply:
_____ Emergency system described in NFPA 70, Article 700
_____ Legally required standby described in NFPA 70, Article 701
_____ Optional standby system described in NFPA 70, Article 702, which also meets the performance requirements of Article 700 or 701.

(NFPA Inspection and Testing, 2 of 4)

FIGURE 10.6.2.3 *Continued*

PRIOR TO ANY TESTING

NOTIFICATIONS ARE MADE	Yes	No	Who	Time
Monitoring Entity	❏	❏	_____	_____
Building Occupants	❏	❏	_____	_____
Building Management	❏	❏	_____	_____
Other (Specify)	❏	❏	_____	_____
AHJ Notified of Any Impairments	❏	❏	_____	_____

SYSTEM TESTS AND INSPECTIONS

TYPE	Visual	Functional	Comments
Control Unit	❏	❏	_____
Interface Equipment	❏	❏	_____
Lamps/LEDS	❏	❏	_____
Fuses	❏	❏	_____
Primary Power Supply	❏	❏	_____
Trouble Signals	❏	❏	_____
Disconnect Switches	❏	❏	_____
Ground-Fault Monitoring	❏	❏	_____

SECONDARY POWER

TYPE	Visual	Functional	Comments
Battery Condition	❏		_____
Load Voltage		❏	_____
Discharge Test		❏	_____
Charger Test		❏	_____
Specific Gravity		❏	_____

TRANSIENT SUPPRESSORS ❏ _____

REMOTE ANNUNCIATORS ❏ ❏ _____

NOTIFICATION APPLIANCES

	Visual	Functional	Comments
Audible	❏	❏	_____
Visible	❏	❏	_____
Speakers	❏	❏	_____
Voice Clarity		❏	_____

INITIATING AND SUPERVISORY DEVICE TESTS AND INSPECTIONS

Loc. & S/N	Device Type	Visual Check	Functional Test	Factory Setting	Measured Setting	Pass	Fail
_____	_____	❏	❏	_____	_____	❏	❏
_____	_____	❏	❏	_____	_____	❏	❏
_____	_____	❏	❏	_____	_____	❏	❏
_____	_____	❏	❏	_____	_____	❏	❏
_____	_____	❏	❏	_____	_____	❏	❏
_____	_____	❏	❏	_____	_____	❏	❏

Comments: _____
_____
_____
_____

(NFPA Inspection and Testing, 3 of 4)

FIGURE 10.6.2.3 *Continued*

EMERGENCY COMMUNICATIONS EQUIPMENT	Visual	Functional	Comments
Phone Set	❏	❏	
Phone Jacks	❏	❏	_____
Off-Hook Indicator	❏	❏	_____
Amplifier(s)	❏	❏	_____
Tone Generator(s)	❏	❏	_____
Call-in Signal	❏	❏	_____
System Performance	❏	❏	_____

	Visual	Device Operation	Simulated Operation
INTERFACE EQUIPMENT			
(Specify) _____	❏	❏	❏
(Specify) _____	❏	❏	❏
(Specify) _____	❏	❏	❏
SPECIAL HAZARD SYSTEMS			
(Specify) _____	❏	❏	❏
(Specify) _____	❏	❏	❏
(Specify) _____	❏	❏	❏

Special Procedures: _____
_____
_____

Comments: _____
_____
_____
_____

SUPERVISING STATION MONITORING	Yes	No	Time	Comments
Alarm Signal	❏	❏		
Alarm Restoration	❏	❏	_____	_____
Trouble Signal	❏	❏	_____	_____
Supervisory Signal	❏	❏	_____	_____
Supervisory Restoration	❏	❏	_____	_____

NOTIFICATIONS THAT TESTING IS COMPLETE	Yes	No	Who	Time
Building Management	❏	❏		
Monitoring Agency	❏	❏	_____	_____
Building Occupants	❏	❏	_____	_____
Other (Specify)	❏	❏	_____	_____

The following did not operate correctly: _____
_____
_____

System restored to normal operation: Date: _____ Time: _____

THIS TESTING WAS PERFORMED IN ACCORDANCE WITH APPLICABLE NFPA STANDARDS.

Name of Inspector: _____ Date: _____ Time: _____

Signature: _____

Name of Owner or Representative: _____

Date: _____ Time: _____

Signature: _____

(NFPA Inspection and Testing, 4 of 4)

FIGURE 10.6.2.3 *Continued*

Some useful information from Potter Electric Signal:

Water Leaks in fire sprinklers

Water is leaking into the device from the Pipe

1. The hole in the pipe may be the wrong size. 2" & 2 1/2" devices require a 1 1/4" hole. All other sizes require a 2" hole. We have always used these hole sizes for every VSR version.

2. The device may not be installed correctly. The bushing in the saddle must be completely in the hole in the pipe. If the bushing gets smashed against the side of the hole, it could separate the bushing from the saddle and create a leak. The device probably needs to be replaced.

3. In rare cases, the orange seal around the trip rod could be bad. The device needs to be replaced.

Installation & Location

1. Vane type flow switches can be installed on horizontal or vertical sections of pipe. If installed on a horizontal section they must be installed on the top half of the pipe. They can be installed on the side of the pipe or between the side and the top.

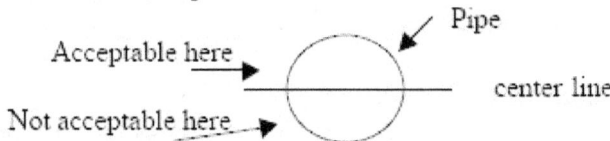

2. Flow switches can be installed to detect water flowing down a section of pipe, (from ceiling to floor instead of floor to ceiling). The retard times will be longer, possibly by as much as 50%.

3. Potter literature states that the flow switches should not be installed within 6" of a change in pipe direction or 24" from a valve. This is only a recommendation, not a requirement. Valves, (especially Butterfly valves), & changes in pipe direction can create turbulence in the water which can affect the sensitivity of the flow switch. It should not damage the switch. There are many devices installed closer than we recommend and they work. If the device works when the inspectors test valve is opened it can be considered an acceptable installation.

4. The VSR-F is for steel pipe, schedule 10 through 40.
   The VSR-CF is for Copper or Plastic pipe
There are no flow switches made for ductile iron pipe, the inside and outside diameters are too different than steel. The saddle may not seal against the pipe and the paddle may drag on the inside.

5. All of Potters flow switches are NEMA 4, they can be installed outdoors, but they cannot be submerged.

6. There is a specific flow switch for every size pipe. The size of the flow switch is stamped on the saddle next to where the "U" bolt goes through. 1 side shows the metric size, the other side shows the inch size.

If the pipe size, (diameter), is unknown try to find a fitting or valve, the size is usually stamped on them, or use this formula:

Circumference ÷ pi = diameter.   (pi = 3.1416)

The circumference is the distance around the pipe. The diameter is the distance across the pipe.

Pipe size (flow switch size)	Outside diameter of pipe	Pipe size (flow switch size)	Outside diameter of pipe
2"	2.375"	5"	5.563"
2 1/2"	2.875"	6"	6.625"
3"	3.5"	8"	8.625"
3 1/2"	4"	10	10.75"
4"	4.5"		

7. The flow switches only detect flow in one direction. There is an arrow stamped on the saddle or brass bushing indicating the direction of waterflow. If water flows in the opposite direction it will not damage the flow switch, but the device will not trip.

8. The VSR-SF and VS-SP screw into Tee fittings for installation. They have a 1" brass bushing and must screw into a tee that has a 1" threaded insert. The devices fit 1"-2" pipe. The portion of the tee that the flow switch screws into MUST be 1" threaded, (example, for installation on 2" pipe the tee would have to be 2"x2"x1"). It is not permissible to put a reducing bushing into the tee in order to fit the flow switch because now the paddle will not be at the proper depth in the tee.

9. There are 10 different paddles included with the flow switch. The proper paddle for the size and type of tee being used must be placed on the flow switch. The flow switches are shipped with a paddle for 1" threaded tees installed.

120 VAC Bells on Fire Sprinkler Systems

Older sprinkler systems used mechanical water gongs – bells driven mechanically by water pressure. These were high maintenance and often failed due to corrosion.

The modern approach has been to install electric bells. While these are usually supplied by the fire alarm contractor and are low voltage (12 or 24 volts DC); they are sometimes supplied by the sprinkler contractor and powered by 120 VAC (high voltage)

Wire a flowswitch to ring a bell and/or connect to a fire panel

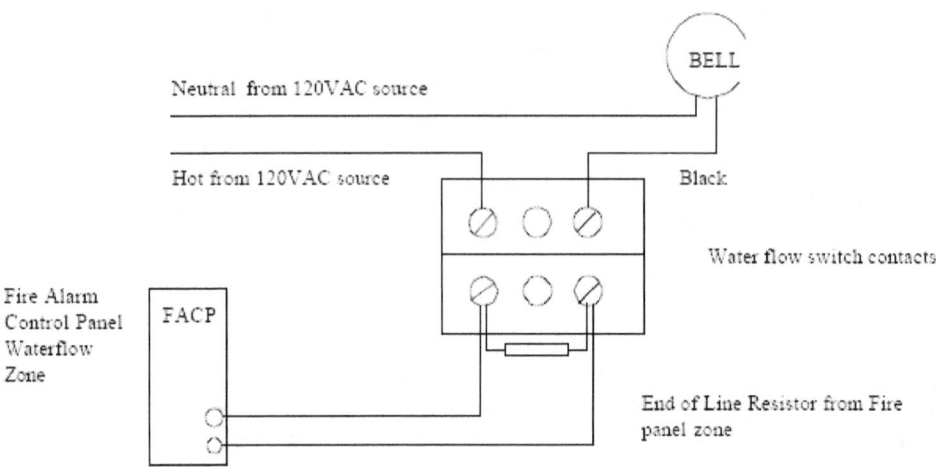

USE CAUTION WHEN WORKING ON SPRINKLER BELLS IN CASE THEY ARE HIGH VOLTAGE!

QTY	DEVICE	STANDBY	TOTAL	ALARM	TOTAL
	STANDBY BATTERY CALCULATIONS				
QTY	DEVICE	STANDBY	TOTAL	ALARM	TOTAL
1	XR200 FIRE CONTROL PANEL	0.080	0.080	0.080	0.080
2	ACTIVE ZONES ON XR200	0.002	0.003	0.002	0.004
1	893 DUAL PHONE MODULE	0.012	0.012	0.050	0.050
1	472 INTERFACE MODULE	0.085	0.085	0.085	0.085
1	690 KEYPAD	0.100	0.100	0.100	0.100
1	714 LOOP EXPANDERS	0.007	0.007	0.007	0.007
4	ACTIVE ZONES ON EXPANDERS	0.004	0.016	0.030	0.120
1	SMOKE DETECTOR	0.009	0.009	0.028	0.028
1	PULL STATION	0.001	0.001	0.001	0.001
1	WATERFLOW SWITCH	0.001	0.001	0.001	0.001
3	VALVE TAMPER	0.001	0.003	0.001	0.003
1	HORN / STROBE	0.001	0.001	0.175	0.175
	TOTALS		0.318		0.654
		HOURS	**CURRENT**	**TOTAL AH**	
	STANDBY	24	0.318	7.632	
	ALARM	1	0.654	0.654	
	TOTAL AMP HOURS REQUIRED			**8.286**	
	BATTERY AMP HOURS	7.000			
	TOTAL BATTERIES REQUIRED	2.000			
	ACTUAL BATTERY USED	14.000		**14.000**	
	BATTERY RESERVE	41%			

Typical Standby Battery Calculation

		SEQUENCE OF OPERATIONS					
	WATER	MANUAL	AREA	DUCT	VALVE	POWER	SYSTEM
	FLOW	PULL	SMOKE	SMOKE	TAMPER	FAILURE	TROUBLE
ANNUNCIATE AT FACP/KEYPAD	YES	YES	YES	YES	YES	YES	YES
INDICATE AT REMOTE ANNUNCIATOR	YES	YES	YES	YES	YES	YES	YES
SOUND AUDIBLE DEVICES / VISUALS	YES	YES	YES	NO	NO	NO	NO
TRANSMIT ALARM TO CENTRAL STATION	YES	YES	YES	YES	NO	NO	NO
TRANSMIT SUPERVISORY TO CENTRAL STATION	NO	NO	NO	NO	YES	NO	NO
TRANSMIT TROUBLE TO CENTRAL STATION	NO	NO	NO	NO	NO	YES	YES
ACTUATE FIRE DAMPERS/ SHUTDOWN HVAC	YES	YES	YES	YES	NO	NO	N/A
RECALL ELEVATORS	YES	YES	YES	YES	NO	NO	N/A

Sample Sequence of Operations

CONDUIT FILL CALCULATIONS

BELDEN FORMULA -

SQUARE THE O.D. OF EACH WIRE AND TOTAL

MULTIPLY THE TOTAL * .7854

FACP PANEL STUB UP

WIRE TYPE	WIRE DIAMETER	O.D SQUARE	WIRE QTY	WIRE TOTAL
22-4	0.2	0.04	1	0.04
18-2	0.234	0.054756	3	0.164268
18-4	0.257	0.066049	2	0.132098
18-6	0.42	0.1764		0
14-2	0.206	0.042436	1	0.042436
RG59	0.237	0.056169		0
RG6	0.27	0.0729		0
		0		
		TOTAL		0.378802
FACTOR	0.7854	AREA	7	0.2975111
	SIZE	SIZE	MAX	MAX FILL
CONDUIT	0.75	3/4"	40%	0.30
	1	1"	40%	0.40
	1.5	11/2"	40%	0.60
	2	2"	40%	0.80

Sample Conduit Capacity Calculation

GENERAL NOTES

1. THE SYSTEM SHOWN IS INTENDED TO MEET THE FOLLOWING CODES AND STANDARDS:

   HEALTH & SAFETY CODE SECTION 13145

   CALIFORNIA CODE OF REGULATIONS (CCR) TITLE 19

   CCR TITLE 24, PART 2, 2001 EDITION CALIFORNIA BUILDING CODE (CBC)

   CCR TITLE 24, PART 3, 2001 EDITION CALIFORNIA ELECTRICAL CODE (CEC)

   CCR TITLE 24, PART 4, 2001 EDITION CALIFORNIA MECHANICAL CODE (CMC)

   CCR TITLE 24, PART 9, 2001 EDITION CALIFORNIA FIRE CODE (CFC)

   NFPA 72, NATIONAL FIRE ALARM CODE, 1999 EDITION

   AS AMENDED IN CBC 2001 EDITION, CHAPTER 35

2. THE EQUIPMENT AND MATERIALS USED ARE APPROVED BY THE CA STATE FIRE MARSHALL TRANSMISSION OF SIGNALS IS ACCOMPLISHED ACCORDING TO NFPA 72 STANDARDS

3. THE FIRE ALARM CONTROL PANEL / COMMUNICATOR IS INHERENTLY POWER LIMITED AND SIGNALING AND INITIATING CIRCUITS DO NOT REQUIRE OVERCURRENT PROTECTION.

4. THE FIRE ALARM CONTROL PANEL / COMMUNICATOR SHALL BE EQUIPPED WITH TWO PHONE LINES AND PROGRAMMED FOR TWO PHONE NUMBER DIALING. LOCAL TROUBLE ALARM WILL SOUND IF FAILURE OCCURS IN EITHER PHONE LINE.

5. THE FIRE ALARM CONTROL PANEL / COMMUNICATOR SHALL BE PROGRAMMED TO INITIATE A TEST SIGNAL TRANSMISSION AT LEAST ONCE EVERY 24 HOURS.

6. WATER FLOW INITIATING CIRCUITS SHALL COMPLY WITH NFPA 72 3-5.6.3.1 FOR SIGNALING AND ALARM DURING TROUBLE CONDITIONS.

7. TESTS WILL INCLUDE MEETING THE MAXIMUM TIME FRAMES IN NFPA 72 5-2.6.1

8. IF AN 800 (WATTS) LINE IS USED AT THE CENTRAL STATION TO RECEIVE ALARMS FROM THIS LOCATION THEN THE SECOND PHONE NUMBER SHALL BE A DEDICATED LOCAL LINE.

9. THE CENTRAL STATION SHALL BE UL AND FM APPROVED.

Typical Notes on a Fire Alarm Plan Submittal
(This one is in California)

INSTALLATION NOTES

1. DEDICATED 120 VAC POWER SHALL BE PROVIDED FOR THE FIRE ALARM CONTROL PANEL. IN ACCORDANCE WITH NPFA 72 1-5.2.5.2

2. POWER LIMITED WIRING SHALL BE SEPARATED FROM NON POWER LIMITED WIRING BY A MINIMUM OF TWO INCHES PER NFPA 70, 760-54

3. ALL WIRING AND CABLING METHODS SHALL COMPLY WITH NFPA 70, 760-52 AND SHALL BE PROTECTED WITHIN SEVEN FEET OF THE FINISHED FLOOR BY CONDUIT OR CONCEALED WITH IN WALLS.

4. FIRE DEPARTMENT STAMPED AND APPROVED PLANS MUST BE PRESENT AT THE JOB SITE.

5. AS BUILT PLANS MUST BE SUBMITTED TO THE FIRE DEPARTMENT IMMEDIATELY AFTER THE FINAL INSPECTION AND TEST IF ANY WIRING OR EQUIPMENT CHANGES WERE MADE AFTER THE ORIGINAL PLANS WERE APPROVED.

6. A DIGITAL MULTIMETER SHALL BE USED DURING THE FIRE DEPARTMENT INSPECTION TO VERIFY COMPLIANCE.

7. THE SYSTEM SHALL BE PLACARDED AT THE FIRE CONTROL PANEL IN ACCORDANCE WITH NFPA INDICATING THE CONTRACTOR AND CENTRAL MONITORING STATION.

8. AN NFPA 72 FIRE ALARM COMPLETION FORM SHALL BE PROVIDED AT TIME OF FINAL INSPECTION.

9. ALL FIRE ALARM CIRCUITS SHALL BE IDENTIFIED AT TERMINAL AND JUNCTION LOCATIONS

10. RESETTING OF THE FIRE ALARM SHALL BE VIA ALPHANUMERIC KEYPAD BY THE USE OF THE ONTARIO FIRE DEPT CODE OF 36170

10. GROUND FAULT DETECTION SHALL BE PROGRAMMED OR TURNED ON AT ALL TIMES.

11. ALL KEYS OR TOOLS FOR FIRE PANELS AND/OR NECESSARY FOR RESETTING THE SYSTEM SHALL BE PROVIDED IN THE KNOX BOX AT TIME OF FINAL INSPECTION.

12. THE FIRE ALARM CONTRACTOR SHALL PROVIDE A VALID COPY OF THE SERVICE CONTRACT WHICH SHALL SPECIFY THE LEVEL OF SERVICE, RESPONSE TIME, MAINTENANCE AND TESTING FREQUENCY ACCORDING TO NFPA 72

Typical Notes on a Fire Alarm Plan Submittal

(This one is in California)

Burglar (Intrusion) Alarm Systems

Burglar alarms come in every flavor from a local bell to million dollar systems protecting vast government facilities. Burglar alarms have a rich, marvelous history which few outside of the industry are aware. For instance, did you know that as early as 1871 alarm companies built the first telephone exchanges? ADT, the largest security company in the world, used to be known as American District Telegraph; because they built the infrastructure to support transmitting burglar alarms. In early New York city wires ran from street corner call boxes to central exchanges sending telegraph like signals to notify "operators" that a messenger was needed. Early accounts tell of so many wires running overhead that they actually blotted out the sky.

While communication technology has caught up, alarms are in fact, still very similar to those early efforts. The basic "model" for an alarm system has not changed much. Many people are surprised to learn that the alarm signal is actually transmitted from the business or residence to a central monitoring site where "operators" interpret the signal and then notify the police.

An alarm still needs a "**control panel**", some type of arming device (keypads these days), and a manner for transmitting the alarm signal to the central station. The control panel contains the intelligence of the system. These days, that panel packs quite a lot of intelligence indeed. The least inexpensive panel (some as low as $40), has more features and abilities than most customers will ever use.

Typical Control panel with accessories

Control panels manage many more functions than just the burglar detection. They contain a power supply including a backup battery and charger. They monitor the actual wires in your system to maintain integrity. They manage the communications- including dialing multiple numbers repeated times until the signal gets through. Beyond these functions, the control panel also maintains the audible warnings (bells, sirens, etc.), **entry / exit delay** (which we'll explain shortly, and remembers the PIN numbers or keypad combinations for multiple users.

Controls panels transmit much more than just alarm signals. They can log power loss, when the system is armed or disarmed, and which user did it. This last feature can be invaluable to managers and owners to have an audit trail of their employees.

The higher end **keypads** all have displays that provide information to the user. Alpha-numeric displays are much preferred over simple LED lights, and are more than worth the extra money. Besides just making it easier to arm or disarm the system, these keypads display the exact "**zone**" or detection device status, previous history, and diagnostics. They are also generally used for programming the alarm system by the alarm company technicians.

Security System Keypad

One program item is the entry / exit delay time. Since the keypad should always be located within the protected area, a method is needed to allow the user to get in and disarm it before the alarm trips. This is called the entry delay and is simply a time period in seconds while the system waits for a disarm code to be entered. The sequence goes like this: the user opens a door, the system detects the door opening and begins a countdown timer (usually 30- 60 seconds). If the system is disarmed within the time period no alarm occurs. If no code (or the wrong code) is entered, the control panel then transmits an alarm signal- and likely sounds some audible device like a siren.

The exit delay is the opposite and allows the user to arm the system and then walk through the door. As long as the door is closed within the allotted time the system is then armed and no alarm occurs. While this method is quite effective, especially in small systems, it is not foolproof. The keypad should always be located at the door users enter and leave through. Often, the keypad is mistakenly placed at a main entry but employees actually use a rear door. If the path of travel is long to get to the keypad, the chance of false alarms due to late disarming is increased dramatically.

Another major cause of false alarms is the "I just popped back in for a minute because I forgot something". In other words, the employee arms the system and goes to his or her car and realizes they forgot something in the office. They go back in and get it without disarming and rearming and leave again. By the time the entry delay runs out, they are long gone home but the police have a false alarm. This is probably one of the biggest causes of false alarms and consequently, poor police response.

We should mention here that although the keypad should be mounted inside the protected area, it is more for weather protection than anything else. With modern keypads it is not really possible to disarm the system by taking it apart and touching wires together- that's another Hollywood myth. The keypad uses data to communicate with the control panel.

The system communicates to the central monitoring station by phone lines. Residences can use the phone line already there but many alarm companies prefer businesses install a **dedicated phone**

line just for the alarm. This is not bad advice. Although it increases your total monthly cost, a dedicated line reduces the chance the alarm control won't be able to get through to the central station. If the intrusion system can't dial out and deliver the alarm message, the central station won't be aware you have an alarm condition.

Newer alarm systems (and more advanced monitoring companies) now offer "internet" monitoring. Instead of the traditional phone line they use broadband Internet access such as DSL or cable. Some systems continuously monitor the condition of the line and can warn if the connection is lost. These are highly recommended because of their speed and security. The cost is usually very much in line with dedicated voice phone lines. Plus if you already have Internet access, the alarm transmission is essentially free.

Whichever type of communication you use, ensure the phone line is protected where it enters the building. This is something to be especially aware of in residential applications. You don't want the phone line exposed where burglars can easily cut it.

EOL (End of Line) Supervision
Just a word on "supervision"- this is a term used to describe how a fire or intrusion panel insures that all the wiring in a security system is intact. Supervision makes sure that no wires are cut when the system is disarmed or armed. A resistor of a specific value- usually 1000 ohms or 3000 ohms- is placed across the circuit at each detection device then the control panel sends a constant voltage through this circuit and measures it. If the voltage drops or the current increases, the panel senses the change as either a short or open and alerts the user or transmits a trouble signal.
Some alarm company installers have been known to circumvent this feature by placing the resistor at the panel connection side instead of the device connection point. While this is a code violation on a fire alarm, it is just very bad practice on an intrusion system. You can readily test this feature by simply disconnecting one wire at any detection device (contact, PIR, or glass beak) and within a few minutes the control panel should display a message indicating the zone if bad.

Contacts
We've talked about the burglar alarm control panel but what about the actual items that detect intrusion? The first line of defense is, and always has been, the **door contact**. Nearly 99% of the time, this consists of a two part unit- a magnet and a reed switch. The magnet goes on the moveable door and the switch is mounted on (or in) the door frame (which doesn't move). The wires are connected to the switch, while the magnetic doesn't require any connection so it's free to move open and closed.

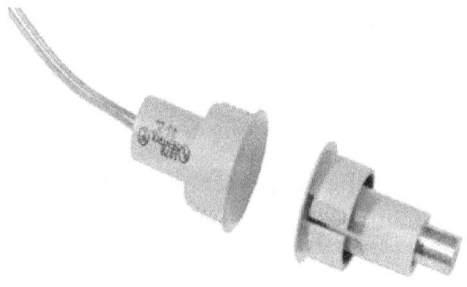

Concealed type of Door Contact

When the door is closed, the magnet is brought up next to the switch and it's magnetism holds the reed switch closed, completing a circuit. Almost all burglar alarms depend on this closed circuit principal, this is so if a burglar attempts to cut any wires anywhere while the system is armed, it will trip and transmit an alarm signal. The control panel also monitors this wiring while the system is off or disarmed by the way. If a wire is open when you go to arm the system, the control panel will warn you.

Once the system is armed, any opening of the door either by key or by force, will trip the alarm. Notice we do not say, "unlocked". The alarm cannot detect whether the door is locked or unlocked- only if it is open or closed. Many customers mistake this. Sometimes they forget to lock their door and when they return realize it was unlocked all night and blame the alarm company. If the alarm company did not receive any alarm signals over night, it means no one actually opened the door- even though it was unlocked, (consequently, a lucky occasion for the customer).

Most door contacts are fairly sensitive and if the door is opened more than an inch or so, it will set off the alarm. There is somewhat of a fine line here- the contact must be sensitive enough that the door cannot be opened too far but forgiving enough not to alarm on wind and rattles.

Garage doors, roll up doors, and overhead doors all function the same way. Large garage doors use larger and sturdier magnets and switches. Overhead doors are subject to much more abuse however. Forklifts can run over switches or damage them in other ways. Some doors can be contacted at the top instead of the bottom and this is always advisable if possible. Contacting the doors at the top will shorten the wiring while keeping switches out of harm's way.

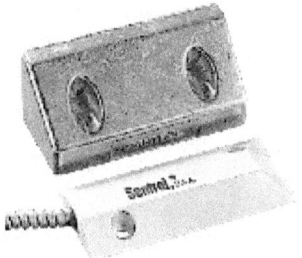

An alarm contact for an overhead or rollup door

Contacts come in many sizes and configurations for specialized applications. One special type is the "biased" or high security contact. These have a special magnet that is matched to the switch. Once in place, if any other magnet is brought close to the contact, it will sense the wrong magnet and send an alarm. These are especially useful where the contact is subject to tampering- such in a warehouse with remote fire exit doors. It can prevent dishonest employees from bypassing the switch and opening the door to place stolen merchandise outside for later pickup.

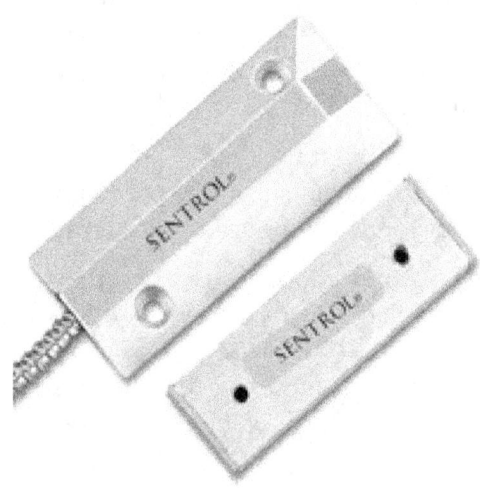

Motion Detectors

PIR

The next most common detection devices are motion detectors, and the most common motion detector by a wide margin is the PIR or Passive Infrared. Over the years many other technologies have come and gone, (ultrasonic and microwave were most prevalent), but the PIR has maintained it's place as the most common and widely used motion detector.

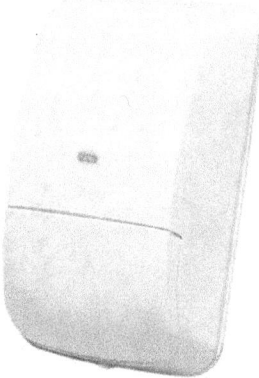

Wall Mount PIR by Bosch / Detection Systems

As it's name implies the PIR is a passive device. It does not emit any beam, it simply "looks" at an area and senses temperature changes. Imagine a room at an ambient temperature of 78 degrees Fahrenheit, the PIR senses and remembers this temperature. If a foreign object enters the room in the field of view of the PIR's sensor, the temperature will change. The PIR is very sensitive and even a change as small as tenths of a degree will be detected.

Of course if the PIR were just pointed at a room it would be alarming constantly from normal variations in temperature. Since infrared is in fact a wavelength, optics can be utilized to "focus" the infrared energy onto the sensor. Most PIRs employ mirrors to divide the room or area to be monitored into 4 or more zones. The PIR is them programmed to look at a temperature change between these zones. If all four zones remain equal- as in a change in room temperature from heaters, then no alarm is generated.

However if a rapid change is detected between zone 1 and zone 2 then the PIR assumes an intruder has entered the area and signals an alarm. This is the reason PIRs are only effective at detecting intruder moving *across* their field of view. If the PIR is incorrectly installed so the intruder only moves towards it, then no alarm will be generated because it will not sense the temperature change between two or more zones.

Unfortunately, pets and birds also move readily across rooms and are known to generate false alarms. Pets are handled by limiting the downward detection zones to about three feet off the floor depending on the pets encountered. There is no solution for birds except to limit the PIR use to areas without the possibility of flying birds.

PIRs do have a unique weakness, which is both an advantage, and a weakness. Infrared energy does not penetrate glass. It is not recommended to ever mount an PIR actually looking directly at glass for other reasons- namely bright lights can interfere with the optics; but they will not sense a temperature change outside through glass.

Glass Break Detectors

Since the earliest alarms there has been a need to deal with glass windows. For the first three quarters of the 20th century foil was pretty much the only method available. This involved gluing fragile tin foil to the window in a continuous pattern to form a closed loop. If the glass was broken the foil broke as well and interrupted the circuit causing an alarm.

Technology finally stepped in and glass break detectors or **GBD**s came in use. Glass Break detectors come in two basic types- vibration (shock) or acoustic.

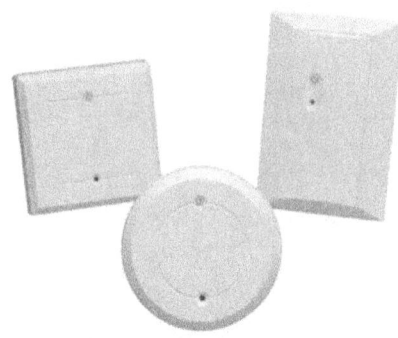

Various styles of Glass Breaks by Bosch

Acoustic type glass break detectors contain a microphone and actually listen for the sound of breaking glass. Since there are so many different types of glass these detectors must be capable of detecting both plate glass (which is noisy and high frequency) and tempered (which is relatively quiet and low frequency). This presents significant issues since many other common sounds fall into these frequencies such as keys, ringing phones, cleaning equipment, and many other items.

While acoustic detectors are fairly adept at detecting breaking glass, they also are very prone to false alarms due to the issues above. Manufacturers have built in processing power to circumvent the false alarm issues such as combining vibration or passive infrared detection. Unfortunately, the combination technologies tend to work too well and can result in no alarm when the glass is actually broken.

Vibration / shock type GBDs typically do not suffer as many false alarms because they are more focused. These devices employ a piezo crystal structure which generates voltage when undergo sufficient vibration. Although they don't directly detect breaking glass per se, they are very effective at detecting break ins through windows, walls, or nearly any structural part of a building.

Like anything else, vibration sensors have their own set of drawbacks, the biggest of which are limited range (the vibrations only travel short distances) and the fact they must be rigidly attached to frames or glass (which many owners do not like due to aesthetics).

Beams

Beams are the active counterparts of passive infrareds (PIRs). Since these are active infrareds, they require two parts: a transmitter and a receiver. The transmitters only require power and send an invisible *modulated* infrared to a receiver. The receiver, once powered up, expects to "see" the modulated infrared energy. If the receiver does not see the beam for any reason, if signals an alarm to the control panel.

Active Beams by Bosch / Detection Systems

Beams come in many configurations and ranges from single beams for up to a 100 foot line to double and quad sets which can go as far as 1000 feet. A characteristic of infrared beams is their black housing and lenses. Since infrared easily penetrates even very, very dark red; the observer (or thief) cannot determine which way the beams are pointing. This is especially useful when there are multiple sets of beams converging. Active beams can be used outdoors with no problem.

Drawbacks of beams are exactly what you might imagine, when used outdoors they are prone to alarms from animals, blowing debris, and very heavy rain or snow. Indoors it can be difficult to maintain a clear path, especially if the beams are far apart. Beams do remain a very viable option to cover long distances, but when used outdoors we recommend they be used in conjunction with cameras to allow responders or security to observe the areas when an alarm occurs.

Video Motion Detection (VMD)

As of the writing of this document, the only Video Motion Detection devices available are part of Digital Video Recorders (DVR). We anticipate that in the near future standalone cameras will include VMD circuits and relay outputs to interface with intrusion alarm panels. With the ongoing advances in digital storage technology and processing power, video motion detection (VMD) will become the standard type of motion detection. Video motion works by "memorizing" the scene (in pixels) and comparing any new pixels to what is in memory. Once the threshold of new pixels exceeds the old ones, an alarm is generated. The most superior aspect of VMD is of course, that you can actually see what caused the alarm!

Due to the terrorist threat, VMD is receiving much attention and research. VMD systems can already accomplish amazing tasks such as determining which way an object is heading, whether an object is stationary for a specific length of time, when an object is moving too fast or too slow, and it can determine objects of specific sizes. Companies have even demonstrated VMD systems which can determine an individual's characteristics such as color of clothes and even height and weight!.

If you are already planning to install cameras, then a complete video motion detection system in lieu of PIRs or glass breaks is a viable option. VMD can be configured to "look" at specific areas of the picture and to have different sensitivity at different times of the day. Again, the bonus is the fact that by playing back the video you will have a picture of exactly what or whom caused the alarm.

What about darkness you might ask? New cameras as so sensitive they can pretty much see in the dark now. But burglars must be able to see as well, so the chances are they will be using a flashlight. In total darkness, a flashlight is like a beacon to a VMD system. We successfully demonstrated a VMD system in a museum where the cameras were focused on paintings. This presented an extremely low key detection method for the public visitors while maintaining a very high level of security should they venture too close. A bonus was when the museum turned off the lights and tried to approach a painting- the would-be intruder was detected every single time. In turns out if a human can't see the camera still could! But when the human required more light, the VMD detected them even further in advance.

Wireless Alarm Systems
No discussion of intrusion alarms would be complete without mentioning wireless alarm systems. For many years manufacturers sought to alleviate the high labor portion of installing intrusion alarms with limited success. Eliminating wiring, especially in residential applications, has significant impact on the total cost of security systems. But the early wireless systems were a poor compromise at best.

Modern advances in wireless technology- especially the availability of higher frequencies in the gigahertz range- have tilted the chart towards wireless in certain applications. Unfortunately, wireless is not an ideal complete solution because wireless equipment and devices tend to be much more expensive than standard devices. There is a certain point where wireless loses any advantage over labor savings and it is usually only in rather small systems.

In smaller applications, such as apartments and condo, wireless can have very significant advantages. Installation is very fast- often much less than one day; in some cases just hours, so disruption is held to the absolute minimum. Damage, and the necessary patch and paint, is also minimal or non existent.

The homeowner does need to be aware of certain aspects of wireless however, which even in small applications may negate its use. For one, the door contacts are much larger and need to be exposed so the wireless can transmit. This may be objectionable to many people.

Also you should be aware that all wireless devices require batteries, and batteries do need to be changed periodically. Another problem is that the batteries are non-standard and usually need to be purchased from the Alarm Company or manufacturer; they are not something you can pick at the local market. Motion detectors are high use devices since they are always sensing motion (even when the system is off) so they consume batteries much faster than door contacts. This is another reason to keep wireless system to small applications.

Wireless alarms are not generally used (nor recommended) in commercial environments except for very specialized uses such as panic and holdup alarms. Wireless panic and holdup buttons (which look and operate just like your car remote) are widely used and effective. Although the battery caveats still applies, modern wireless systems will alert the customer- and the alarm company- when batteries need replacing.

Monitoring

Once the intrusion system is installed it is usually monitored by some outside party. While you could simply just sound a siren or ring a bell upon an alarm, it is pretty clear this wouldn't accomplish much unless you have neighbors that are present 24 hours a day and willing to call the police. The police themselves almost never accept alarms directly, so the only alternative is to contract with a central monitoring station. Usually, the alarm company that installs and services your alarm will monitor it. In some cases they may contract it out to a third party.

In any case, the monitoring company is obviously critically important. Your security ultimately depends on their action or inaction. When an alarm is received at the central station, an operator must interpret it and take the appropriate action- such as notifying the police. Sounds simple doesn't it? The problems arise when the operator must begin to make judgment calls regarding the signals.

If you are prone to causing false alarms, improperly arming or disarming, or forgetting to turn the alarm off; expect the operator to hesitate before doing anything. It's not possible for human beings to do perform the correct action every single time. If you generate a dozen false alarms and then the thirteenth one is real, you can't expect a good outcome. The operator can't read your mind and as of yet may not be able to actually "see" what is going on at the premises. (More on that later).

Likewise, if you request complex special instructions, it makes the operator's job more difficult and increases the chance of mistakes. For example, "send the police every time except on Sunday nights between 5pm and 10pm when the courier goes in and picks up a shipment; and ignore the janitors between 8pm and 11pm Monday, Wednesday, and Fridays."

We have actually seen instructions like that and believe us, the chances of ever actually catching a burglar are slim to none. The more generic and ordinary the operation of your alarm system is, the more likely it will be handled correctly.

Some things you do want to insist on are "Call Lists" and pass codes. The central station will maintain a list of names and phone numbers to call on alarms or other kinds of trouble or questions. Make sure this list is always up to date. It's not fun coming to work on Monday morning to find your business was broken into and no one was notified because all the phone numbers were bad.

Also make sure the pass words or code words are current and sensible. The central station will issue you, and whoever else you request, a pass code word or number to be used when communicating with them. If you need to speak to someone at the central station because you accidentally set off the alarm, they will ask you to identify yourself by this code.

Surveillance (CCTV)

Whether referred to as surveillance, CCTV, video or VMS (Video Monitoring Systems), they all use cameras, monitors and recorders to observe, document, and deter activity around and in your location.

Cameras

There has probably been more advancement in the video area than any aspect of electronic security. Cameras have been completely solid state for years and consequently are extremely reliable. Security cameras are almost exclusively color and we would never allow any black & white cameras to be installed since there is almost no price differential any longer.

Panasonic Fixed Dome Camera

The CCD sensors (Charge Coupled Device –the chip that converts light into a usable picture) are so sensitive that even the most inexpensive cameras can almost see in the dark. Most of the cost difference these days in cameras is the additional processing power for difficult lighting applications such as the extreme dynamic range between lower interior light and bright sunlight. For example if you have an interior camera viewing an exterior door, when someone opens the doors sunlight pours in and used to blind the camera; this is not an issue with more sophisticated cameras.

Brand name cameras tend to be more expensive but worth every penny. Stay away from no-name brands and insist on cameras from Panasonic, Pelco, Bosch, Philips, Sony, Toshiba, etc. – brands you've probably heard of will tend to last longer, be more reliable, and produce a superior picture. Lenses are very important and we recommend the lenses and cameras be from the same manufacturer. This will insure compatibility and quality.

What do cameras look like these days? Well, they come in all shapes and sizes. There are cameras the size of lipstick or a postage stamp and these are generally used for covert or hidden situations.

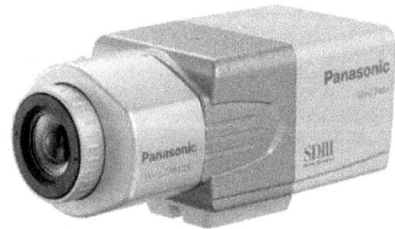

A Panasonic Fixed Camera (sometimes called a brick)

The vast majority of security cameras installed today are in the dome configuration. These are very popular because they are one piece and do not require mounts or enclosures. They are also aesthetically pleasing and have the additional benefit of concealing the actual position of the camera inside. In other words, people will not be able to see which direction the camera is viewing so they in effect cover a much wider "virtual" area.

Dome cameras have gotten smaller and smaller and current models are approximately 5" in diameter. Movable versions are also available in the same size footprint.

IP (Network) Cameras

The latest trend in video is network cameras. Cameras come in two flavors- analog and digital. Analog cameras are the traditional ones which have been around for many years and require a coaxial cable to carry an RF signal- similar to your cable TV.

Digital cameras convert the video signal to digital bits and transmit the signal over Ethernet LAN back to Digital Video Recorders (DVR) or Network Video Recorders (NVR). Most of these digital cameras have the capability of having their own IP (Internet Protocol) address and some even have built in web servers so they can be accessed and viewed from anywhere.

Panasonic Network Digital Camera

There is quite an onrush to deploy IP cameras but beware that IP cameras have severe limitations, which many seem to be blissfully unaware. Number one would be the inherent distance limitation of Ethernet protocol- 328 feet. This means no IP camera can be located more than 328 feet from an IDF room with an active hub or switch. Not a problem for small buildings but a major obstacle in larger facilities.

Another problem with IP cameras is the required bandwidth. If you're running a 10mb Ethernet, forget it. One camera will pretty much bring down the network. Just 4 cameras running at DVD quality (which is actually less than standard analog) requires over 8mb of bandwidth. The only way to reduce the impact of video over network is to run at significantly reduced resolution and speed (frames per second). In the back of this guide is a handy bandwidth calculator.

As of this writing it is still much cheaper to run analog cameras and coax cable which will result in higher quality pictures. That being said, camera manufacturers have generally abandoned further development of analog cameras, and are pushing IP cameras with the idea they are "future proof". The suggestion being that as networks progress, eventually digital camera technology and bandwidth availability will equal out.

Manufacturers have also shifted focus on the design side, suggesting IP cameras and NVRs should be on their own dedicated network. Newer DVRs and NVRs have dual network ports so cameras can be directed to one port and the other used for outside connections for viewing. This effectively segregates the network so high demand bandwidth for video is kept apart from normal everyday data bandwidth. It does require installing more data cabling and in some cases completely duplicating the customer's existing network.

Lastly, once the video is digital, future applications will be able to take advantage of the digital video and do things such switch video under certain conditions anywhere in the world or perform some of the analysis we write about in the section under DVRs..

Monitors

Tube based (CRT) monitors, while still on the market, should be avoided. Insist on LCD monitors and for future compatibility they should be capable of analog and digital (including a PC connector). The larger the monitor the better, up to a point. 17" should be the absolute minimum size but 20" are now so much lower in price, it may be wise to just standardize on them. Sizes larger than 20" still tend to have a much larger price differential but can still be economical if the application calls for it. For example, if you need to display 32 or 64 cameras in a command post, it may be wiser to go to a 42" LCD rather than multiple 17" or 20" monitors.

Recorders (DVR- Digital Video Recorder)

Your video system should always be recorded even if you never think you will need it because you will sooner or later. VHS or analog recorders are still available but have been completely overshadowed by digital recorders. Don't buy a VHS or analog recorder- period. The advantages of digital video recording are so over whelming there is really no comparison.

Digital video recorders are essentially computers with hard drive storage. The video signal from the camera is "captured" and converted to digital through hardware and software, compressed to smaller file sizes, and then written onto the hard drive. Since computers are very intelligent, the DVR always knows exactly where the video is stored *by time*. This means you can instantly find any event or time instead of endlessly rewinding and fast forwarding.

Although convenience alone would dictate going digital, the biggest plus is the video quality does not degrade from recording to recording, it is always as good from the first second to the 30th day. Which brings us to another advantage- the ability to keep an entire months worth of video at your fingertips- no more putting in a different tape for each day!

DVRs also manage multiple cameras because they have built in multiplexers. This means DVRs grab frames from each camera and stores as many as 16 or 32 cameras on a single hard drive. Most DVRs are also capable of displaying the cameras in a multi-screen format as well.

Since the DVR is a computer and has intelligence it can do many more things. Video Motion Detection (VMD)is one of the most important. This one feature has many uses. First, VMD allows the DVR to record only *on motion*. There's no sense recording views that don't change- empty rooms for instance. With VMD activated, only images that change are recorded which greatly increases the amount of *time* that is stored on a given hard drive. So it becomes much easier to size your DVR hard drives to store at least 30 days worth of video.   Secondly, VMD can be used to activate intrusion alarms when actual motion is detected. Third, the recording speed can be increased when motion is detected for higher quality video.

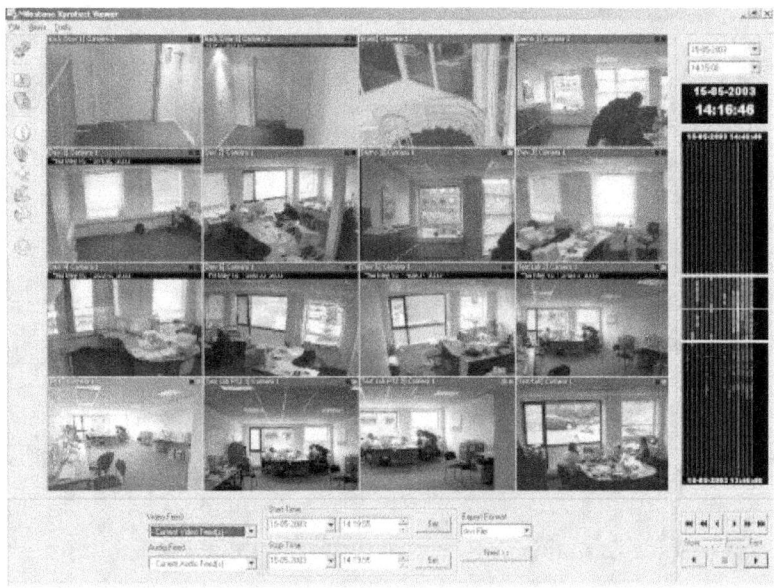

Most DVRs have multi-screen capability

A word about video quality is probably a good idea at this point. Digital video at this writing is not quite up to par with analog VHS but it comes close if properly configured. Broadcast (or DVD) quality video is considered to be 20 frames per second (FPS) at about 720 X 480 pixels. This is also known as 4 CIF (pronounced SIF). DVRs can usually approach this but only on one camera or for shorter storage periods. The reason being is that 20 FPS at 720 X 480 requires tremendous processing power and huge file sizes.

The lower end DVRs usually state specifications that look good until you realize that the spec is for *one* camera. Additional cameras simply divide up the total processing power and storage. So if one camera can be recorded at 20 FPS at 4 CIF, four cameras will actually be recorded at 5 FPS and 1 CIF (352 X 240 pixels). There are very sophisticated DVRs that can do much higher rates but are considerably more expensive.

Another huge advantage of DVRs is their ability to be connected to networks. This has two important uses: one, it means if you have multiple buildings (or multiple areas in one large building), then cameras are connected in relatively short runs to the nearest DVR and then the DVRs are connected together via the network. This allows the user to manage and view multiple DVRs (and possibly hundreds of cameras) from one central location. Another use for the network is for the owner/ manager to be able to view any of his cameras from anywhere he has an internet connection.

Recorders (NVR- Network Video Recorder)

An NVR is usually defined to mean a computer with storage and software to record digital video directly from either IP video cameras or digital video *encoders*. In reality the line between DVRs and NVRs can be somewhat indistinct. DVRs usually contain the analog to digital converters necessary to change NTSC camera video to digital bits and then store it on the hard drive. NVRs on the other hand usually do not and expect to only receive digital video which has already been converted. NVRs are designed to reside on a network and receive digital video over that network and store it.

 The most popular systems right now employ encoders at the remote side near the analog cameras which do the conversion and then transmit that digital video stream over the network (either LAN Local Area Network or WAN Wide Area Network) to the NVR computer. As stated NVRs can also take digital video direct from IP cameras.

The actual NVR is usually just an off-the-shelf computer with large hard drive storage. A RAID (Random Access Intelligent Disk) array in the neighborhood of one terabyte (one trillion bytes) is the norm but systems can go lower or higher in storage capacity.

NVRs also usually come with a software client or application to manage the video playback and searching. A recent development is video forensics. These are software tools to analyze the video once it has been stored. This area is developing so rapidly that whatever we write will probably be obsolete by the time you read this but such tools can already do amazing things.

Some common tasks are:

Object left too long (an object remains in the view for more than a programmed time period)

Object missing (an object has disappeared from the view)

Object going wrong way (usually a human- is traveling a different path from a programmed one.

Object too fast or too slow (moving through the view beyond programmed parameters)

Analytic video systems can even determine a person's height, weight and color of clothes and search for that person among other video sources. Facial recognition software can be integrated with NVRs to search for and identify persons in stored digital video.

Very soon it will be routine to grab a snapshot of a person of interest- such as a known terrorists, thief or passer of bad checks and alert a command center when that person enters a location anywhere with networked video cameras.

Access Systems

An Access system does pretty much what the name implies- it controls access to a facility (or just a room). In order to accomplish this, the systems needs to be able identify the persons attempting to gain access. The identification can be by **Card**, **PIN** combination, or **Biometrics** (a unique human characteristic such as a fingerprint).

In order to control access, the system will also need a means of unlocking and locking doors. This is accomplished by electrifying the door locks. Standard locking hardware can be replaced with similar appearing locksets that have an electric solenoid. Electric strikes (the area in the door frame where the lock plunger goes) can be added. Or Magnetic (**Mag**) locks can be installed which consist of very powerful electro magnets which can hold the door closed with up to 2000 lbs of force.

Each of these solutions has advantages and disadvantages. One important aspect is to maintain ADA (Americans with Disabilities Act) compliance. Most jurisdictions require that any person be able to exit the building with *no prior knowledge*. Usually this is interpreted that the levers and push bars remain operational so a person can exit without doing anything out of the ordinary.

Locks

While electrified locks and strikes easily comply, mag locks present some challenges. Mag locks are typically used in situations such as full height glass doors where no other hardware is available. Since mag locks "unlock" by removing power, some means must be installed to allow people to exit electronically. This is generally accomplished by a REX (Request to Exit) detector. A REX is an PIR which looks for people approaching the door from the inside and releasing the mag lock when motion is detected.

Locks make up a significant part of the total cost of an access system- usually as much as 50%. Electrified lock sets are the most expensive, followed by mag locks, with electric strikes being the least expensive. As you might expect, the reliability of each is a direct function of the cost- strikes being the least reliable and easiest to circumvent.

It is highly recommended that whatever type of locks you install; do *not* distribute any hard keys! If anyone retains a mechanical key after the access system is installed, the access is essentially worthless. Also, using a key instead of the reader *will* cause a false alarm.

Door Position Sensor (Door Contacts)

Unlike an intrusion alarm system, the access control system always knows whether a door is locked or unlocked since it obviously controls this function. However, for the access system a means is also needed to indicate when the door is open or closed. The door position sensor accomplishes this, and it is identical to a door contact used for intrusion purposes.

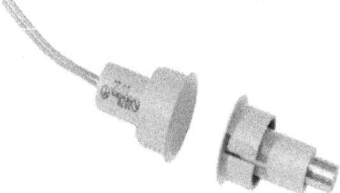

The Door Position Sensor is the same as the contact used for Intrusion

In normal operation a person wishing to gain access presents their card to a reader and the system unlocks the door. The access system has a programmed time to keep the door unlocked to allow the person to pull the door open (this is called the **Door Unlock Time**). If the reader is close to the door, this time can be as short as 5 seconds but if the reader is farther away or people tend to bring large packages through, it may need to be as long as 30 seconds. The problem is that if the time is too long, another person can come behind them and simply pull open the door before the time runs out. This is known as **Tail Gating**.

To avoid this, the door position sensor is used to monitor when the door opens and closes. The access system can be programmed to automatically relock the door as soon as it sees the door go open – (or closed depending on the type of locking hardware.) This cancels the unlock time period and prevents people from tail gating.

Another use of the DPS (Door position sensor) is to monitor **Door Held Open** or door open too long. Obviously if a door is propped open, your security and the access system is worthless. This is another programmable time in the access system. Once the system senses the door open, it starts a timer and expects the door to close within this period. If the door is still open after the time expires, the system usually generates an audible warning at the door alerting someone to close the door. If the door is still open after another period, a Door Held Open alarm is generated. Janitors and smokers are usually the biggest offenders of this so be sure to account for them in your plan. Janitors should be issued cards and smokers should have a designated door they can exit and smoke near.

The last and certainly one of the most important functions of the DPS is **Door Forced** monitoring. This is equivalent to an intrusion alarm. As we mentioned previously, the access system expects to receive a card read before if unlocks the door. Makes sense right? But if the system senses the door opening *without* a card read then there are only two possibilities- either the door was broken into (forced open) or someone used a key instead of a card- either way a security violation- one slightly more critical than the other.

This is one of the reasons all hard keys should be collected from employees- and management. A difficult and sometimes delicate task so most often the locks are simply changed out rendering all existing keys un-useable.

REX (Request to Exit)

Special PIRs called REX detectors are used to unlock and bypass alarms when a person leaves a through a secured door. If REX detectors are used, they must be installed very carefully and set up properly. There have been instances where people have inserted long sticks from outside through the gap in the doors and caused the REX to unlock the door. REXs are designed to detect anything approaching the door, so they are very "loose" and have a wide pattern. While this makes them more useful for detecting authorized people exiting, it can also result in unauthorized entrances. The best solution is to install two REXs on double doors- one over each leaf and narrow the pattern so it can't be manipulated form outside.

Pushbuttons can also be used in some circumstances but local inspectors will probably not approve them because of the "no prior knowledge" requirement. There have been situations where Fire Manual Pull stations painted yellow have been used as emergency door releases. Your security vendor should be aware of local regulations and provide a system that complies.

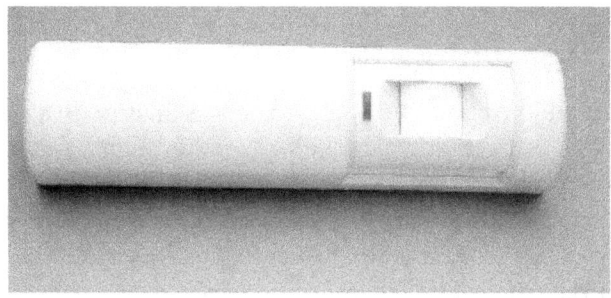

Request to Exit Detector by Bosch / Detection Systems

Readers

Although it is certainly possible to use keypads and PINs to identify users on an access system, it is neither recommended nor convenient. PINs are often shared among employees and pretty soon you find everyone using the same number which completely negates your control and documentation.

Card readers are the current preferred method. Among the reader technologies- only **proximity** is recommended. If any company tries to sell you any type of swipe or insert reader- find someone else. There is no cost differential any longer. Proximity readers are sealed and have no moving parts. There is nothing to wear out and once installed and working will probably continue to work forever. In fact most manufacturers provide a lifetime warranty.

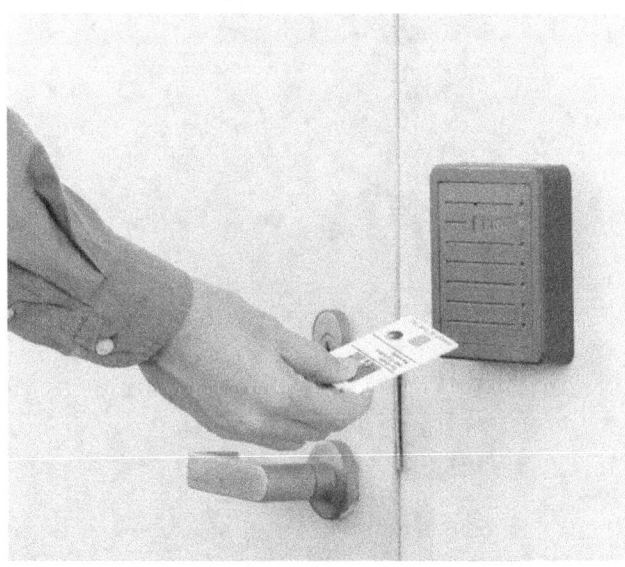

Proximity Reader from HID

Proximity readers, as the name implies, only require that the card be brought into close proximity with the reader, usually about 3 to 4 inches is the reading distance. Some readers go can much further, some are slightly less. The card does not have to be inserted or swiped, just held within the range of 3-4 inches for a brief period.

Proximity readers work by radio frequency. The card acts as an antenna, the reader is the transmitter and receiver. The card modifies the radio signal in such a way as to be uniquely identified as a number. The number is made up of bits (digital computer language). The higher the bit format of the card, the greater number of digits it can represent to the system. As of this writing, 37 bit cards are the norm. We do not recommend lesser number of bits or other formats. 37 bit cards are quite flexible and the number of digits will suffice for many years to come. Be wary of odd formats, some companies like to lock their customers into proprietary formats which only they can supply.

Smart Card Readers

Another type of reader is for "Smart Cards". Smart cards have an embedded read / write memory chip. This means systems now have the ability to add information to cards and read variable data. Smart card readers function just like proximity readers but the data exchange can be two way versus one way (read only) as in prox cards. MIFARE is the current standard but there are numerous types depending on the application and requirements. (More on this in the Card section.)

Smart Card Reader by HID

If you are about to invest in a new card access system, it makes sense to go to Smart Cards. The cards themselves are relatively cheap in large quantities and you will be future proofing your facility.

Biometric Readers

Biometrics is the science of using unique human characteristics for identification purposes. Common biometrics are fingerprints, hand geometry, and retinal patterns. The least intrusive and most reliable and well understood are fingerprints of course. Fingerprint readers are readily available and the least expensive of the three- although still about 4-5 times more than standard proximity or smart card readers.

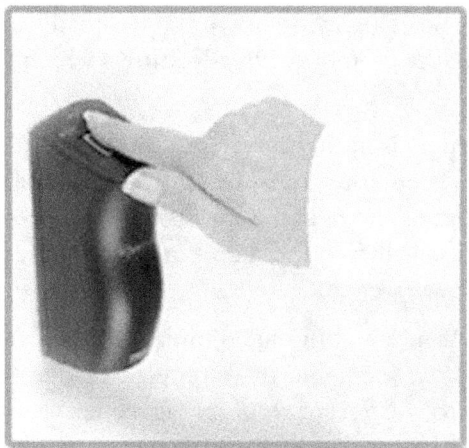

Biometric Fingerprint Reader by Bioscrypt

Although there is some psychological resistance to fingerprint readers they are still much more convenient than hand geometry and especially retinal scanning devices. Once you explain to users that the "fingerprint" is not actually stored and can't be used by the FBI, their use is generally accepted.

Currently there are two technologies in use for fingerprint readers; while they both use a form of optical scanning they differ in producing the actual template. The minutiae-based system is very similar to that used by law enforcement and forensics in that it records the ridges and swirls of the finger. The pattern based system can not be used for forensics since it concentrates on a "picture" of the finger. The image is encoded and stored as a template to compare against a live finger scan. This makes the pattern based systems easier to sell to employees and unions. Once you explain that such templates can not be recovered and used for outside identification, any resistance usually disappears.

Some pattern based systems were actually originally developed for the U.S. military for smart weapons. Weapons were to have a fingerprint sensor imbedded into them with the idea that only the soldier issued the weapon would be able to fire it. Consequently, fingerprint sensors of the pattern based type are very rugged and reliable. They can scan below the first layer of skin to avoid dirt, cuts, and abrasions. Some sensors can even work under water.

So why would you want to use biometrics? PIN numbers and access cards can be swapped and shared by users but since biometrics is tagged to an individual's unique characteristics, it is a positive means of identification. For instance, if a fingerprint is required to open a drug cabinet, you can be sure it was that person who opened it. Auditing authorities will accept biometrics without question. Many time and attendance (electronic time keeping systems) have gone to biometrics for this very reason.

Biometric readers usually require a second means of identification such as a PIN or card. The reason for this is to reduce the comparison time necessary to look up the biometric template. Understand that on a normal card reader, the only thing to be read is a number, the number is then tied to a database which contains the users personal data. On a biometric system, there is much more data. The person at the reader places his finger on the reader and that fingerprint template must be compared with the stored template. Since they could be potentially hundreds or thousands of users, there needs to be a way of narrowing down the templates to be compared. If the user is required to enter a PIN or card, the biometric already knows which stored template to compare with the live one.

One drawback of biometric readers is in fact this necessity to store the biometric template. When a new user is to be added to the system, they must be "enrolled". Since you can't require users to enroll at every single reader on the system, some means must be provided to download the enrolled template to all the readers. This usually requires additional wiring between each reader to distribute the templates.

Smart cards can provide a solution by writing the template to the card. When the new user enrolls, they are asked to present their smart card and the biometric reader "writes" their template to the card itself. When the user goes to a different reader, that reader "reads" the template from the card and compares it to the live one. This makes a very convenient system which can be deployed over multiple buildings and locations without the need for additional wiring.

Photo ID Badges
It is very popular to place card holder's pictures on badges for positive identification. All access cards can double as photo ID badges- in other words, use the same card for photo ID and for access control. All access systems have the capability to make photo badges with additional hardware such as a camera and printer. You can print on labels which then peel and stick to the card or you can print directly onto the card itself. The access system also includes a badge designer which lets you create different badge designs and add logos and graphics.

The photo is actually stored in the access control system database and can be recalled at any time whether you print a badge or not. This is a very important feature and even if you decide not to use photo ID badges, you are still encouraged to store every user's picture. The system can be set up to automatically bring up a user's photo when they use their card at certain readers. This is a valuable feature for security at main entrances to verify a person's identify.

In very sensitive areas such as cash pickups and drug vaults, you need to be aware of the person's real identity. It's best to use four forms of verification: card, photo on badge, stored photo, and live image of the person. For example, let's say a thief has obtained or stolen one of your access cards. It is possible (although it takes effort) to wipe off the picture and print a new one. This means a person can enter an area with a card that passes muster from the casual observer but is actually using someone else's card number. Your security looks at the badge and at the person and the picture is the same so they accept them. If the original card holder's picture is stored in the database however and security checks that – it will be glaringly obvious something is wrong.

If you need to implement such a system at a sensitive location it is recommended that the area be confined with physical barriers, such as a mantrap. A camera can be directed onto the user's face and the live image be displayed on a screen in an adjoining security office. The person wishing to gain entrance is required to present their access card which brings up their stored picture automatically. Security is then able to compare the live image against the stored on and see the user's personal details all on one screen.

Door Controllers

Door controllers, as the name implies, actually do the physical work of the access control system-locking and unlocking the doors. The readers attach to the door controllers; as well as the locks, door contacts (position sensors), and REX (request to exit). The door controllers then attach to the main database server which contains the database.

Door Controllers come in many shapes and sizes- usually 2 – 4 readers but can go as low as one reader and as many as 16 readers. When first powered up, the door controller is downloaded with it's data from the database server and then can function on it's own without communicating with the main system.

Door controllers can usually perform all decision making as to whether a door should be locked, and if a person is authorized to gain access. Be careful however, some companies may elect to install "slave" or dumb controllers which do not contain any memory on board and which must always be in communication with the main server. This can be very frustrating. If one wire is cut, the whole system stops operating and the facility is left helpless. We always recommend fully intelligent door controllers with full memory on each controllers so if the database server or main controller goes down, the doors and readers will contain to function as if nothing happened. While it may cost a little more, it is more than worth it.

Cards

Do not under any circumstances accept mag stripe, or any card that requires swipe or insertion. Bar codes are to be avoided at all costs and are only suitable for very low security applications- even though they are widely used in time and attendance.

Proximity cards are the standard. HID Corp. is by far the largest manufacturer of proximity cards for access control. Their standard is 125 KHZ. These cards come in many formats or bit capacity. The earliest cards were limited to 26 bits for a maximum card number of 65535. To get around this limitation, Facility or Customer Codes were added from 1- 255. This means each sequence of numbers from 1 to 65535 could be duplicated 255 times. That still meant the total card population without duplicates was just over 16 million- a small number in a world population of billions.

As more powerful processors become available, the card formats were increased to 32 bit and then to 37 bit which resulted in more numbers becoming available without duplicates. If you are set on old style proximity cards, insist on 37 bit cards. 37 bit cards do not require the use of a customer code and as a result are more secure.

Smart cards are an attractive alternative to prox cards and from the user standpoint, function identically. Smart cards present many more options for other uses, now and in the future. Because of their intelligent read/write chip, they can be used for any cashless application such as vending, parking, dining, book stores and libraries; while still performing duty as an access control card. Smart cards can be direct printed with photo for photo ID badges. Barcodes can even be printed on them as well for other purposes. One smart card can serve many, many solutions.

Smart cards come in many different types and the choices can be overwhelming. HID Corp has their own format called iClass. You are not guaranteed total capability with iClass however, so be careful that the iClass card you select is compatible with other applications.

MIFARE is the European standard and is the most widely deployed card type in the world. The MIFARE card has been used for many years in the transportation sector in Europe and so is a fairly safe bet. Other cards such as DESFIRE (ISO 14443A) are made especially for government applications for higher security. These are probably overkill (and much more expensive) for private use but the choice is yours.

Besides the type, there are varying memory sizes available from 1k (1000 bits) to 4k and higher. (At present 16k seems to be the limit.) The memory size strictly depends on your application. Smart cards have multiple sectors (separate areas) which can be partitioned for different applications. For example, one sector can be for parking, while another is for gym membership. Consult your vendors for the optimum size card.

Fobs

Fobs are small versions of cards which are designed to be carried on a keychain for convenience (and so you won't forget to carry it). They are more expensive and have a shorter read range than cards. Of course, you can't print on them either. But almost all access systems allow you to issue multiple cards to the same user so a user can have a photo ID badge card and a fob.

Software (Application)

Our system so far consists of cards, readers, locks, door contacts, and REXs connected to door controllers; but we still need somewhere to store all the information and manage it. This is the purpose of the software application. Although access control software is usually sold as a package, in actuality it usually consists of a proprietary application and a separate open architecture database engine.

In fact, it is very important to insist on an open architecture database engine such as Microsoft SQL or Oracle. This allows you to export your data to a new or different access control system in the future; as well as make it possible to import and export data for other purposes such as custom reports. Not such a concern on systems with a few dozen users but critical on systems with thousands of card holders.

To refresh ourselves on the total system operation, it goes like this: The card is read by the reader which passes the card number to a door controller which makes the decision to unlock the door. The access control software application & database do not come into play during normal system operation. When the system is first installed and programmed however, the software is the part that manages the input of data into the database and also downloads that data into the door controllers. It is also required when changes- adds or deletes, must be done and to obtain reports or perform diagnostics.

While some features vary from one access control manufacturer to another, most access control software is very similar so you should make purchasing decisions based on the dealer's reputation, references, and how comfortable you are using the software. Insist on a demo, and make sure you are able to try it hands on. All software should be intuitive and not require you to read a manual to perform day to day functions. Pay special attention to the Help menus, are they readily available and do they provide clear information and answers?

Card Holder Data

Once you've settled on a system, the real work just begins. It is vital to set up procedures and standards for entering information- especially if you are going to rely on others to operate the system from day to day. Probably the most important caveat is to *enter data consistently*. Always put the same piece of data in the same field in the same format. A good example would be contract employees like janitor and guards. Don't enter "janitors" one time and "cleaners" another. If you enter "guards", don't later enter "security". This will allow you to produce accurate reports which actually reflect the true database.

Let's say you run a multi-tenant office building and want a report showing all the janitors who have cards. It's easy if you always entered Janitors- but you can see a custom report for "janitors" won't include any fields with the name "cleaners".

Never, ever issue cards with names like "Temp", "Vendor", "Contractor" or multiple cards under the same name like John Smith for all of John Smith's employees. Insist on individual names or at the least department names or company names. If you allow a dozen cards to be issued under "Vendor" and have a problem such as a theft, you will never be able to narrow down who exactly was in the building. The preferred method is to issue cards to "Vendor FedEx"; or "Vendor Verizon". Contractors should always be identified by company names- "Contractor ABC Electric". This way there can be no mistake when you look at a transaction history report when something happens after hours.

Access control databases can be integrated to HR databases as well. As long as all the databases are open architecture, XML or ODBC links can be set up to exchange information between systems. This means once new employee data is entered into the HR system, it is automatically entered into the card access database and vice versa if an employee quits or is fired. It takes a high level security integrator to accomplish this so get references on successful jobs.

TIP: Never store a person's Social Security Number. This will help you stay in compliance with data security standards.

Photo ID Badge Software

Although almost all access control systems allow you to store pictures – whether you have photo ID badges or not. You can usually take any digital camera picture, move it onto the access control computer and then import it into the access control database.

If you plan on issuing true Photo ID badges however, almost all access control packages come with a Photo ID badge module. The main purpose of the Photo ID Badge software module is simply to design the badge templates. You can add a company logo, simple graphics, the person's photo, and personal data such as last name, first name, department, employee number and so on. The badge designer allows you to specify what fields from the database will appear on the photo ID badge- another reason to be sure you have consistent, clean data.

You will also need a card printer to print on the cards. These printers start at $2500-$3000 and go up considerably from there. Unfortunately, the ribbons are also very expensive and the printers themselves are not known for their reliability. Depending on your type of cards and application you may find it better to print labels and then attach them to the cards. This can be very tedious with large quantities of cards so choose wisely. Photo ID badges will always be a question of many compromises.

Visitor Management

Another module included with many access systems is Visitor Management. This is simply an electronic means of logging in visitors but with some significant advantages. Electronically logging visitors provides a searchable database of all visitor activity for example. You can add driver license scanners to collect information without manually writing it. Repeat visitors are already in the database so logging them in is much faster. Temporary badges can be printed through the system. Another interesting feature is the ability to have the visitor pre-authorized. This means the company employee the visitor is coming to see can log onto the access control system and input the visitor's name and time of appointment. When that visitor arrives, security or reception already has most of the information they need entered and just enters the time. Since many companies do not allow visitors without prior appointments, this is a very handy feature to keep out unannounced sales people.

Visitor Management systems can also alert security or reception of unwanted visitors. Suppose an employee is in the midst of a domestic dispute; their "partner" can be flagged so if they show up at the building a warning message is displayed once reception or security enters their name into the system.

Your security vendor should point out all these features to you during the sales process. If they don't, be wary of their knowledge.

Turnstiles

One last means of controlling access are **turnstiles**. These are gaining popularity in large office buildings where large amounts of people go in and out every day. These newer turnstiles are usually *optical*, which means they use a beam (just like intrusion alarms) to control access. Turnstiles are almost always used in conjunction with access control systems.

The turnstiles consist of a number of lanes- each lanes being an entrance, an exit or reversible. Picture 3 freestanding pedestals: one on the right, one on the left and one in the middle. A beam built into each pedestal shoots from the right to the middle and from the left to the middle. The left and right have card readers on opposite ends.

Under normal operation, a person wishing to enter the lobby uses their card on the right hand (in lane). If accepted, a light turns green and the visitor walks through breaking the beam. Since there was a valid card read, nothing happens. If a person walks through without using the card or the card was not accepted, when they break the beam an alarm sounds, alerting lobby security.

Turnstiles can be set up to require a card read when leaving the building as well. This can be valuable in the event of a disaster like a bomb threat or earthquake since the management can get a report from the access system of everyone who entered the building and everyone who left and by comparing them, find out who is still in the building.

Web Based Access Control Systems

A recent development has been the advent of web browser based access systems which do away with the traditional client- server based systems. We consider these to be the wave of the future since the IT department is taking on more and more of the security management role as systems move onto networks.

Web based access panels do not employ computers as a part of the system. The hardware contains solid state memory which has a Linux based web server and database running in it. The access system manager uses any computer (Apple or Windows or virtually anything else with a web browser) to log on and manage it. Since you are in effect using a web browser such as Internet Explorer, there is nothing to learn- you already know how to use it.

More importantly, since you are doing it through the world wide web, you can manage your system from anywhere in the world- whether at home, or at the airport or on vacation. These systems represent a tremendous convenience for some people. If you fall into this category, web based access systems are worth investigating. S2 is the market leader in this technology as of this writing; see their web site at s2sys.com

Logical Access

A relatively new system that is very similar to access control and in fact can go hand in hand with it is logical access. These systems employ card or biometric (usually fingerprint) to log onto internal computer systems, networks and even applications.

In the case of logical access, the reader is attached to the employee's computer. Some keyboards even have built in readers for this purpose. Once the user places his card or fingerprint on the reader, they are automatically logged onto whatever systems they are authorized to use. This access is set up by the IT (Information Technology) department through the use of policies.

The main advantage of logical access is that passwords are no longer needed because they are internally stored under the user's profile. Because users no longer need to remember passwords they can be "strong" – as many as 64 characters- making it difficult to impossible for hackers to gain access to company systems.

Logical access can be integrated with physical access control systems so that data only needs to be entered once. For example, the Human Resources department enters a new employee into the HR database. The HR database sends a message to the access control database with the new user data and that in turn sends it to the logical access database- eliminating a great deal of work on your part. The future may see these systems share a *common* database but for now such a system does not exist, mainly because of the resistance between manufacturers.

Last but not least, logical and physical access systems can be set up to exchange information concerning a person's whereabouts. This means you can deny a person from logging onto their computer unless they have physically entered the building. They can also be automatically logged off if the access system sees them exiting an area (assuming you have card readers installed at that exit). The possibilities are quite endless and limited only by your needs and imagination.

Integrated Systems

We have discussed many of the key electronic security systems and hardware and even mentioned some ways these systems can interact. Almost any location or facility with multiple electronic security systems can benefit from some integration between these systems. For example, if you have card access and an intrusion system, wouldn't it be nice to just use your card to enter the facility and disarm the intrusion system at the same time? This is integration.

Card access systems, since they traditionally employ computers, have been at the center of integration. With the right options and equipment, most access systems can seamlessly display video and intrusion information on a unified display; and can perform functions based on input from these other systems.

A good example is the access control system can arm the intrusion system automatically at a specified time and then bypass alarm doors when a card holder enters. A "Door Forced" alarm can also cause a window to pop up and display video from a camera at that door- both *before* and *after* the event! This is invaluable in providing first class security.

Integration is not an easy task, especially on very complicated systems. It takes a very knowledgeable security company (a security integrator) and specialized equipment designed to work together.

Integrating access and video is fairly straightforward and helpful. This generally just involves selecting DVRs or NVRs which are compatible with the access systems software. What usually happens is that the access system knows the IP address of the DVR / NVR and then is able to bookmark and pull video off the recorder. If you happen to have a DVR that is not compatible with the access system, it is probably best just to bite the bullet and replace it with one that is compatible. It will be expensive to write some custom integration script or software.

Some integration of intrusion and access is almost a necessity if both systems are present; otherwise you will undoubtedly end up with false alarms. A very difficult situation to solve is when you have employees working at odd hours. If your business schedule is consistent, then automatic integration works well. But if employees are prone to drop in at midnight to work when inspired, then very careful design is required. For example, the use of PIR motion detectors will not work and most likely glass break detectors which can handle human occupation will be required.

Integrated systems should have a detailed system design up front and approved by both the customer and security contractor in writing so there is no misunderstanding about how the system will function. Such a document will serve to raise red flags to both parties about potential problems. Don't forget to include janitor schedules, couriers, and especially management or employees who are prone to come in at odd times. Customers tend to want too many options (it does this- except when this happens- but not at this time). If the integration is kept fairly simple, you will have a much greater chance of success.

Central Station

What's it like in a central station? Very hectic! Consider that central stations are open and manned 24 hours a day, 365 days a year. Unlike even the phone company, central stations never close. There are no holidays, no down time. Someone always has to be on duty and usually at least two people are there at all times. A central station is very similar in operation- and stress level to an air traffic control center.

Central stations or monitoring companies range in size from small local concerns to nationwide centers with hundreds of employees. Some central stations have only one or two large customers- they may contract with a school district or local government. Some are even run by the company they monitor. For example, some large chains or even school districts run their own central station.

Before computers came into use, alarms were displayed in central stations by mechanical means- dials, meters, lights, buzzers, and even paper tapes. An average central station may have had 5000 or more alarms so operators were kept very busy running from rack to rack handling "openings" and "closings" as well as alarms. Typically when a customer armed his system, the display in the central station would change by lighting up and buzzing. The operator would then turn a dial putting the system into night mode and clock a time card for that customer. No one ever fell asleep in a central station!

If the dial, meter and buzzer indicated an alarm, the operator had to find the correct dial, look up in a book who the customer was and what to do and clock a card with the time. Even though a shift might have 5 or more people on duty, there were many occasions when multiple alarms had to wait for the next available operator

Today, central stations are quieter, with rooms full of computer displays. Systems are more automatic so openings and closings are handled by the computer and logged without the operator having to take action. While that may seem to take a large workload off the operators, the job is in fact tougher than ever. Monitoring companies today may handle 10,000 customers or more.

Incoming alarms, trouble signals and other monitoring points arrive on displays in order of priority and with colors indicating the type or importance of the alarm. The operator or "customer service representative" must determine from a database of information and instructions what action to take. Usually, they will notify the police or fire department dispatch center but often the type of signal dictates other actions such as notifying the customer or a maintenance person.

Unfortunately, the vast majority of signals arriving in the central station are false alarms- as many as 99% of all alarms are false. This means the operators are busy handling false signals when the occasional actual alarm arrives. This is also the area where there is room for error.

There has been much discussion in the monitoring community about "operator judgment calls". Should the central station operator decide whether to notify the police or should they just do it on every alarm? Either way the monitoring company employee is put in a difficult situation. They may indeed call the police time after time on the same alarm from the same customer and endure the wrath of a police dispatcher who won't dispatch patrol cars anyway. But the very time they make a judgment call and not call the police will be the time the alarm is real.

There was an actual case many years ago where an alarm monitoring company received an intrusion alarm from the home of a famous baseball player. The operator duly notified the police. A few minutes later fire alarms and additional intrusion alarms came in from the same location. The operator assumed the police had arrived and all was under control.

About 30 minutes later the operator received a call from the police dispatcher stating the baseball player's home was on fire and asked had she dispatched the fire department!

It was learned later that a small fire in the garage had burned through the burglar alarm wires first causing the initial alarm which she had notified the police about. But the first police car couldn't find the address so they went back on patrol thinking it was just a false alarm.

As the fire grew, it set off the home's fire alarm and burned through more of the burglar alarm wires. Finally, a neighbor noticed smoke and called the fire department. By the time the fire department arrived the home was totally engulfed- and a total loss.

Many legal actions were filed against the alarm company, the wire manufacturer, and the company that made the water heater (where the fire actually started). Even though the alarm company was held up to severe ridicule, it was ultimately limited to a $250 damage payout due to it's rigid limit of liability clause in the monitoring contract.

This should teach you that not only are central stations personnel human but alarm company contracts are very hard to attack in court. Most of them limit liquidated damages from negligence to $250 and this been upheld time and again in court.

The real point is just we don't want the monitoring company to make judgment calls but on the other hand, don't cause false alarms so they are never confused about your business or residence operation. The clearer your system operation is, the less likely any mistakes will be made.

The term central station is not used as often today because the name is confusing to the public, most prefer the term monitoring company. Also traditionally "central station" was used to denote a UL Listed facility with guard response.

It was quite common up to the 1990's for central stations to dispatch armed guards to investigate the cause of alarm. UL in fact demanded response on certain types of burglar and fire systems in a specific time period. Certain high grade burglar alarms (Grade A) required response within 15 minutes.

Alarm company guards routinely carried keys to the customer's premises with the idea that guards and police would be able to gain entry and search the premises. Even as far back as the mid 70's police response was erratic or slow and many time the alarm company guards searched the buildings by themselves.

As populations, traffic, and liability concerns grew, armed response by central stations began to decline until today when it is very, very rare. At best, the central station or the customer will contract with a patrol service to respond. This adds considerable cost but at least it guarantees action will be taken on alarms the police will likely ignore.

Interestingly enough, we are not aware of any instances where the central station itself was attacked. UL has always recognized that possibility and has strict standards for securing the building. In fact, UL specifies the monitoring area itself should not have windows if it is on the ground floor, and doors must be locked and controlled at all times.

Attacking the monitoring company would render the alarms they monitor useless since no police would be notified of any alarms. There have been instances of evacuations due to bomb threats or hazardous spills in the neighborhood and we have always suspected these may have been caused for ulterior motives but nothing was ever proven.

Human Security (Guards)

The term guard usually conjures up an unflattering image of a tired old man sleeping at his post. In fact many security guards are retired – from the military or police department. Some security guards are even off duty policemen seeking to earn extra money. It is also true they can be incompetent and lazy. Just like any other employee, there are good ones and bad ones.

It has been our experience that about 50-75% of the typical guard force is alert, competent and well trained. It does depend greatly on the company employing them too. A good guard company will provide training and roving supervisors to check on their people. If you plan on contracting for guards, insist on seeing their personnel files detailing their past employment, training and experience. Ex-military are preferred due to the extreme sense of responsibility and maturity instilled during military service.

Keep in mind that the lower your cost to hire the guard, the lower the quality will ultimately be. Don't forget, the guard company is making a profit on the difference between what you pay and what they pay the guard. You can also insist on high quality guards if you're willing to negotiate a higher rate. One big advantage of contracting out for guards is that you pay a fixed rate (unless you want extra hours in an emergency). The guard company is responsible for benefits and overtime. You should seek out a reputable guard company that pays their people well and provides good benefits such as health insurance and vacations. Some provide nothing and consequently have poor employees with low morale and high turnover.

In large systems and facilities, human security personnel can be considered an essential part of the integration. Security supervisors should be brought in at the earliest stages to provide input and suggestions. Frequently you will be amazed at some detail or operating procedure security is aware of that significantly impacts the overall security design.

Modern electronic security systems have several enhanced features aimed at human security. Almost any type of security signal can be directed to portable, wireless laptops, PDAs, or smart phones. This includes video. Imagine a roving guard patrol, either on foot or in a vehicle, receives an intrusion alarm signal on his smart phone indicating a door intrusion on the rear of the warehouse. Either automatically or manually he commands a video stream of the affected area and knows immediately if there is a problem or perhaps it's just a false alarm. No matter what type of system you ultimately have installed, insist that the security contractor thoroughly trains the security staff.

Should you have your own in house security?

Guards are very expensive, a big selling point of electronic security is to reduce or eliminate guards. Do the math- having just one guard on duty 24 hours a day = 168 total hours each week; that's 8736 hours per year. If you only pay $15 per hour, that's a total annual cost of $131,040! You can buy a lot of electronic security equipment for that amount.

If you employee your own guards you will have to have extra people to handle days off and vacations- and you will have to add taxes, benefits, and overtime. Add radios, uniforms, and other vital equipment and this could easily increase your annual cost to more than $200,000.

Many companies do not take these costs into consideration until their bottom line starts to suffer and they start looking closely at expenses. If you employ guards or have a contract with a guard company, you can save major amounts of expense by just eliminating one shift and relying on electronic security.

While employing your own security does allow you to control quality, very high quality people will undoubtedly cost more than $15 per hour. If your business dictates guards, then look to contract to a security guard company.

Don't make the mistake of assigning security duties to regular employees either. This is a recipe for disaster. Not only can untrained "guards" result in liability against the company but virtually handing employees the keys to your business is just asking for theft and collusion.

Physical Barriers

Bars

Truck and vehicle gates

Crash barriers

These days, physical barriers again present a good solution to many security threats. Bars over vulnerable windows or skylights can deter or slow down burglars allowing the electronic intrusion system time to notify police and have them respond.

Vehicle gates can help prevent auto theft and petty theft and vandalism. Access systems can control such gates just as easily as doors. Generally the security contractor will work with your gate company to interface the systems. It is usually cheaper to control a gate than a door because the hardware is already there. The access system just sends a signal to the gate operator.

If threats from car and truck bombs exist in your particular situation then there are extensive solutions with vehicle crash barriers which can stop five ton trucks approaching at 30 mile per hour. Obviously, these are very specialized and very expensive but they do exist.

Can alarms be defeated? Strengths & Weaknesses

You are considering the suggestions put forth in this guide and are ready to make a major purchase but then you see a movie demonstrating how burglars completely get around the high tech security system. Hollywood has perpetrated the myth that alarms can be defeated but like most things in Hollywood, the reality is quite different.

With current technology, a well designed, maintained, and tested intrusion system is in itself almost impossible to defeat. The cable television show "Mythbusters" devoted at least two episodes to defeating various intrusion technologies and discovered just how difficult it was.

The key is a well designed system. All doors should be alarmed, and backed up by motion detectors. Motion detectors should be infrared sensing and must be placed at no more than eight feet high and always so that the intruder must pass across their field of detection- never facing. The alarm door contacts and the PIRs (Passive Infrared) motion detectors act as back ups to each other. There are many variations on alarm contacts to suit different installation requirements. Your alarm company will choose the right one for each application- such as overhead doors.

Should a burglar get through a wall or window, the PIR will detect them and vice versa. PIRs generally have an effective range of 40- 50 feet. While there are models that have longer range, we recommend staying away from them due to issues with false alarms. It is simply very difficult to control the environment hundreds of feet away from the detector.

PIRs should never face glass. Although infrared does not pass through glass- the intense light from the sun or headlights can cause the sensor to alarm. Glass is in fact the PIR's only weakness, don't expect a PIR to detect motion on the other side of internal office windows or showroom display windows. And it is true that if a burglar could somehow place a sheet of glass in front of a PIR it would no longer detect motion, that just isn't likely to be possible.

The best defense to avoiding any problems with PIRs is just to test them. All PIRs have a "walk test light", an LED on front that lights up when it senses motion. Make it a point to walk in front of your PIRs periodically and ensure the LED is coming on. This will also alert you if somehow the power is cut to the unit- although the PIR should be powered from the alarm control panel- and *it* should detect any problems with power immediately.

Longer distances such as hallways or warehouses can be protected with active infrared beams (also know as PECs – Photo Electric Cells a holdover term from the older days). Although some people refer to these as "lasers" they are not. These consist of a modulated transmitter and receiver pointed at each other. As Mythbusters so rightly proved, these cannot be seen with powder or special goggles- despite what you've seen in movies. They are completely invisible and it is impossible to use a mirror to reflect the beam back on itself. One reason is that no one knows which side is the transmitter since both transmitter and receiver appear identical.

Glass break sensors are very popular but we only recommend them as a last resort and never, ever as primary protection- only as a backup. The only really *effective* glass breaks are based on vibration or piezo effect and are mounted to window frames or glued directly onto the glass.

All other glass breaks are acoustic, these actually listen for the sound of breaking glass. These are generally either a false alarm nightmare or fail to detect breakage at all. Even worse, the latest trend is to combine a PIR and an acoustic microphone in the same detector so that if the PIR senses motion, the glass break is disabled. This is supposed to eliminate false alarms from janitors or employees but it more likely to result in no alarm during a real burglary.

Never allow the alarm company to install ultrasonic or microwave type detectors or "dual technology" sensors. Ultrasonic can easily be defeated, (ultrasonic waves can be deflected by a bed sheet), and are almost never used any more. Microwaves pass through walls too easily and are a major source of false alarms. Some alarm manufacturers have attempted to get around this by combining microwave and infrared into so called "dual technology" detectors. Unfortunately, what ends up happening is you get the worst of both. The microwave stays in alarm all the time and the system falls back only on the infrared. Dual technology detectors end up just being expensive PIRs. Save your money.

There are some serious considerations with the alarm control panel and *communication*. All alarm panels must communicate with the outside world in some manner to transmit an intrusion signal. This is one of the major weaknesses of most alarm systems. Traditionally, the alarm transmission is over voice grade telephone lines. The alarm panel actually dials the phone number of the central monitoring station and transmits an encoded data stream. Once the central monitoring station receives the alarm, their computers automatically bring up your account in the database and they then notify the police.

Obviously, if the phone line is cut then the alarm signal will not go through. For this reason, it is extremely important that the phone line be protected or hidden. The larger the facility the less the chance of burglars cutting phone lines because there are so many. There have been instances however, when thieves cut ALL the lines entering a building to make certain they disabled the alarm.

In any case, phone lines for alarms should never be marked or identified with tags. They should be in conduit from the point of entry to the alarm control. This can be very difficult when lines are fed from overhead poles since the phone company is just going to drop the line down the side and into your building.

A new alternative to dial up alarm transmission is internet monitoring. The alarm uses a broadband internet connection such as DSL or a cable modem to contact the central station. The big advantage of this scheme is that is can be *two way*. The central station's computers can be programmed to automatically and periodically contact the alarm panel to make sure it is there. If the line is cut or disabled, the central station can detect this in as little as 90 seconds.

Some very high risk businesses such as jewelry stores are usually required by their insurance companies to have a UL Listed alarm system. Depending on the UL Listing, they will likely require this two way form of communication. This is often referred to as "**Line Security**". The advantage is this is now available to anyone with the right alarm control panel and an internet connection.

The consideration in all cases must be however, what to do if the line is disrupted? The central station gets a trouble message indicating communication was lost with the alarm control panel. UL usually requires a police dispatch but in reality the police would not even know what to look for, if there was no outward evidence of a burglary they would simply chalk it up to another false alarm and move on to the next call.

You would be notified but is there really anything you could do or would want to do? If you are concerned about this, the only real solution is to subscribe to some sort of alarm response service. Many alarm companies and some guard companies will provide an armed response. Although it can be somewhat costly, it could be worth the peace of mind and you will never have to worry about police response.

So assuming that you have good alarm detection equipment and good alarm communication, can the alarm system be defeated? Human error becomes the single biggest weakness- as in most things.

The alarm detection devices have to correct for the application. They have to be installed correctly and they must be serviced and tested. But this will still not be enough.

Human error will still enter the picture. The alarm system must be armed for one thing. People often forget to arm the system when they leave! You can purchase an additional level of monitoring from the alarm company called "**Late to Close**". You provide a schedule to the monitoring company and if the alarm system is not armed by the specified time, they will notify you. In most cases, the alarm company can remotely arm the system if you give them permission.

There is also room for human error on the part of the alarm monitoring company. If the alarm company operators are overwhelmed with too many variations of schedules and special instructions it becomes easier for them to misinterpret a situation. The best way to guard against this is to maintain a routine. If you arm and disarm the system at approximately the same time every day and don't vary, they will be much more likely to notice when something is wrong.

You can also have your system programmed with "**Duress codes**". This is a special unique PIN combination that differs from your normal arm/ disarm code. If you are under duress and forced to disarm your system by thieves, using the special duress code disarms the system as usual but also sends a special message to the central station indicating you are being forced to open your business or home. Be sure to discuss this at length with your alarm company, and your employees or family. The worst thing you can do is use the duress code by mistake.

This brings us back to the major weakness of alarm systems- human error. If you, your employees, or family constantly (or even occasionally) cause false alarms, your system is as good as worthless. Police departments not only keep records of false alarms (usually for fines) but the patrolmen are very aware of them. If they recognize your location as having had false alarms in the past, they are not going to get there with any particular speed. On the opposite side, if there has never been a false alarm at your location, the police are much more likely to respond quickly.

We have also seen numerous instances of repeated false alarms leading up to actual burglaries. Professional burglaries have been known to cause alarm after alarm until the police grow tired of responding, then they can break in at their leisure with the knowledge they have extra time inside.

Causing false alarms can be done in various ways on poorly designed systems: shining powerful spotlights on PIRs pointed towards windows, rattling windows until acoustic glass break detectors go into alarm, shaking loose doors, etc. The best way to combat this problem is to make sure none of these problems exist and to demand immediate service of any false alarms. One false alarm is cause for serious concern.

But of all the actions you can take as a manager, business owner or homeowner regarding day to day operations of your security system, the most important one is to make sure you or others are not causing false alarms. Once any false alarms occur it can be months before that memory fades from the alarm monitoring company and the police department.

So, there are ways to defeat an alarm. If one has physical access to the system it is possible for an expert to bypass detection devices and then return after the system is armed and gain entry-assuming the owner did not test the system before leaving. It is also possible that an inside person, such as a security guard, acts to aid accomplices to defeat the system from within.

An alarm can also be defeated by disabling communications to the monitoring center – as long as there is no line security in place to detect this.

An alarm can also be defeated by human error on the part of the owner or the monitoring company, and this is the most likely scenario but it would require the burglar know in advance that the owner often fails to arm the system- or the monitoring company is lax or overworked and frequently makes mistakes.

Intrusion systems that are backed by armed guard response and monitored by diligent professionals are extremely difficult if not impossible to circumvent. This is why you rarely hear of a large burglary of expensive items. When you do, it is very likely an inside job where the system was bypassed from within by "authorized" personnel.

If you happen to manage a high risk facility, one step you can do to help protect yourself is to insure that plans for security system are under lock and key. There are no requirements that mandate security plans be submitted to any city department. Fire alarms yes, but not security. No security plan should be a matter of public record (except unfortunately public buildings which are done under bid and therefore part of public records).

Your security plans should be in your possession. Insist that the security company turn over all copies to you and have them sign a release confirming that fact. As long as your have the plans available for technicians there should be no argument. By the way- always confirm the identity of alarm technicians by calling the security company before admitting them!

How to Defeat Burglar Alarms (not)!

Having been in the security and alarm business since 1973, I have always been aware of an intense interest in alarms on the part of Hollywood- (and some tech geeks), as well as business and home owners.

I decided to write this section to punch holes in popular myths and things you see in the movies- but more importantly to educate, in order to protect yourself against potential weaknesses in your security system. I firmly believe that if some of you are aware of the possible defects of your alarm system, you are better prepared to correct those problem areas.

Finally, as I 'm sure you will discover upon reading this book, actually defeating a modern alarm system is a whole lot harder than some would lead you to believe!

The people that design and manufacture alarm systems are not stupid; they know every trick and how to counteract them. As in any other system, cost and time are the bigger factors in defeating it. The cost factor goes hand in hand with the time factor. The lower the cost of the system, the faster it can be defeated. If one buys a cheap alarm system, they will get less protection and a system easier to defeat. On the other hand, given enough time one can defeat almost anything. Modern alarm systems balance these two factors quite well.

So can you defeat a burglar alarm?

In order to be aware of or exploit the weaknesses of a system, you need to understand the system. With that in mind we will explore and explain each component of alarms and security systems.

Please note that some material is duplicated here to relieve you from having to flip back to earlier sections.

Perhaps first we should explain the terms 'alarm' and 'security' as used in this guide.

'Alarm' will be used to designate an intrusion system designed to deter and detect burglars.

'Security' on the other hand will describe any other system designed to detect, deter, control, and document intruders or unauthorized persons. Some examples of these systems are:

Video Surveillance (CCTV, digital video, DVRs, etc.)

Card Access (key cards, card keys, access cards, etc.)

Biometric Identity Systems (fingerprint, hand geometry, retinal scan)

Metal Detectors

Human Security

Finally, we will explain about Central Monitoring Stations.

With the above in mind, we will cover each system and each component, detailing how it works, its strengths and weaknesses, and potential ways to bypass or defeat it.

Before we start however, you need to get some things out of your mind- like everything you've ever seen in a movie or on television! I have yet to see any movie or TV show that actually portrays an alarm or security system accurately. In fact, security professionals always get a good laugh at what they see on the silver screen. Some scenarios are so ludicrous it's astounding how even uninformed people could fall for them.

But that's Hollywood and the reasons they do what they do are strictly visual. I worked closely with producers, directors, and set decorators on quite a few movies and they are not the least bit interested in reality- only how something looks on screen.

One case in point- how many times have you seen actors slide, swipe, or insert access key cards when trying to get through a high security door? The truth is, the real security industry abandoned that technology almost twenty years ago. These days, 99% of card readers are of the "proximity" type; which means the card just has to be held within four inches of the reader. Modern readers are contactless and can even read through clothes, purses and briefcases. Although I have pointed this fact out to numerous movie production people, they don't want them because they don't "look cool". Movie people think it looks a lot better if the actor has to do something- like sliding a card through a reader.

Another great myth is the fire sprinkler system. Again, how many times have you seen a movie where the actor lights a match and sets off every sprinkler in the building? In reality- only the specific sprinkler head which senses the fire will discharge water. But the truth just doesn't look good or advance the story.

So get all that Hollywood baloney out of your mind and we'll explain how alarms really work! The fact is, although some individual components of alarms and security systems do have weaknesses, when they are put together in a complete system those potential weaknesses are for the most part counteracted. The truth is, a modern alarm system is extremely hard to defeat.

While this book won't make your movie experience more enjoyable, it will give you plenty of ammunition to argue with your friends and it will help you make your own security system better.

The Alarm System

An alarm system consists of many individual pieces which are designed to work together as an intrusion detection system. The typical alarm system consists of a control panel, a keypad, detection devices (door contacts and motion detectors), and a sounder such as a bell or siren. These are parts you are probably somewhat familiar with but there are many more devices which manage the system and are designed to complete the overall detection system.

The Control Panel

The control panel serves as the brains of the alarm. It monitors the keypad and the detection devices and makes if-then decisions based on programming. Alarm control panel programs can be quite complex and perform many functions such as managing communications, entry & exit delays, monitoring the integrity of all the wiring, storing user PINs and activity- as well as handling all different types of alarm events. Programs can easily run into as many as 500 entries and as a result are often entered through a laptop or by remote download.

Control panels manage many more functions than just the burglar detection. They contain a power supply including a backup battery and charger. They monitor the actual wires in your system to maintain integrity. They manage the communications- including dialing multiple numbers repeated times until the signal gets through. Beyond these functions, the control panel also maintains the audible warnings (bells, sirens, etc.), entry / exit delay (which we'll explain shortly, and remembers the PIN numbers or keypad combinations for multiple users.

Another responsibility of the control panel is backup power. All systems contain at least one standby battery which is usually capable of running the system at full efficiency for at least 24 hours and often as long as 72 hours.

Besides just sounding a bell or siren locally, the control panel is also responsible for transmitting the actual alarm signal to the monitoring station. Very few, if any, police departments these days will receive alarms directly; they are just too busy. 99% of all alarms go to a private central monitoring station which decodes the alarm signals and then human operators take the appropriate action- notify the police or the customer.

Controls panels transmit much more than just alarm signals. They can log power loss, when the system is armed or disarmed, and which user did it. This last feature can be invaluable to managers and owners to have an audit trail of their employees.

The system usually communicates to the central monitoring station by phone lines. Residences can use the phone line already there but many alarm companies prefer businesses install a dedicated phone line just for the alarm. This is not bad advice. Although it increases the total monthly cost, a dedicated line reduces the chance the alarm control won't be able to get through to the central station. If the intrusion system can't dial out and deliver the alarm message, the central station won't be aware of an alarm condition- another important point.

Newer alarm systems (and more advanced monitoring companies) now offer "internet" monitoring. Instead of the traditional phone line they use broadband Internet access such as DSL or cable. Some systems continuously monitor the condition of the line and can warn if the connection is lost. These are highly secure because of their speed and security. Internet communication is two-way- the alarm monitoring company can actually detect if the customer's panel is not replying because it is off-line.

Whichever type of communication is used, the phone line is the weak link and must be protected from cutting. This is something to be especially aware of in residential applications. If the phone line exposed then burglars can easily cut it. This is one of the primary weaknesses of the modern alarm system- the communications path.

Manufacturers have recognized this and several alternatives are available. Wireless transmission comes in the form of cellular or radio. Neither are widely used mostly due to the extra expense and difficulty of setting them up. Although cellular would seem the perfect choice in fact it is the most difficult due to the ever changing cell network. The recent switch from analog to digital left many alarm cellular transmitters in the dust. The industry is just now catching up but the point remains that a fixed cellular antenna is not the best solution for a perfect signal. After all you can move around when talking on your cell- the alarm system can't.

Radio is a viable option but requires a private radio network. Some companies have tried to get around this by using other customers as "repeaters" (which relay your signal along down the network) but this never caught on because of poor market penetration.

The vast majority of alarms use standard phone lines and if they are cut the alarm simply won't be effective except as a local alarm which will simply trigger the siren or bell. All alarm systems using phone lines do test them by sending an automatic signal to the central monitoring station- but only once every 24 hours. Then, of course, the monitoring company has to do something if the test signal does not arrive.

The alarm system can also protect itself against someone calling and trying to keep the line busy- the system will constantly hang up to keep the line clear- and it can do it must faster than one can call it. Also, many systems have two phone lines- the second for backup.

The best way to protect against phone line tampering is to simply make it impossible or difficult to cut. All telephone lines should enter underground and never be exposed. Don't assume this is impossible just because you don't have underground lines presently- the phone company will bury them- at your expense of course- in many areas.

If underground lines just can't be done then have the lines installed inside metal conduit and the terminal connections inside a locked and secured metal box. This box can be tampered so that the alarm triggers if the box is opened. Effectively protecting the telephone lines is the most important thing you can do to prevent defeat of the alarm system.

Other than cutting off the alarm control panel's communications path, the industry itself has worried about the possibility of thieves "substituting" their own control panel to mimic the target's alarm. This actually occurred a few times in the seventies- but that was when alarm controls were very crude- before the microprocessor.

Today, ultra high security UL Grade AA rated alarms communicate via encrypted signals making substitution nearly impossible- assuming the burglar could get their hands on one to begin with. But Underwriter's Laboratories does consider the possibility, which goes like this: the thieves find out what kind of alarm control their target has and then go out and find another location with the exact same panel, which they then steal. The stolen panel is reprogrammed to the same address and "identity" as the target panel. The stolen panel replaces the target panel but since no detection devices are connected to it, the thieves have free reign of the target.

To counteract this threat, high security alarm control panels have built in initialization codes. When the panel's memory is erased to reprogram it and it communicates with the monitoring receiver the first time, the central monitoring station receiver recognizes this as a brand new panel it has never seen before and alerts the operators with a warning message "New Panel On Line".

The Keypad

These is essentially a human interface device allowing the user, (and service technician) to interact with the system and program it The higher end keypads all have displays that provide information to the user. Alpha-numeric displays are much preferred over simple LED lights, and are more than worth the extra money. Besides just making it easier to arm or disarm the system, these keypads display the exact "zone" or detection device status, previous history, and diagnostics. They are also generally used for programming the alarm system by the alarm company technicians.

One program item is the entry / exit delay time. Since the keypad should always be located within the protected area, a method is needed to allow the user to get in and disarm it before the alarm trips. This is called the entry delay and is simply a time period in seconds while the system waits for a disarm code to be entered. The sequence goes like this: the user opens a door, the system detects the door opening and begins a countdown timer (usually 30- 60 seconds). If the system is disarmed within the time period no alarm occurs. If no code (or the wrong code) is entered, the control panel then transmits an alarm signal- and likely sounds some audible device like a siren.

One huge potential avenue to explore in defeating an alarm system is this entry delay. People being people, they tend to want the entry delay programmed very long. Obviously if this delay is set as long as three to five minutes, it gives a potential burglar a long time inside before the alarm goes off.

The way entry delay works is that the first time a delay door opens (each zone or device can be programmed as either delay or instant), the countdown starts. The alarm control waits the amount of entry delay until generating an alarm. Any additional devices tripped during that time period, such as motion detectors, are also ignored (as long as they are programmed as delay devices) until the alarm is either disarmed or the time delay runs out. It doesn't matter if the door is closed behind you or not, once the cycle starts it cannot be stopped unless the system is disarmed.

The exit delay is the opposite and allows the user to arm the system and then walk through the door. As long as the door is closed within the allotted time the system is then armed and no alarm occurs. While this method is quite effective, especially in small systems, it is not foolproof. The keypad should always be located at the door users enter and leave through. Often, the keypad is mistakenly placed at a main entry but employees actually use a rear door. If the path of travel is long to get to the keypad, the chance of false alarms due to late disarming is increased dramatically.

The important point for the owner is to keep the entry and exit delays as short as possible while still allowing enough time to enter and leave. While 30-45 seconds may seem short, it is actually quite long- as long as the keypad is located correctly. At least one keypad must be located near the door employees or owners actually use to enter the building- not necessarily the front entrance.

Another major cause of false alarms is the "I just popped back in for a minute because I forgot something". In other words, the employee arms the system and goes to his or her car and realizes they forgot something in the office. They go back in and get it without disarming and rearming and leave again. By the time the entry delay runs out, they are long gone home but the police have a false alarm. This is probably one of the biggest causes of false alarms and consequently, poor police response.

We should mention here that although the keypad should be mounted inside the protected area, it is more for weather protection than anything else. With modern keypads it is not really possible to disarm the system by taking it apart and touching wires together- that's another Hollywood myth. The keypad uses data to communicate with the control panel- shorting wires together will only damage the keypad and render it useless.

While electrically speaking the keypad is pretty secure, it does have inherent weaknesses from human nature. Although most alarm systems can store hundreds of PINs (allowing audit trails of exactly who armed or disarmed the alarm) many owners end up only using one PIN for everyone. This makes it much easier for a bad guy to obtain the PIN if a disgruntled employee leaves since the owner or manager will usually fail to change the PIN since everyone uses it.

Another weakness with one PIN for many users is that the numbers on the keypad can actually be worn from constant use making it possible to narrow down the PIN. Since most people only use 4 digit pins – and like combinations with lower numbers first, it may be possible to guess the PIN by the wear on the keypad.

Of course, there is always the possibility of simply observing a user entering their PIN. If the keypad is located in a highly visible area, it may be possible to observe it- whether from outside, by remote camera or telescope or even by following a person in on some pretext. Keypads should never be located opposite windows or glass doors for this reason and avoid placing them in public areas at all if possible.

Alarm users- don't be lazy or stupid- use different 6 digit PINs for every person using the alarm system!

EOL (End of Line) Supervision

Just a word on "supervision"- this is a term used to describe how an intrusion panel insures that all the wiring in a security system is intact. Supervision makes sure that no wires are cut when the system is disarmed or armed. If the panel senses the change it then alerts the owner and/or transmits a trouble signal.

Some alarm company installers have been known to circumvent this feature by placing the resistor at the panel connection side instead of the device connection point. While this is a code violation on a fire alarm, it is just very bad practice on an intrusion system. One can readily test this feature by simply disconnecting one wire at any detection device (contact, motion detector, or glass beak) and within a few minutes the control panel should display a message indicating the zone if bad.

The Sounder (Sirens & Bells)

Although almost all systems have some sort of sounding device like a bell or more commonly a siren; they are really of little benefit <u>except to warn the burglar he has tripped the alarm</u>. I tend to favor extremely loud, penetrating sirens which serve mostly to un-nerve the burglar and hurt his ears. There are peizo type sounders which can be so piercing that the average person can't stand to be in the area for more than a few minutes.

Unfortunately, many alarm system owners get upset at the sounder being too loud so they tend to want something low key- until they actually experience a break-in.

All sounders are generally supervised, by the way. Cutting wires to sounders will only serve to transmit an alarm to the central monitoring station and warn the police even earlier.

By the way- shooting the sounder or covering it with sticky foam will not silence it- or prevent the alarm from being transmitted anyway. Sorry Hollywood!

Contacts

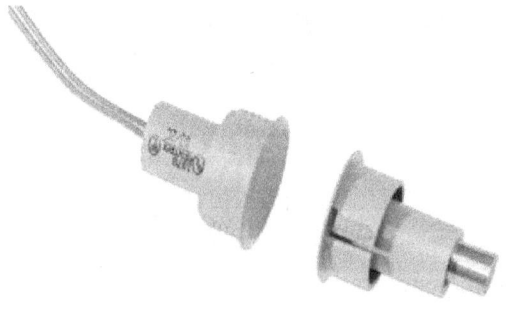

Concealed type of Door Contact

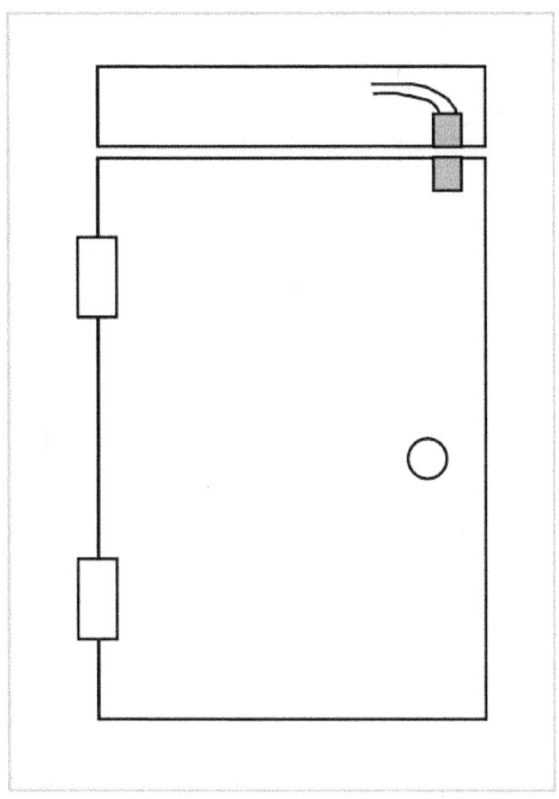

A typical hidden door contact

The door contact consists of two parts- a magnet and a switch. The magnet is installed into a hole bored in the door itself (the lower swinging part). The switch is installed in the frame (the upper part) since the frame doesn't move the wires are run from the switch to the alarm control panel. A big feature of the hidden or concealed contact is that the wires are by design also concealed or hidden- making it nearly impossible to attempt to bypass the contact by interfering with the wiring.

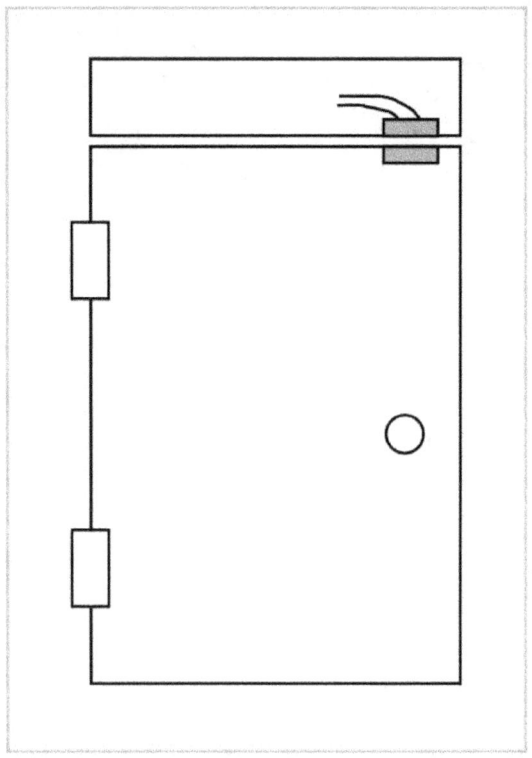

A typical surface door contact

Older systems and cases where the door is set in solid concrete often use surface mount contacts. The big flaw here is that the wires (and the switch) <u>are exposed to tampering</u>.

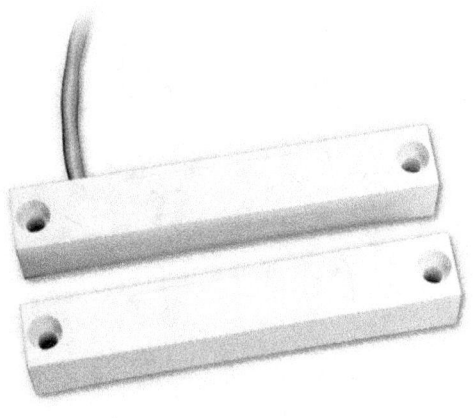

An example of a surface mount contact

Another type of surface contact where even the terminals are exposed.

The bottom part is a cover that is designed to protect the terminals but is rarely used. This type of contact should be avoided. If your system has them- have them replaced with the type above that at least have "pigtails" instead of open terminals.

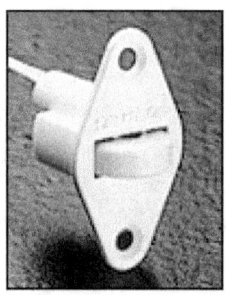

This is an infamous plunger contact

Cheap alarm systems (or installers) sometimes put in plunger contacts like that above. These go in the door jam so that when the door is closed the plunger is pushed in and the switch inside is then held closed. This type of contact is the worst of all and is ridiculously easy to circumvent by simply pressing them in as the door is opened. If you value your security- don't ever allow contacts like this to be installed.

Nearly 99% of the time, this consists of a two part unit- a magnet and a reed switch. The magnet goes on the moveable door and the switch is mounted on (or in) the door frame (which doesn't move). The wires are connected to the switch, while the magnetic doesn't require any connection so it's free to move open and closed.

When the door is closed, the magnet is brought up next to the switch and it's magnetism holds the reed switch closed, completing a circuit. Almost all burglar alarms depend on this closed circuit principal, this is so if a burglar attempts to cut any wires anywhere while the system is armed, it will trip and transmit an alarm signal. The control panel also monitors this wiring while the system is off or disarmed by the way. If a wire is open when you go to arm the system, the control panel will warn you.

Once the system is armed, any opening of the door either by key or by force, will trip the alarm. The alarm cannot detect whether the door is locked or unlocked- only if it is open or closed. Many customers mistake this. Sometimes they forget to lock their door and when they return realize it was unlocked all night and blame the alarm company. If the alarm company did not receive any alarm signals over night, it means no one actually opened the door- even though it was unlocked, (consequently, a lucky occasion for the customer).

Most door contacts are fairly sensitive and if the door is opened more than an inch or so, it will set off the alarm. There is somewhat of a fine line here- the contact must be sensitive enough that the door cannot be opened too far but forgiving enough not to alarm on wind and rattles.

Garage doors, roll up doors, and overhead doors all function the same way. Large garage doors use larger and sturdier magnets and switches. Overhead doors are subject to much more abuse however. Forklifts can run over switches or damage them in other ways. Some doors can be contacted at the top instead of the bottom and this is always advisable if possible. Contacting the doors at the top will shorten the wiring while keeping switches out of harm's way.

Since alarm contacts are by their very nature magnetic, they have an inherent weakness in this regard. The typical basic alarm contact cannot differentiate between "it's" magnet and a foreign magnet. If the switch is the exposed surface variety, it is possible to bypass the contact with another magnet. We have seen many instances of this in warehouses and distribution centers where employees tape their own magnet to the alarm contact so they can open the door during the day without setting off alarms. Of course, this requires access to the alarm contact from *inside* the building.

It is also possible to slip some magnetic material through the door frame from outside the building in the vicinity of the contact and bypass it. Thin magnetic material such as used in refrigerator magnets will sometimes do the trick- assuming the gap between the door and the frame is wide enough to insert it.

This is extremely tricky since you have to insert the magnetic in exactly the right place and hold the magnet strip in place while forcing or jimmying the door. Even if you succeed that far, you must continue to magnet while opening the door and then secure it while inside to prevent it from falling off and tripping the alarm anyway. While I have not seen this successfully accomplished, it does remain a possibility.

Even if you are able to insert a foreign magnet, you are not always safe. Contacts come in many sizes and configurations for specialized applications. One special type is the "balanced" or high security contact. These have a special magnet that is matched to the switch. Once in place, if any other magnet is brought close to the contact, it will sense the wrong magnet and send an alarm. These are especially useful where the contact is subject to tampering- such in a warehouse with remote fire exit doors. It can prevent dishonest employees from bypassing the switch and opening the door to place stolen merchandise outside for later pickup.

While these types of contacts are not common, they are used on high-risk, high security applications- the very kind of place it would be worthwhile to break into.

Of course, there is still the possibility of encountering a place using exposed surface mount alarm contacts where the wires are exposed. It is true that alarm contacts can be bypassed by shorting these wires since most contact set off the alarm by "opening" the circuit. Be aware however, that EOL resistors are typically used to supervise such contacts and any attempt to short the contact will cause an alarm.

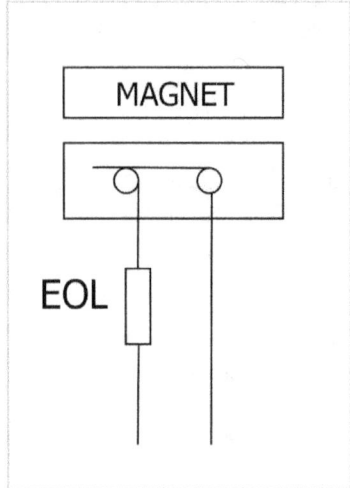

This diagram shows the magnetic holding the switch closed (door is closed). The control panel "sees" a steady voltage through the 1000 ohms EOL resistor. If the circuit opens, an alarm is generated; if the resistance changes an alarm is generated. The only way to bypass this contact is by shorting it directly at the switch *before* the EOL.

On good quality, well designed alarm systems you will never see exposed contacts or wiring for this reason. It is also possible to add another EOL across the contact and have "four state" supervision. This will also detect direct bypassing of the contact.

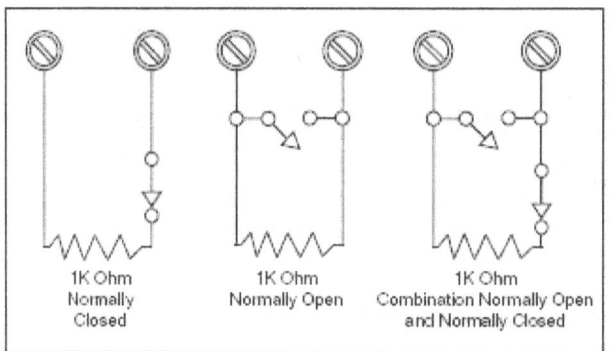

1K Ohm
Normally
Closed

1K Ohm
Normally Open

1K Ohm
Combination Normally Open
and Normally Closed

Motion Detectors

PIR

The next most common detection device is the motion detector, and the most widely used motion detector by a wide margin is the PIR or Passive Infrared. Over the years many other technologies have come and gone, (ultrasonic and microwave to name two), but the PIR has maintained its place as the most common motion detector.

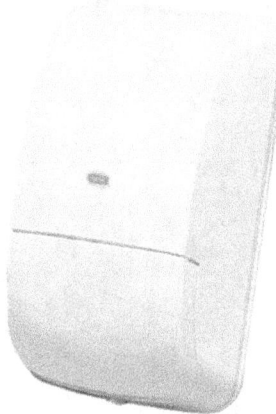

Wall Mount PIR

The walk test LED is in the middle

As its name implies the PIR is a passive device. It does not emit any beam; it simply "looks" at an area and senses temperature changes. Imagine a room at an ambient temperature of 78 degrees Fahrenheit, the PIR senses and remembers this temperature. If a foreign object enters the room in the field of view of the PIR's sensor, the temperature will change. The PIR is very sensitive and even a change as small as tenths of a degree will be detected.

Of course if the PIR were just pointed at a room it would be alarming constantly from normal variations in temperature. Since infrared is in fact a wavelength, optics can be utilized to "focus" the infrared energy onto the sensor. Most PIRs employ mirrors to divide the room or area to be monitored into 4 or more zones. The PIR is them programmed to look at a temperature change between these zones. If all four zones remain equal- as in a change in room temperature from heaters, then no alarm is generated.

However if a rapid change is detected between zone 1 and zone 2 then the PIR assumes an intruder has entered the area and signals an alarm. This is the reason PIRs are more effective at detecting intruder moving *across* their field of view. If the PIR is incorrectly installed so the intruder only moves towards it, then is less likely an alarm will be generated because it will not sense the temperature change between two or more zones.

Unfortunately, pets and birds also move readily across rooms and are known to generate false alarms. Pets are handled by limiting the downward detection zones to about three feet off the floor depending on the pets encountered. There is no solution for birds except to limit the PIR's use to areas without the possibility of flying birds.

Since the PIR is at heart an optical device, it is possible to set some of off with an extremely bright light (such as headlights). We have also been lights to lull police into slow response and then commit a burglary. This was even demonstrated on a television show which has since gone off the air. More expensive PIRs have circuitry to prevent this but such lights can be suspect when investigating causes of false alarms.

PIRs do have a unique weakness, which is both an advantage, and a potential flaw. Infrared energy does not penetrate glass. It is not recommended to ever mount a PIR actually looking directly at glass for other reasons- namely the bright lights that can interfere with the optics; but they will not sense a temperature change outside through glass. Be suspicious of high false alarm activity prior to burglaries- it could be burglars purposely tripped the PIR alarm with bright lights.

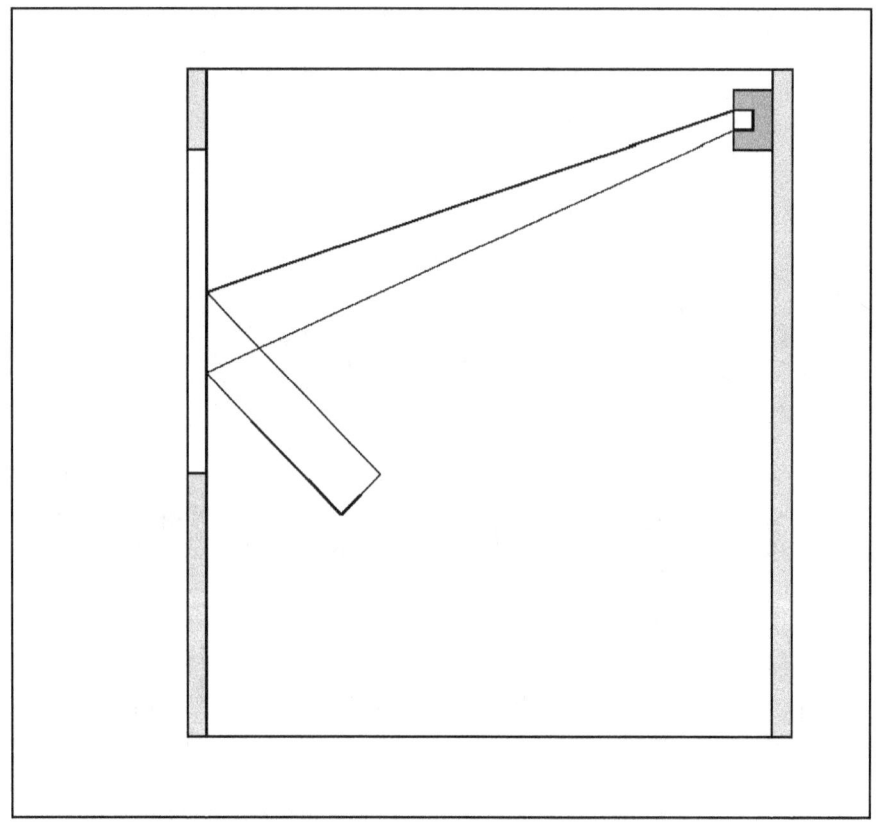

Infrared bounces off glass

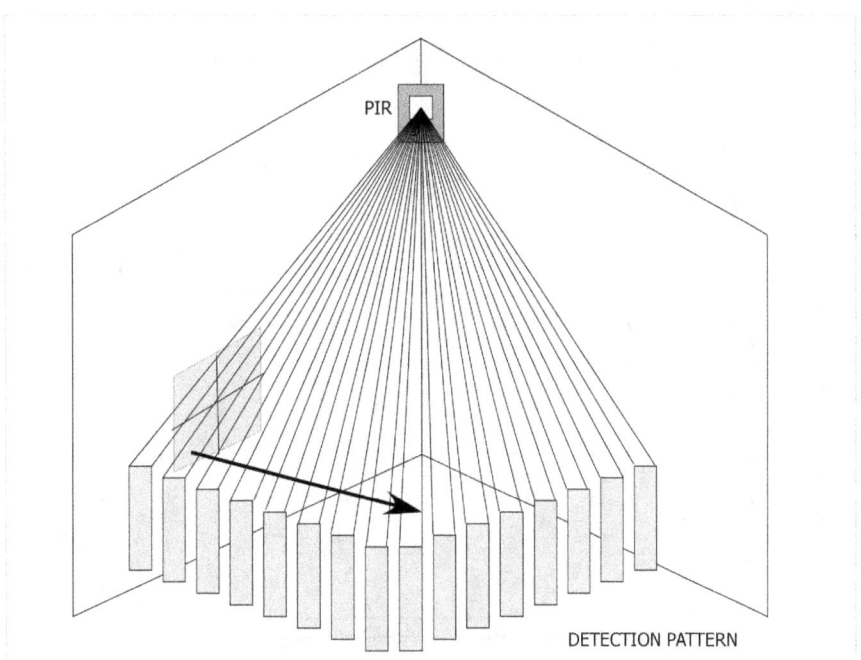

PIR detection "fingers" or zones

PIRs are always more effective at detecting motion moving across their pattern because each zone must sense temperature change. They are by design not as effective when moving directly towards the sensor. Usually however, the fingers are close enough that a body coming towards the PIR will still be detected- just not as quickly.

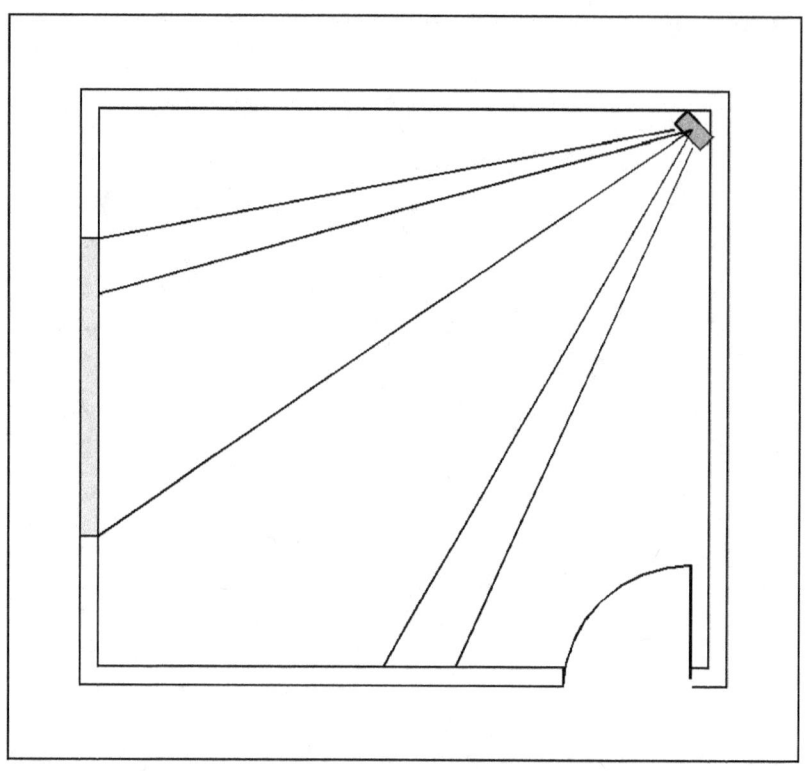

Incorrect PIR location

Notice the PIR is vulnerable from the door and it points towards the window- both bad ideas. A burglar, knowing the PIR's location could break through the bottom on the door and crawl under the PIR.

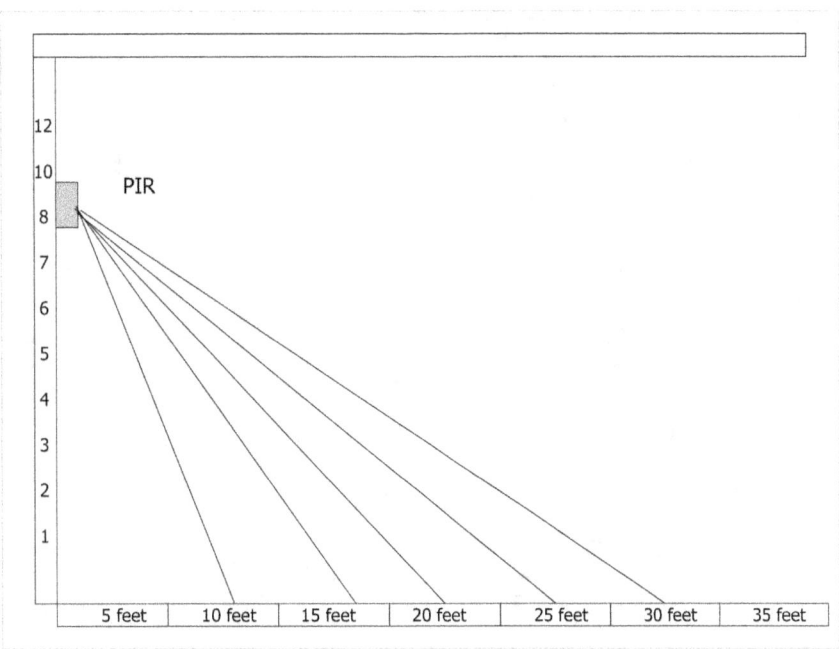

A typical PIR detection pattern side view

Notice there is a gap under the detector because it can't "look" straight down. It is possible to exploit this weakness if the PIR is improperly installed- such as on a side wall too close to a window or door. The PIR should always be installed in a corner so crawling underneath it –from a door or window- for any distance is impossible.

Observe the installation, an intruder should not be able to gain access through a window or door and be able to duck under the PIR without being detected.

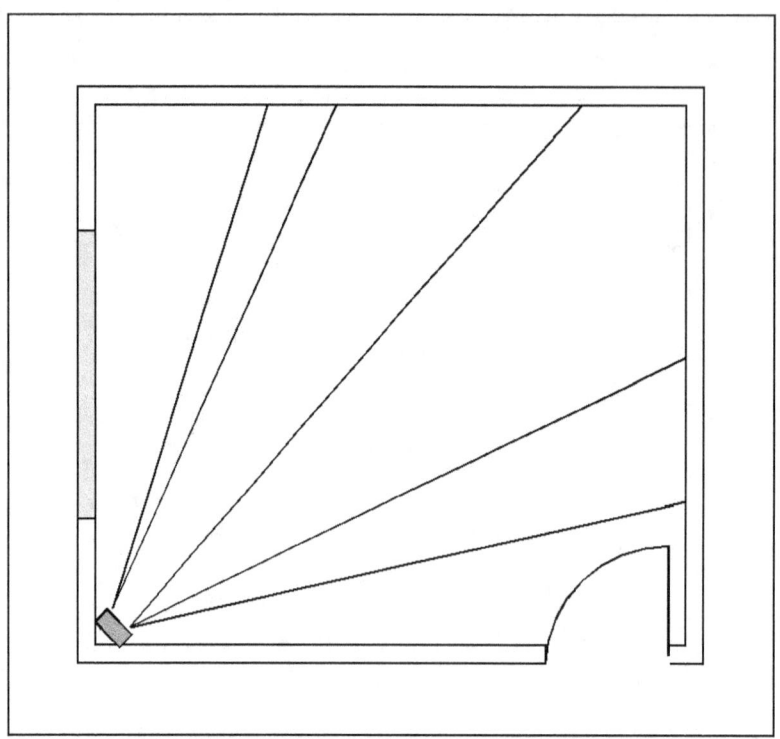

Correct PIR Location

This location is the best overall. It forces any intruder to move across the PIR either from the door or the window while avoiding looking at the glass.

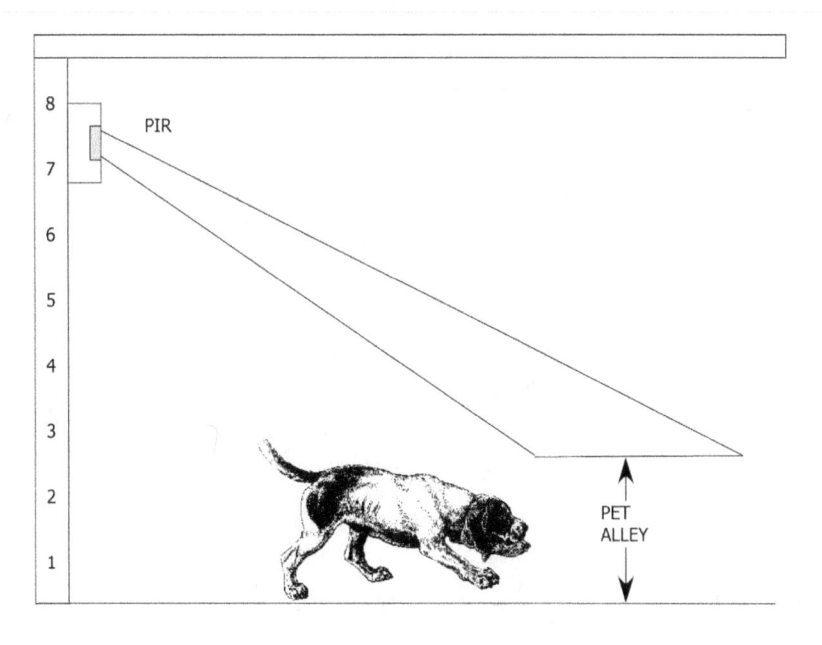

The "pet alley" is a significant weakness of some PIR installations

PIRs have a "pet option" which adjusts the optics so the detection pattern is about two- three feet off the floor so pets can move around freely and not cause false alarms. This is a real weakness. If the homeowner has pets it is very likely a burglar could crawl all around the home without being detected as long as they stay very low.

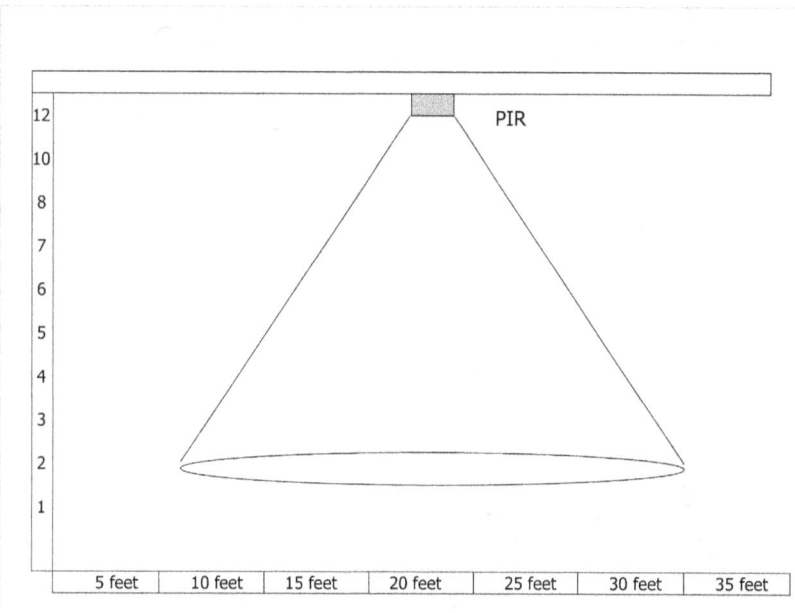

A ceiling mount PIR detection pattern

Ceiling mount PIRs are popular because they can cover large areas without being blocked by furniture or equipment. They also have a gap in coverage if installed too high. Most PIRs are completely ineffective if the ceiling height is over 12 feet. At a height of 8 feet however they are killer good- except if the owner has pets of course- then the same problem applies.

Short of crawling around on the floor which is a not a guarantee of success, there is only one real way to defeat a good quality PIR. A popular television show devoted several episodes to defeating alarm systems. Using an infrared camera to check their work they attempted several methods to circumvent a PIR.

First, the room was warmed to 98 degrees to offset the PIR's sensitivity. The result when a person entered was still an immediate alarm. The fact is, a PIR is much more sensitive than it needs to be. It can easily measure temperature in hundredths of a degree.

The next approach was to cool a person down. One of the crew members was dressed in a "wet suit" and then chilled down with a CO_2 fire extinguisher. Although the infrared camera showed almost no heat signature the PIR was still able to pull him out of the background and trip the alarm.

Next the person was encased completely in cool, wet mud- the PIR still tripped. No matter how slow or how fast, or from what direction- the PIR always detected the intruder. They finally found the only way to defeat the PIR was to place a sheet of glass in front of it.

This is not very practical of course but it does raise an issue. If some other coating (such as clear lacquer) was applied to PIR it could be masked. This would still require the burglar have prior inside access to the PIR in order to defeat it.

While we have not actually ever encountered this method, it is always advisable for the owner to check all their PIRs on a regular daily basis. Simply walking by each one and observing to make sure the walk test LED comes on will circumvent any possibility of defeat. Have your alarm company technician show you how to test your motion detectors if in doubt.

Ultrasonic & Microwave

While these two technologies are never used anymore, it is possible they are still installed in older locations. Ultrasonic works by sound waves transmitted and received back. If the sound waves don't return in a precise time, the detector assumes there is intruder and trips the alarm. Ultrasonic can easily be defeated, since ultrasonic is essentially just sound waves it be deflected by most materials- even a bed sheet.

Never allow the alarm company to install ultrasonic or microwave type detectors or "dual technology" sensors. Microwaves pass through walls too easily and are a major source of false alarms. Some alarm manufacturers have attempted to get around this by combining microwave and infrared into so called "dual technology" detectors. Unfortunately, what ends up happening is you get the worst of both. The microwave stays in alarm all the time and the system falls back only on the infrared. Dual technology detectors end up just being expensive PIRs.

Beams

Beams are the active counterparts of passive infrareds (PIRs). Since these are active infrareds, they require two parts: a transmitter and a receiver. The transmitters only require power and send an invisible *modulated* infrared to a receiver. The receiver, once powered up, expects to "see" the modulated infrared energy. If the receiver does not see the beam for any reason, if signals an alarm to the control panel.

Beams come in many configurations; they can vary from single beams for up to a 100 foot line to double and quad sets which can go as far as 1000 feet. A characteristic of infrared beams is their black (really very dark red) housing and lenses. Since infrared easily penetrates even very, very dark red; the observer (or thief) cannot determine which way the beams are pointing. This is especially useful when there are multiple sets of beams converging. Active beams can be used outdoors with no problem -except as we'll discuss next.

Outdoor Beams with their distinctive black housings

Drawbacks of beams are exactly what you might imagine, when used outdoors they are prone to alarms from animals, blowing debris, and very heavy rain or snow. Indoors it can be difficult to maintain a clear path, especially if the beams are far apart. Beams do remain a very viable option to cover long distances, but when used outdoors they are often used in conjunction with cameras to allow responders or security to observe the areas when an alarm occurs.

Beams represent my all time favorite movie myth. I must have seen fifty films where the burglars put on some special headgear or goggles and are then magically able to "see" the red beams crisscrossing some protected high value area. Sorry guys, no such goggles exist. Active infrared beams are not lasers and do not emit pencil then beams like you see in the movies. You can't hold up a mirror or replace the beam with another.

Beams are quite effective but they do have weaknesses. There are often gaps in coverage- especially at corners where two sets of beams coincide. Even more likely there will be gaps under the beams- purposely so to avoid false alarms by animals. Whether one can exploit these gaps depends a great deal on their agility and is similar to the gaps in indoor PIR coverage, which are technically possible but extremely difficult in real life.

Outdoor beams usually have a "fog" cutout. If dense fog blocks the beams to a certain percentage, the beam is temporarily disabled. Intruders could take advantage of this feature if they are willing to wait for a foggy evening.

Another approach used by intruders when trying to defeat outdoor beams is to simply cause false alarms- repeatedly and constantly until the owner ignores them or disconnects them. I would guess from experience that easily 50% of all outdoor beams are disconnected and just remain as a visual deterrent. Intruders will often just trip one and hide to see if the police respond.

Outdoor beams can be combined with digital video technology to make them more effective so don't give up on them.

Video motion combined with beams so that both have to trip before generating an alarm can solve many outdoor protection problems. In this setup, a camera is dedicated to view the same area as one set of beams and it's video motion grid is then set to alarm along the beam. The output of the video motion is connected to the alarm system and "cross-zoned" with that beam. Both devices have to trip before the alarm control transmits the alarm. A great advantage of this is that the video will show exactly what caused the alarm- and can be viewed remotely by the monitoring company or event eh owner.

Inside beams are another matter entirely for a potential intruder. They can be very difficult to spot in the dark since they may be shooting hundreds of feet across a warehouse but if you know where they are you can usually easily slid underneath them. Then again they are also prone to blockage from boxes, forklifts, and other material so often internal beams are also ignored or disconnected due to laziness.

Indoor beams are meant to act as "traps" preventing burglars from "hiding inside" until everyone leaves for the day and / or transiting wide areas should they gain entry. For these reasons it is important not to let the general public wander around where they can map out beam locations during the day. Also don't share too much of the system design with employees who may sell the information to burglars.

Glass Break Detectors

Since the earliest alarms there has been a need to deal with glass windows. For the first three quarters of the 20th century foil was pretty much the only method available. This involved gluing fragile tin foil to the window in a continuous pattern to form a closed loop. If the glass was broken the foil broke as well and interrupted the circuit causing an alarm. Foil was extremely effective, by the way, it was very difficult to bypass and almost always worked.

Technology finally stepped in and glass break detectors or GBDs came in use. Glass Break detectors come in two basic types- vibration (shock) or acoustic.

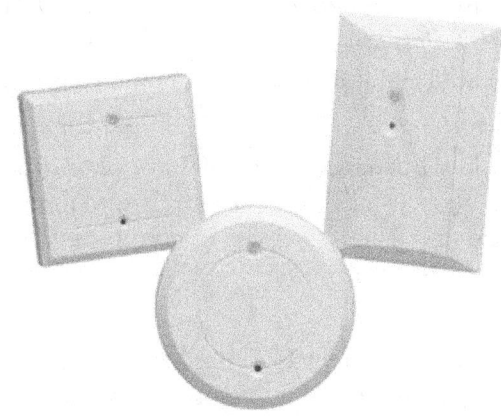

Various styles of Glass Breaks

Acoustic type glass break detectors contain a microphone and actually listen for the sound of breaking glass. Since there are so many different types of glass these detectors must be capable of detecting both plate glass (which is noisy and high frequency) and tempered (which is relatively quiet and low frequency). This presents significant issues since many other common sounds fall into these frequencies such as keys, ringing phones, cleaning equipment, and many other items.

While acoustic detectors are fairly adept at detecting breaking glass, they also are very prone to false alarms due to the issues above. Manufacturers have built in processing power to circumvent the false alarm issues such as combining vibration or passive infrared detection. Unfortunately, the combination technologies tend to work too well and can result in no alarm when the glass is actually broken.

Cheaper glass breaks are subject to false alarms and are often misadjusted or improperly installed resulting in poor coverage. Insist on a thorough test of the glass beaks in your presence when they are installed or call out your alarm company and have them retested in you have any doubts.

Most glass breaks need to be located within 12 feet or so of the glass they are protecting. That means you may need a lot of them if your building has an abundance of glass.

The most effective glass break detection is the type that attached to the glass or frame and detects the vibration of the glass shattering rather than the sound of it breaking. These are much less prone to false alarms as well. This type is considerably more expensive to install since there must be a minimum of one per window or window frame and there is more wiring which must be concealed.

Vibration / shock type GBDs typically do not suffer as many false alarms because they are more focused. These devices employ a piezo crystal structure which generates voltage when undergo sufficient vibration. Although they don't directly detect breaking glass per se, they are very effective at detecting break ins through windows, walls, or nearly any structural part of a building.

Like anything else, vibration sensors have their own set of drawbacks, the biggest of which are limited range (the vibrations only travel short distances) and the fact they must be rigidly attached to frames or glass (which many owners do not like due to aesthetics). If you are truly concerned about detecting glass breakage however, this are highly preferred over the acoustic type.

In case you were wondering- cutting a perfect hole in a glass window in next to impossible- despite what you see in the movies. Most glass windows and especially glass doors and surrounding glass fronts are tempered glass- by law. Tempered glass has a tendency to shatter in thousands of pieces when any pressure is put on it and usually can only be cut on a special machine.

Sure, there's a possibility that older buildings could still have plate glass installed but we once challenged several professional glass installers to cut a circle into a plate glass window to test several glass break detectors- three tried and failed. One was able to get a large circular cut but the glass finally shattered and tripped the detectors anyway.

Pressure Sensors
So called "pressure sensors" which can detect a burglar lifting off the glass case protecting some valuable object are very popular in the movies. In reality, I have never seen one. I suppose one could rig up something similar but I know of no commercially available device.

There are such things as "mats" which are designed to be placed under carpet under windows so that if a thief entered through the window, the pressure of his feet hitting the floor would trip the alarm. Mats were only used in residential and have fallen out of favor.

High value art objects are better protected with concealed contacts, beams or even digital video. Jewelry cases usually just have contacts to detect opening the rear doors, very rarely will you see any type of alarm on the glass itself but this easily accomplished with vibration type glass break detectors.

Safes & Vaults

If you happen to have a safe of vault, there is very specialized protection available. A typical safe protection package consists of balanced safe contacts (which sense if foreign magnets are introduced near them), shock sensor, vibration detectors, audio listening devices (which alarm on the sound of drills), and heat detectors (to sense attempt to burn through the safe or vault).

In previous times, there was also a proximity detector which could sense someone just touching the safe. These capacitance alarms were very similar to the touch lamps you see sometimes. The capacitance control was adjusted or "balanced" via an sensitivity control. After that anyone just touching the metal safe or vault would trip the alarm.

While these were very effective (when they worked) they were also prone to mis-adjustment and false alarms, the main reason being environmental. While the adjustment would be perfect for 72 degrees and 50% humidity, as soon as the room temperature or humidity changed, so would the sensitivity! Often it changed to more sensitive and anything would set it off. As a result capacitance alarms are mostly a relic of the past.

These days safes and vaults are protected by Electronic Vibration Detection (EVD) and Vaults Sound Alarm (VSA) with high security triple biased contacts backed by PIR motion detectors covering the safe or vault area. A minimum of two PIRs should be used so they can back each other up. This provides a very superior, almost foolproof intrusion system.

Sophisticated safe and vault alarms are extremely effective and nearly impossible to defeat in any way despite what you might have seen. These alarms are almost always (and certainly should be) on separate areas or zones so that even if the main alarm system is disarmed or bypassed the safe or vault is still armed and active. The slightest vibration from a drill or heat from a burning bar or torch will trip these alarms long before a burglar can get the door open.

EVDs are able to monitor multiple vibration sensors but even one on a safe will detect the slightest attempt at drilling.

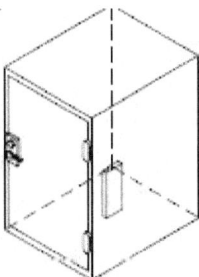

EVD placement on side of safe

 VSAs also are capable of monitoring multiple microphones and can protect very large vaults. Sound detection is the perfect medium for vaults- after all, vaults are by their very nature extremely quiet environments.

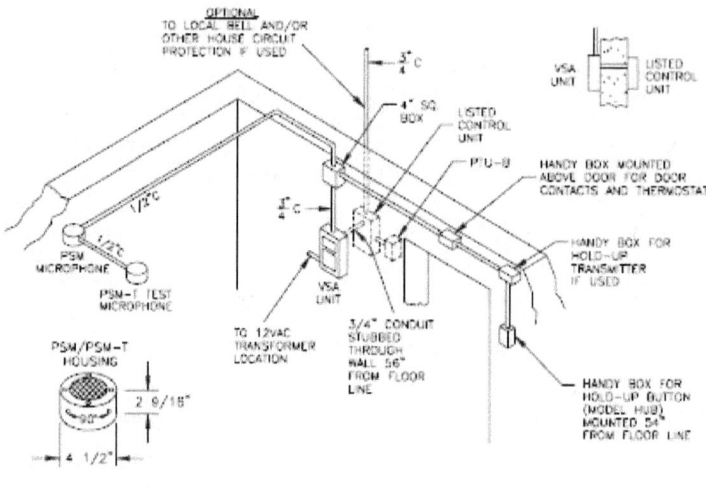

VSA

VSAs will pick up the tiniest sound long before a burglar could gain entry.

Of course, safes and vaults have played a huge role in many movies. There have been numerous heart pounding scenes of burglars performing elaborate schemes to get inside a vault. If you think back though, you'll remember that the story line almost always involved breaking into the safe or vault - some of them quite ingenious – but not actually bypassing the alarm. By the way, my favorite was the movie where the burglar used water to fill the vault and then blew the door off from high pressure build up inside. The same cable television show tried that one too- with little success.

While this is all in good fun, people with real vaults are not usually stupid enough to leave some major weakness in their system. Safes and vaults don't exist by themselves; they are surrounded by the rest of the building which also have alarms. Every safe and vault not only has its own internal alarm but numerous motion detectors pointing at it, not to mention all the rooms leading to it.

The biggest danger to vaults is in fact their location. If the location is old, the surrounding building may have changed considerably over the years- potentially leaving open a weakness that can be exploited.

Some examples would be nearby tenants who have left leaving their adjoining space unoccupied and a haven for burglars to work all weekend to gain entry into the back of your vault. Another would be underground parking which is directly below the vault and can be used to gain entry through the vault floor.

A thorough assessment of your situation will point out these loopholes and if they exist, corrective action should be taken immediately. Have your alarm system temporarily extended next store until a new tenant moves in or block off parking spaces below the vault permanently.

Breaking into a vault requires heavy equipment and lots of knowledge- that's the best way to counteract such attempts. The fact that safe cracking and vault break-ins are so difficult is demonstrated by how rarely it actually happens. When is the last time you read about such a break-in in the newspapers?

Burglars are for the most part very lazy and too not bright. They favor "smash and grab" techniques and will usually move on to targets that are not protected by alarms.

Wireless Alarm Systems

Eliminating wiring, especially in residential applications, has significant impact on the total cost of security systems. Modern advances in wireless technology- especially the availability of higher frequencies in the gigahertz range- have tilted the chart towards wireless in certain applications.

Also you should be aware that all wireless devices require batteries, and batteries do need to be changed periodically. Another problem is that the batteries are non-standard and usually need to be purchased from the Alarm Company or manufacturer; they are not something you can pick at the local market. Motion detectors are high use devices since they are always sensing motion (even when the system is off) so they consume batteries much faster than door contacts. This is another reason to keep wireless system to small applications.

Wireless alarms are not generally used (nor recommended) in commercial environments except for very specialized uses such as panic and holdup alarms. Wireless panic and holdup buttons are widely used and effective. Although the battery caveats still applies, modern wireless systems will alert the customer- and the alarm company- when batteries need replacing.

Modern "digital" wireless systems are fairly sophisticated and nearly impossible to jam with any readily available equipment. The control panel checks in on all it's wireless devices at least once a day –and sometimes every few minutes- to make sure they are functional and reporting back. Probably the only practical way to defeat one is act on the battery weakness. Wireless PIRs draw a lot of power and can wear down batteries faster than other wireless devices. One could conceivably exploit this by tripping a PIR constantly until the battery goes at which point it will probably take at least a day to get the alarm company out to replace it leaving a window open for intrusion. Of course again you must have daytime access to the location.

Video Motion Detection (VMD)

As of the writing of this document, the only Video Motion Detection devices available are part of Digital Video Recorders (DVR) or Network Video Recorders (NVR). We anticipate that in the near future standalone cameras will include VMD circuits and relay outputs to interface with intrusion alarm panels. With the ongoing advances in digital storage technology and processing power, video motion detection (VMD) will become the standard type of motion detection.

Video motion works by "memorizing" the scene (in pixels) and comparing any new pixels to what is in memory. Once the threshold of new pixels exceeds the old ones, an alarm is generated. The most superior aspect of VMD is of course, that you can actually see what caused the alarm!

Due to the terrorist threat, VMD is receiving much attention and research. VMD systems can already accomplish amazing tasks such as determining which way an object is heading, whether an object is stationary for a specific length of time, when an object is moving too fast or too slow, and it can determine objects of specific sizes. Companies have even demonstrated VMD systems which can determine an individual's characteristics such as color of clothes and even height and weight!

If you are already planning to install cameras, then a complete video motion detection system in lieu of PIRs or glass breaks is a viable option. VMD can be configured to "look" at specific areas of the picture and to have different sensitivity at different times of the day. Again, the bonus is the fact that by playing back the video you will have a picture of exactly what or whom caused the alarm.

What about darkness you might ask? New cameras as so sensitive they can pretty much see in the dark now. But burglars must be able to see as well, so the chances are they will be using a flashlight. In total darkness, a flashlight is like a beacon to a VMD system. We successfully demonstrated a VMD system in a museum where the cameras were focused on paintings. This presented an extremely low key detection method for the public visitors while maintaining a very high level of security should they venture too close. A bonus was when the museum turned off the lights and tried to approach a painting- the would-be intruder was detected every single time. In turns out if a human can't see the camera still could! But when the human required more light, the VMD detected them even further in advance.

Your video system should always be recorded even if you never think you will need it because sooner or later- you will. The only thing to consider these days is digital video. The advantages of digital video recording are so over whelming there is really no comparison.

Digital video recorders are essentially computers with hard drive storage. The video signal from the camera is "captured" and converted to digital through hardware and software, compressed to smaller file sizes, and then written onto the hard drive. Since computers are very intelligent, the DVR always knows exactly where the video is stored *by time*. This means you can instantly find any event or time instead of endlessly rewinding and fast forwarding.

Although convenience alone would dictate going digital, the biggest plus is the video quality does not degrade from recording to recording, it is always as good from the first second to the 30th day. Which brings us to another advantage- the ability to keep an entire months worth of video at your fingertips- no more putting in a different tape for each day!

DVRs also manage multiple cameras because they have built in multiplexers. This means DVRs grab frames from each camera and stores as many as 16 or 32 cameras on a single hard drive. Most DVRs are also capable of displaying the cameras in a multi-screen format as well.

Since the DVR is a computer and has intelligence it can do many more things. Video Motion Detection (VMD) is one of the most important. This one feature has many uses. First, VMD allows the DVR to record only *on motion*. There's no sense recording views that don't change- empty rooms for instance. With VMD activated, only images that change are recorded which greatly increases the amount of *time* that is stored on a given hard drive. So it becomes much easier to size your DVR hard drives to store at least 30 days worth of video. Secondly, VMD can be used to activate intrusion alarms when actual motion is detected. Third, the recording speed can be increased when motion is detected for higher quality video.

A word about video quality is probably a good idea at this point. Digital video at this writing is not quite up to par with analog VHS but it comes close if properly configured. Broadcast (or DVD) quality video is considered to be 20 frames per second (FPS) at about 720 X 480 pixels. This is also known as 4 CIF (pronounced SIF). DVRs can usually approach this but only on one camera or for shorter storage periods. The reason being is that 20 FPS at 720 X 480 requires tremendous processing power and huge file sizes.

The lower end DVRs usually state specifications that look good until you realize that the spec is for *one* camera. Additional cameras simply divide up the total processing power and storage. So if one camera can be recorded at 20 FPS at 4 CIF, four cameras will actually be recorded at 5 FPS and 1 CIF (352 X 240 pixels). There are very sophisticated DVRs that can do much higher rates but are considerably more expensive.

Another huge advantage of DVRs is their ability to be connected to networks. This has two important uses: one, it means if you have multiple buildings (or multiple areas in one large building), then cameras are connected in relatively short runs to the nearest DVR and then the DVRs are connected together via the network. This allows the user to manage and view multiple DVRs (and possibly hundreds of cameras) from one central location. Another use for the network is for the owner/ manager to be able to view any of his cameras from anywhere he has an internet connection.

Recorders (NVR- Network Video Recorder)

An NVR is usually defined to mean a computer with storage and software to record digital video directly from either IP video cameras or digital video *encoders*. In reality the line between DVRs and NVRs can be somewhat indistinct. DVRs usually contain the analog to digital converters necessary to change NTSC camera video to digital bits and then store it on the hard drive. NVRs on the other hand usually do not and expect to only receive digital video which has already been converted. NVRs are designed to reside on a network and receive digital video over that network and store it.

The most popular systems right now employ encoders at the remote side near the analog cameras which do the conversion and then transmit that digital video stream over the network (either LAN Local Area Network or WAN Wide Area Network) to the NVR computer. As stated NVRs can also take digital video direct from IP cameras.

The actual NVR is usually just an off-the-shelf computer with large hard drive storage. A RAID (Random Access Intelligent Disk) array in the neighborhood of one terabyte (one trillion bytes) is the norm but systems can go lower or higher in storage capacity.

NVRs also usually come with a software client or application to manage the video playback and searching. A recent development is video forensics. These are software tools to analyze the video once it has been stored. This area is developing so rapidly that whatever we write will probably be obsolete by the time you read this but such tools can already do amazing things.

Cameras

We must think of VMD in the context of cameras since VMD cannot work without them. These days cameras come in both analog & "digital" versions. The term digital really means an IP based camera which streams the video over Ethernet- similar to a web cam. Analog cameras use coax cable (RG-59) which must be home run from the camera to the recording device and / or monitor.

You've probably seen quite a few movies in which the bad guys "insert" a pre-recorded empty scene into the video security system while they then walk unseen in front of the cameras. There are two variations on this myth- one involves hanging a still picture in front of the camera and the other inserting a recording into the video stream.

The 'hanging still picture' trick is not going to work because of focusing issues- something that close to the camera lens will be completely blurred out- CCTV cameras do not currently have auto-focus capabilities. But "inserting" a video recording does have possibilities; of all the Hollywood myths and tricks, this one is actually technically feasible but only under exactly the right conditions.

If a facility has a human security force, they are not watching recorded video – there would be no reason to do so. The security force will be viewing live video at all times so inserting a pre-recorded blank scene will be noticed- whether they take any action on it or not is a question. Inserting such video can only be done on an analog video signal by the way; this little trick won't work on digital video without a heck of a lot of expertise.

On an analog video system with coax cable you would have to insert the video signal at a point where a connector is available (such as the camera itself or a junction box) or else it would take too long to cut the cable, separate the shield and signal and connect into it. This is difficult since cameras are usually installed inside housing which often have tamper proof screws. Junction boxes are often equipped with tamper switches which may set off other alarms.

The best way to protect yourself against attacks of this type is to in fact make sure all housings, enclosures and junction boxes are tampered and that your security force investigates all momentary camera problems by going out to the area and visually inspecting it.

The main weakness of a digital video recording system is again- cheap equipment and poor installation or design along with human error. Although an area may be recorded via digital video recorder, it is not always a sure thing that the recording will be usable. If the owner tries to save money by installing fewer cameras or a cheap DVR, it is likely the resulting recording will be of such poor quality that the intruder will not be recognizable.

We have seen numerous instances of recordings showing a suspect vehicle entering or leaving a facility but the license number couldn't be determined because the camera was too far away or the video was being recorded in too low quality. You've probably seen movies or television shows where such pixilated video was run through some magic program that cleared it up to a sharp image- another myth. You can't get information out of nothing. If you have a low resolution image such as 240 X 352 you are not able to increase it to 800 X 600, you'll just end up with more blobs. If you want a high resolution picture at the end, you have to start with a high resolution image at the recording. There are program which can enhance a recording with too much contrast or too little brightness but that's about it.

Another potential flaw is the amount of frames being recorded. If this number is too high (30 frames per second is real time) then the hard disk storage will be used up quickly. If this frame rate is too low then the hard disk storage will last much longer but it's likely the recorder will miss something.

We mentioned previously that the recorder grabs frames from as many as 16 or 32 cameras. What many people fail to understand is that the effective frame rate being recorded is a function of how many cameras are connected to the DVR. For example, if the DVR is recording at 30 frames per second but has 16 cameras then the effective record rate is only 30 / 16 or 1.875 frames per second. A lot can happen between the time the first camera and the last camera is being recorded. More expensive DVRs and NVRs can record 30 frames per second per camera so the lesson is once again- you get what you pay for. Don't scrimp on the video recorder or the hard drive space if you want real security.

Also of course, if the recorded video is not being viewed or played back, then all the video storage in the world is not going to enhance your security. Many people make the mistake of wanting to record everything or too much then complain it takes too much time to review it!

Set your system to record on motion only- and make certain it's only recording significant scene changes. That way you'll have less but much more meaningful video to view when something actually happens. Motion events will then be displayed in the alarm screen and you can just click on the alarm time and play back the video.

Access Control Systems

An Access system does pretty much what the name implies- it controls access to a facility (or just a room). In order to accomplish this, the systems needs to be able identify the persons attempting to gain access. The identification can be by Card, PIN combination, or Biometrics (a unique human characteristic such as a fingerprint).

Gone are the days of magnetic stripe and "swipe" cards. These were too user intensive and inconvenient, not to mention caused excessive service issues. The security industry has pretty much switched to "proximity" cards and many are now in the process of switching over yet again to "Smart" cards.

The typical access control system consists of several components: locks, door position sensors (contacts), request to exit devices, card readers, door controllers, power supplies and a database (usually on a server).

In order to control access, the system will also need a means of unlocking and locking doors. This is accomplished by electrifying the door locks. Standard locking hardware can be replaced with similar appearing locksets that have an electric solenoid. Electric strikes (the area in the door frame where the lock plunger goes) can be added. Or Magnetic (Mag) locks can be installed which consist of very powerful electro magnets which can hold the door closed with up to 2000 lbs of force.

Each of these solutions has advantages and disadvantages. One important aspect is to maintain ADA (Americans with Disabilities Act) compliance. Most jurisdictions require that any person be able to exit the building with *no prior knowledge*. Usually this is interpreted that the levers and push bars remain operational so a person can exit without doing anything out of the ordinary.

While electrified locks and strikes easily comply, mag locks present some challenges. Mag locks are typically used in situations such as full height glass doors where no other hardware is available. Since mag locks "unlock" by removing power, some means must be installed to allow people to exit electronically. This is generally accomplished by a REX (Request to Exit) detector. A REX is an PIR which looks for people approaching the door from the inside and releasing the mag lock when motion is detected.

Mag locks cannot be defeated by pulling force. Most mag locks can exert 2000 lbs or more so it's likely the door frame would come down before the mag lock releases. We have seen instances however, where intruders place tape or thin spacers between the mag lock and the door frame. This can weaken the magnetic field considerably and allow intruders to return later and open the door. Of course, the burglar would have to have had prior access to the open door- and the alarm will still sound once the door is opened because no valid card was used.

It is highly recommended that whatever type of locks you install; do *not* distribute any hard keys! If anyone retains a mechanical key after the access system is installed, the access is essentially worthless. Also, using a key instead of the reader will cause a false alarm.

Unlike an intrusion alarm system, the access control system always knows whether a door is locked or unlocked since it obviously controls this function. However, for the access system a means is also needed to indicate when the door is open or closed. The door position sensor accomplishes this, and it is identical to a door contact used for intrusion purposes.

In normal operation a person wishing to gain access presents their card to a reader and the system unlocks the door. The access system has a programmed time to keep the door unlocked to allow the person to pull the door open (this is called the Door Unlock Time). If the reader is close to the door, this time can be as short as 5 seconds but if the reader is farther away or people tend to bring large packages through, it may need to be as long as 30 seconds. The problem is that if the time is too long, another person can come behind them and simply pull open the door before the time runs out. This is known as Tail Gating.

To avoid this, the door position sensor is used to monitor when the door opens and closes. The access system can be programmed to automatically relock the door as soon as it sees the door go open – (or closed depending on the type of locking hardware.) This cancels the unlock time period and prevents people from tail gating.

Another use of the DPS (Door position sensor) is to monitor Door Held Open or door open too long. Obviously if a door is propped open, your security and the access system is worthless. This is another programmable time in the access system. Once the system senses the door open, it starts a timer and expects the door to close within this period. If the door is still open after the time expires, the system usually generates an audible warning at the door alerting someone to close the door. If the door is still open after another period, a Door Held Open alarm is generated. Janitors and smokers are usually the biggest offenders of this so be sure to account for them in your plan. Janitors should be issued cards and smokers should have a designated door they can exit and smoke near.

The last and certainly one of the most important functions of the DPS is Door Forced monitoring. This is equivalent to an intrusion alarm. As we mentioned previously, the access system expects to receive a card read before if unlocks the door. Makes sense right? But if the system senses the door opening without a card read then there are only two possibilities- either the door was broken into (forced open) or someone used a key instead of a card- either way a security violation- one slightly more critical than the other.

Special PIRs called REX detectors are used to unlock and bypass alarms when a person leaves a through a secured door. If REX detectors are used, they must be installed very carefully and set up properly. There have been instances where people have inserted long sticks from outside through the gap in the doors and caused the REX to unlock the door. REXs are designed to detect anything approaching the door, so they are very "loose" and have a wide pattern. While this makes them more useful for detecting authorized people exiting, it can also result in unauthorized entrances. The best solution is to install two REXs on double doors- one over each leaf and narrow the pattern so it can't be manipulated form outside.

Although it is certainly possible to use keypads and PINs to identify users on an access system, it is neither recommended nor convenient. PINs are often shared among employees and pretty soon you find everyone using the same number which completely negates your control and documentation.

Card readers are the current preferred method. Among the reader technologies- only proximity is recommended. If any company tries to sell you any type of swipe or insert reader- find someone else. There is no cost differential any longer. Proximity readers are sealed and have no moving parts. There is nothing to wear out and once installed and working will probably continue to work forever. In fact most manufacturers provide a lifetime warranty.

Proximity readers, as the name implies, only require that the card be brought into close proximity with the reader, usually about 3 to 4 inches is the reading distance. Some readers go can much further, some are slightly less. The card does not have to be inserted or swiped, just held within the range of 3-4 inches for a brief period.

Proximity readers work by radio frequency. The card acts as an antenna, the reader is the transmitter and receiver. The card modifies the radio signal in such a way as to be uniquely identified as a number. The number is made up of bits (digital computer language). The higher the bit format of the card, the greater number of digits it can represent to the system. As of this writing, 37 bit cards are the norm. We do not recommend lesser number of bits or other formats. 37 bit cards are quite flexible and the number of digits will suffice for many years to come. Be wary of odd formats, some companies like to lock their customers into proprietary formats which only they can supply.

Do not under any circumstances accept mag stripe, or any card that requires swipe or insertion. Bar codes are to be avoided at all costs and are only suitable for very low security applications- even though they are widely used in time and attendance.

What are the weaknesses of card access systems? People worry about duplicating these cards (it is extremely difficult to copy a proximity card) but the real problems lay in other areas. Once again, human error rears its ugly head. On older systems with low bit range cards like 26 bit, you'll find the facility code we talked about is often ignored through programming. This results in the distinct possibility that cards from other facilities or businesses will work in your system- and appear as a person in your database! For example, if your system it set to ignore the all important facility code and if a card number of 12345 is assigned to John Smith in your facility and someone with another 12345 card from somewhere else comes it- your system will still show John Smith as using his card! Not a happy situation for either of you.

Another all too common occurrence is for the system administrator to issue multiple cards to generic people like "temp", "vendors", "contractors", and "visitors". We have seen as many as a hundred cards issued to "temp" which results in a complete lack of security since any time any one of those cards is used it will show up on reports as simply TEMP. Even worse, if one or several are lost it is difficult to figure out which one or audit them on a periodic basis. All an intruder would have to do it get a hold of one of these temp cards and then have free rein of your building.

Another weakness of which you should be really aware is the Request to Exit detector or REX. As we previously explained, these are essentially PIRs in a special configuration. The problem is that since they are over the door, they are too close to the outside world and subject to defeat. A common trick is for a burglar to insert a thing metal rod or hangar from the outside through the gap in double doors and trip the REX- which then unlocks the door!

This problem can be solved by installing two REXs- one over each door- and modifying their pattern so that they do not detect in the center gap of the double doors. You should also insure that the REXs do not actually unlock the doors. Most double doors exiting a building have panic bars which can be mechanically released by the person exiting so usually it is not required to have the REX actually unlock the doors.

Biometric Readers

Biometrics is the science of using unique human characteristics for identification purposes. Common biometrics are fingerprints, hand geometry, and retinal patterns. The least intrusive and most reliable and well understood are fingerprints of course. Fingerprint readers are readily available and the least expensive of the three- although still about 4-5 times more than standard proximity or smart card readers.

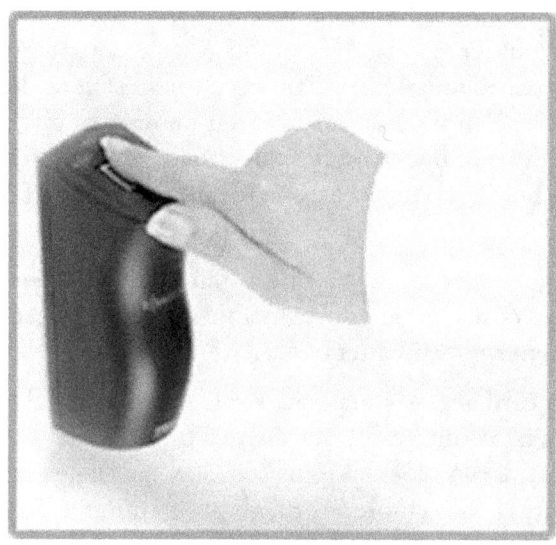

Biometric Fingerprint Reader

Currently there are two technologies in use for fingerprint readers; while they both use a form of optical scanning they differ in producing the actual template. The minutiae-based system is very similar to that used by law enforcement and forensics in that it records the ridges and swirls of the finger. The pattern based system can not be used for forensics since it concentrates on a "picture" of the finger. The image is encoded and stored as a template to compare against a live finger scan. This makes the pattern based systems easier to sell to employees and unions. Once you explain that such templates can not be recovered and used for outside identification, any resistance usually disappears.

Some pattern based systems were actually originally developed for the U.S. military for smart weapons. Weapons were to have a fingerprint sensor imbedded into them with the idea that only the soldier issued the weapon would be able to fire it. Consequently, fingerprint sensors of the pattern based type are very rugged and reliable. They can scan below the first layer of skin to avoid dirt, cuts, and abrasions. Some sensors can even work under water.

So why would you want to use biometrics? PIN numbers and access cards can be swapped and shared by users but since biometrics is tagged to an individual's unique characteristics, it is a positive means of identification. For instance, if a fingerprint is required to open a drug cabinet, you can be sure it was that person who opened it. Auditing authorities will accept biometrics without question. Many time and attendance (electronic time keeping systems) have gone to biometrics for this very reason.

Biometric readers usually require a second means of identification such as a PIN or card. The reason for this is to reduce the comparison time necessary to look up the biometric template. Understand that on a normal card reader, the only thing to be read is a number; the number is then tied to a database which contains the users personal data. On a biometric system, there is much more data. The person at the reader places his finger on the reader and that fingerprint template must be compared with the stored template. Since they could be potentially hundreds or thousands of users, there needs to be a way of narrowing down the templates to be compared. If the user is required to enter a PIN or card, the biometric already knows which stored template to compare with the live one.

One drawback of biometric readers is in fact this necessity to store the biometric template. When a new user is to be added to the system, they must be "enrolled". Since you can't require users to enroll at every single reader on the system, some means must be provided to download the enrolled template to all the readers. This usually requires additional wiring between each reader to distribute the templates.

Smart cards can provide a solution by writing the template to the card. When the new user enrolls, they are asked to present their smart card and the biometric reader "writes" their template to the card itself. When the user goes to a different reader, that reader "reads" the template from the card and compares it to the live one. This makes a very convenient system which can be deployed over multiple buildings and locations without the need for additional wiring.

Hollywood has had a lot of fun with fingerprint and retinal scanners. That popular cable television show we mentioned previously also took a crack at a fingerprint reader- and successfully defeated it! However, in this case there were almost as many holes in their methods as there was in the fingerprint reader.

First, all biometric readers have a programmable threshold of accuracy. If you set the probability of accuracy high you will get more misreads (false denials – a person that is authorized but is denied) since the system is looking for a very high standard of match before it grants access.

Conversely, if you set this threshold low, you will get very few misreads or false denials but more false positives- allowing a person that should have been denied access. Lowering this accuracy threshold could also give a burglar more of a chance to defeat the reader by using a scanned picture of someone else's finger.

Biometric readers also usually require a PIN number along with the fingerprint or other biometric before entry is granted. If you turn off this PIN feature –as apparently was done on the television show- you again make it much easier to defeat the reader. The reader being used on the show also appeared to be of lower cost and quality.

Most sophisticated biometric fingerprint readers also look for the warmth of a human finger and some even expect to detect blood pressure as well. These make it extremely difficult to defeat them using optical gimmicks.

One major weakness of biometric readers does remain however, as you may have seen in the movies, it is possible to cut off the finger (or remove the eye) of an authorized person and then use it on the biometric reader for a few hours or until it cools too much. The perpetrator would still have to have a PIN number though- another good reason to require one.

Metal Detectors

Metal detectors such as commonly seen at airports are growing in popularity in schools and high security buildings. Such detectors are extremely effective and work by creating a magnetic field which is then excited by metal on a person's body, in turn creating a voltage which then sets off the alarm. This principle is based on an electrical generator. The motion of the person walking through the detector along with the metal in their pocket creates the voltage. An important point to consider is that the metal must usually be ferrous to be detected- that is, it must be able to be attracted by a magnet.

While a properly programmed metal detector set to high sensitivity is nearly impossible to defeat, one can mitigate the effects simply by walking through very slowly and not swinging your arms. I have tested this many times. If you walk through very fast, it takes a significantly less amount of metal to set off the alarm. Conversely, if you walk very slowly, you can get a significantly larger amount of metal through the detector with setting it off.

A knowledgeable operator will spot this trick and tell you to walk faster or search you manually. But in ten years of going through airports only once have I had an operator do this to me.

Human error comes into play here as well. In commercial settings it is quite common to turn the sensitivity down due to false alarms. This is very dangerous since many weapons these days have little ferrous metal and could easily slip through detection.

Human Security Guards

The term "guard" usually conjures up an image of an old man sleeping at his post. In fact many security guards are retired – from the military or police department. Some security guards are even off duty policemen seeking to earn extra money. It is also true they can be incompetent and lazy. Just like any other employee, there are good ones and bad ones.

It has been our experience that about 50-75% of the typical guard force is alert, competent and well trained. It does depend greatly on the company employing them too. A good guard company will provide training and roving supervisors to check on their people. If you plan on having guards, insist on seeing their personnel files detailing their past employment, training and experience. Ex-military are preferred due to their sense of responsibility instilled by military service.

Keep in mind that the lower your cost to hire the guard, the less the guard will be paid and the lower the quality of that guard will ultimately be. Don't forget, the guard company is making a profit on the difference between what you pay and what they pay the guard. You can insist on high quality guards if you're willing to negotiate a higher rate.

Guards are very expensive, a big selling point of electronic security is to reduce or eliminate guards. Do the math- having just one guard on duty 24 hours a day = 168 total hours each week; that's 8736 hours per year. If you only pay $15 per hour, that's a total annual cost of $131,040! You can buy a lot of electronic security equipment for that amount.

If you employee your own guards you will have to have extra people to handle days off and vacations- and you will have to add taxes, benefits, and overtime. Add radios, uniforms, and other vital equipment and this could easily increase your annual cost to more than $200,000.

While employing your own security does allow you to control quality, very high quality people will undoubtedly cost more than $15 per hour. If your business dictates guards, then look to contract to a security guard company.

Don't make the mistake of assigning security duties to regular employees either. This is a recipe for disaster. Not only can untrained "guards" result in liability against the company but virtually handing employees the keys to your business is just asking for theft and collusion.

Human security guards have many potential flaws –some of which can be counteracted and some not. Part of your CCTV video surveillance system should always include at least one camera watching the watchers! We always recommend that guard posts, security offices, and command centers be equipped with card readers and cameras.

At the very least these will document the guards are performing their duties. If something happens, these will provide invaluable evidence of what went wrong. Lastly, these devices will also keep the guards on their best behavior since they will know they are being watched.

Such cameras and card readers should never be under the control of the guards. Partition such systems so only the management can observe, playback, or re-program such devices.

Another large threat to the guard force is bribery. Guards are usually, and unfortunately, low paid individuals which open them up to offers of cash from professional thieves to look the other way or provide inside information on the security systems.

Although there isn't much defense against this scheme, thankfully the person offering a potential bribe can never be entirely certain that they won't be reported when they try to offer one. The best way to keep your guards honest is to do everything possible to make sure they were honest in the first place.

As we stated previously, insist on rigid and complete background checks. Obtain copies of their personnel files and refuse to accept any guards with gaps in their backgrounds. Try to only allow only guards with prior military or police experience. Be very wary of "temporary" guards assigned to your facility because your regular people were sick or off. If you have high turnover, it will be very difficult to keep up with backgrounds checks- not to mention they will never be familiar with your company and operations.

Finally, try to always have at least two guards on duty at all times- this way this is much less likelihood both guards can be subverted.

Central Monitoring Stations

To be effective the alarm system must be monitored either by in house / on site security guards or by some outside party. While you could simply just sound a siren or ring a bell upon an alarm, it is pretty clear this wouldn't accomplish much unless you have neighbors that are present 24 hours a day and willing to call the police. The police themselves almost never accept alarms directly, so the only alternative is to contract with a central monitoring station. Usually, the alarm company that installs and services your alarm will monitor it. In some cases they may contract it out to a third party.

Even if you do have on site security guards, we always recommend the alarm system also be monitored by a central station as a backup. This serves many purposes. First, if the guard should become incapacitated or disabled, the alarm will still be handled. Secondly, if the guards should be subverted (paid off) by burglars, then the alarm monitoring company will still be there to notify the police.

In any case, the monitoring company is obviously critically important. Your security ultimately depends on their action or inaction. When an alarm is received at the central station, an operator must interpret it and take the appropriate action- such as notifying the police. Sounds simple doesn't it? The problems arise when the operator must begin to make judgment calls regarding the signals.

If you are prone to causing false alarms, improperly arming or disarming, or forgetting to turn the alarm off; expect the operator to hesitate before doing anything. It's not possible for human beings to do perform the correct action every single time. If you generate a dozen false alarms and then the thirteenth one is real, you can't expect a good outcome. The operator can't read your mind and cannot know what is going on at the premises.

Likewise, if you request complex special instructions, it makes the operator's job more difficult and increases the chance of mistakes. For example, "send the police every time except on Sunday nights between 5 pm and 10 pm when the courier goes in and picks up a shipment; and ignore the janitors between 8 pm and 11 pm Monday, Wednesday, and Fridays."

We have actually seen instructions like that and consequently the chances of ever actually catching a burglar are slim to none. The more generic and ordinary the operation of your alarm system is, the more likely it will be handled correctly.

Two of the most important items you, the owner, needs to handle are "Call List" and pass codes. The central station will maintain a list of names and phone numbers to call on alarms or other kinds of trouble or questions. Make sure this list is always up to date. It's not fun coming to work on Monday morning to find your business was broken into and no one was notified because all the phone numbers were bad.

Also make sure the pass words or code words are current and sensible. The central station will issue you, and whoever else you request, a pass code word or number to be used when communicating with them. If you need to speak to someone at the central station because you accidentally set off the alarm, they will ask you to identify yourself by this code.

Unfortunately, the vast majority of signals arriving in the central station are false alarms- as many as 99% of all alarms are false. This means the operators are busy handling false signals when the occasional actual alarm arrives. This is also the area where there is room for error.

There has been much discussion in the monitoring community about "operator judgment calls". Should the central station operator decide whether to notify the police or should they just do it on every alarm? Either way the monitoring company employee is put in a difficult situation. They may indeed call the police time after time on the same alarm from the same customer and endure the wrath of a police dispatcher who won't dispatch patrol cars anyway. But the very time they make a judgment call and not call the police will be the time the alarm is real.

The real point is just we don't want the monitoring company to make judgment calls but on the other hand, don't cause false alarms so they are never confused about your business or residence operation. The clearer your system operation is, the less likely any mistakes will be made.

Interestingly enough, we are not aware of any instances where the central station itself was attacked. UL has always recognized that possibility and has strict standards for securing the building. In fact, UL specifies the monitoring area itself should not have windows if it is on the ground floor, and doors must be locked and controlled at all times.

Attacking the monitoring company would render the alarms they monitor useless since no police would be notified of any alarms. There have been instances of evacuations due to bomb threats or hazardous spills in the neighborhood and we have always suspected these may have been caused for ulterior motives but nothing was ever proven.

So can alarms be defeated?

You've probably seen many a movie demonstrating how burglars defeat high tech security systems. Hollywood has perpetrated the myth that alarms can be defeated but like most things in Hollywood, the reality is quite different.

With current technology, a well designed, maintained, and tested intrusion system is in itself almost impossible to defeat. A cable television show devoted several episodes to defeating various intrusion technologies and discovered just how difficult it was.

The key is a well designed system. All doors should be alarmed, and backed up by motion detectors. Motion detectors should be infrared sensing and must be placed at no more than eight feet high and always so that the intruder must pass across their field of detection- never facing. The alarm door contacts and the PIRs (Passive Infrared) motion detectors act as back ups to each other. There are many variations on alarm contacts to suit different installation requirements. Your alarm company will choose the right one for each application- such as overhead doors.

Should a burglar get through a wall or window, the PIR will detect them and vice versa. PIRs generally have an effective range of 40-50 feet. While there are models that have longer range, we recommend staying away from them due to issues with false alarms. It is simply very difficult to control the environment hundreds of feet away from the detector.

PIRs should never face glass. Although infrared does not pass through glass- the intense light from the sun or headlights can cause the sensor to alarm. Glass is in fact the PIR's only weakness; don't expect a PIR to detect motion on the other side of internal office windows or showroom display windows. And it is true that if a burglar could somehow place a sheet of glass in front of a PIR it would no longer detect motion, that just isn't likely to be possible.

The best defense to avoiding any problems with PIRs is just to test them. All PIRs have a "walk test light", an LED on front that lights up when it senses motion. Make it a point to walk in front of your PIRs periodically and ensure the LED is coming on. This will also alert you if somehow the power is cut to the unit- although the PIR should be powered from the alarm control panel- and *it* should detect any problems with power immediately.

Longer distances such as hallways or warehouses can be protected with active infrared beams (also know as PECs – Photo Electric Cells a holdover term from the older days). Although some people refer to these as "lasers" they are not. These consist of a modulated transmitter and receiver pointed at each other. As the television show so rightly proved, these cannot be seen with powder or special goggles- despite what you've seen in movies. They are completely invisible and it is impossible to use a mirror to reflect the beam back on itself. One reason is that no one knows which side is the transmitter since both transmitter and receiver appear identical.

Glass break sensors are very popular but we only recommend them as a last resort and never, ever as primary protection- only as a backup. The really effective glass breaks are based on vibration or piezo effect and are mounted to window frames or glued directly onto the glass.

All other glass breaks are acoustic, these actually listen for the sound of breaking glass. These are generally either a false alarm nightmare or fail to detect breakage at all. Even worse, the latest trend is to combine a PIR and an acoustic microphone in the same detector so that if the PIR senses motion, the glass break is disabled. This is supposed to eliminate false alarms from janitors or employees but it more likely to result in no alarm during a real burglary.

Don't allow the alarm company to install ultrasonic or microwave type detectors or "dual technology" sensors. Ultrasonic can easily be defeated, (ultrasonic waves can be deflected by a bed sheet), and are almost never used any more. Microwaves pass through walls too easily and are a major source of false alarms. Some alarm manufacturers have attempted to get around this by combining microwave and infrared into so called "dual technology" detectors. Unfortunately, what ends up happening is you get the worst of both. The microwave stays in alarm all the time and the system falls back only on the infrared. Dual technology detectors end up just being expensive PIRs. If you have either of these detectors- have them replaced.

There are some serious considerations with the alarm control panel and communication. All alarm panels must communicate with the outside world in some manner to transmit an intrusion signal. This is one of the major weaknesses of most alarm systems. Traditionally, the alarm transmission is over voice grade telephone lines. The alarm panel actually dials the phone number of the central monitoring station and transmits an encoded data stream. Once the central monitoring station receives the alarm, their computers automatically bring up your account in the database and they then notify the police.

Obviously, if the phone line is cut then the alarm signal will not go through. For this reason, it is extremely important that the phone line be protected or hidden. The larger the facility the less the chance of burglars cutting phone lines because there are so many. There have been instances however, when thieves cut ALL the lines entering a building to make certain they disabled the alarm.

In any case, phone lines for alarms should never be marked or identified with tags. They should be in conduit from the point of entry to the alarm control. This can be very difficult when lines are fed from overhead poles since the phone company is just going to drop the line down the side and into your building.

A new alternative to dial up alarm transmission is internet monitoring. The alarm uses a broadband internet connection such as DSL or a cable modem to contact the central station. The big advantage of this scheme is that is can be two way. The central station's computers can be programmed to automatically and periodically contact the alarm panel to make sure it is there. If the line is cut or disabled, the central station can detect this in as little as 90 seconds.

Some very high risk businesses such as jewelry stores are usually required by their insurance companies to have a UL Listed alarm system. Depending on the UL Listing, they will likely require this two way form of communication. This is often referred to as "Line Security". The advantage is this is now available to anyone with the right alarm control panel and an internet connection.

The consideration in all cases must be however, what to do if the line is disrupted? The central station gets a trouble message indicating communication was lost with the alarm control panel. UL usually requires a police dispatch but in reality the police would not even know what to look for, if there was no outward evidence of a burglary they would simply chalk it up to another false alarm and move on to the next call.

You would be notified but is there really anything you could do or would want to do? If you are concerned about this, the only real solution is to subscribe to some sort of alarm response service. Many alarm companies and some guard companies will provide an armed response. Although it can be somewhat costly, it could be worth the peace of mind and you will never have to worry about police response.

So assuming that you have good alarm detection equipment and good alarm communication, can the alarm system be defeated? Human error becomes the single biggest weakness- as in most things.

The alarm detection devices have to correct for the application. They have to be installed correctly and they must be serviced and tested. But this will still not be enough.

Human error will still enter the picture. The alarm system must be armed for one thing. People often forget to arm the system when they leave! You can purchase an additional level of monitoring from the alarm company called "Late to Close". You provide a schedule to the monitoring company and if the alarm system is not armed by the specified time, they will notify you. In most cases, the alarm company can remotely arm the system if you give them permission.

There is also room for human error on the part of the alarm monitoring company. If the alarm company operators are overwhelmed with too many variations of schedules and special instructions it becomes easier for them to misinterpret a situation. The best way to guard against this is to maintain a routine. If you arm and disarm the system at approximately the same time every day and don't vary, they will be much more likely to notice when something is wrong.

You can also have your system programmed with "Duress codes". This is a special unique PIN combination that differs from your normal arm/ disarm code. If you are under duress and forced to disarm your system by thieves, using the special duress code disarms the system as usual but also sends a special message to the central station indicating you are being forced to open your business or home. Be sure to discuss this at length with your alarm company, and your employees or family. The worst thing you can do is use the duress code by mistake.

This brings us back to the major weakness of alarm systems- human error. If you, your employees, or family constantly (or even occasionally) cause false alarms, your system is as good as worthless. Police departments not only keep records of false alarms (usually for fines) but the patrolmen are very aware of them. If they recognize your location as having had false alarms in the past, they are not going to get there with any particular speed. On the opposite side, if there has never been a false alarm at your location, the police are much more likely to respond quickly.

We have also seen numerous instances of repeated false alarms leading up to actual burglaries. Professional burglaries have been known to cause alarm after alarm until the police grow tired of responding, then they can break in at their leisure with the knowledge they have extra time inside.

Causing false alarms can be done in various ways on poorly designed systems: shining powerful spotlights on PIRs pointed towards windows, rattling windows until acoustic glass break detectors go into alarm, shaking loose doors, etc. The best way to combat this problem is to make sure none of these problems exist and to demand immediate service of any false alarms. One false alarm is cause for serious concern.

But of all the actions you can take as a manager, business owner or homeowner regarding day to day operations of your security system, the most important one is to make sure you or others are not causing false alarms. Once any false alarms occur it can be months before that memory fades from the alarm monitoring company and the police department.

So, there are ways to defeat an alarm. If one has physical access to the system it is possible for an expert to bypass detection devices and then return after the system is armed and gain entry- assuming the owner did not test the system before leaving. It is also possible that an inside person, such as a security guard, acts to aid accomplices to defeat the system from within. An alarm could also be defeated by disabling communications to the monitoring center – as long as there is no line security in place to detect this.

An alarm can also fail due to human error on the part of the owner or the monitoring company, and this is the most likely scenario but it would require the burglar know in advance that the owner often fails to arm the system- or the monitoring company is lax or overworked and frequently makes mistakes.

Intrusion systems that are backed by armed guard response and monitored by diligent professionals are extremely difficult if not impossible to circumvent. This is why you rarely hear of a large burglary of expensive items. When you do, it is very likely an inside job where the system was bypassed from within by "authorized" personnel.

If you happen to manage a high risk facility, one step you can do to help protect yourself is to insure that plans for security system are under lock and key. There are no requirements that mandate security plans be submitted to any city department. Fire alarms yes, but not security. No security plan should be a matter of public record (except unfortunately public buildings which are done under bid and therefore part of public records).

Your security plans should be in your possession. Insist that the security company turn over all copies to you and have them sign a release confirming that fact. As long as your have the plans available for technicians there should be no argument. By the way- <u>always</u> confirm the identity of alarm technicians by calling the security company before admitting them!

Do you need a consultant?

The truth is, probably not. If you are interested in doing security for a fairly small location or some large ones with simple needs, this guide will tell you everything you need to know.

You should also take advantage of security vendors. All security companies and alarm companies will provide a system design for free in the form of a written proposal. **Security Integrators** will provide more sophisticated designs free of charge. Of course, no one likes to be taken advantage of, but well run security companies will happily provide their take on a system design free of charge.

The best way to handle this is to ask colleagues and neighbors to recommend a company they used. Call three of these security firms and invite them in for a meeting. You can do this as a group or separately but in the case of the latter, be up front and inform them that you are getting three bids. If you can't find three companies then ask the one to suggest one or two others. You'd be surprised but they are going to suggest reputable competitors.

Be prepared to walk each security representative through your location. You should not have to point out potential problem areas, they should be telling you. Although you can be open with problems you have had or why you're interested in a system, a good security rep will know what you need. If they don't, or keep asking you what you need, then they aren't right for you. Find another company instead.

During the walk through, it's very helpful to provide them with a floor plan and or site plan of your facility. This can either be CAD drawings or just a simple block diagram. The better you provide though, the better the result. If you have blue prints (you only need floor plans and a site plan) then it will be worthwhile to have several copies made so you can give one set to each bidder.

The security company should come back to you with a written proposal clearly outlining a security solution and concise pricing. Some companies will even provide a graphic plan or blue print with the proposed equipment so you can better understand the solution and what you are buying. If you have provided floor plans as mentioned above, you should at least expect a neat, marked up plan in return.

The proposals you get back will likely be quite different and the cost will vary considerably depending on the size of the job. Smaller security systems should be fairly comparable in price. Medium systems with card access, CCTV, and alarms can vary quite a bit.

You should then invite each company in again to discuss their bid and answer any questions. Don't hesitate to ask why their price differs either lower or higher from another bidder. One bidder may have missed a major component the others included. Another bidder may be adding too much that you really don't need. The two bidders that are closest are probably the best choices.

At the end you will have three versions of a security solution. You can combine parts of each as you desire to come up with the right solution for your needs. If you decide to pick and choose, be sure to have the security company you think came up with the best proposal re-bid the job based on your new plan.

Consultants *are* necessary sometimes. Usually if your needs are very unique, or you don't feel comfortable making a decision, or you simply don't have time to deal with it; a security consultant can be a big help.

The consultant should interview you and do an extensive security survey. Check out the section on Risk Assessment for an idea of what should be included in the survey. The consultant should then prepare a detailed report and some preliminary budget.

Once you and the consultant decide on what the security plan will be, they will prepare a specification to send out for bid. An RFP (Request for Proposal) will be sent to reputable security companies inviting them to bid. The consultant will probably choose the recipients based on previous experience with them.

The consultant should stay involved with the process and help evaluate the bids received. It's always a good idea to insist the consultants also handle the submittal documents from the successful bidder and oversee the installation and testing of the finished system.

One caveat with consultants- some tend to use old specifications they recycle from previous jobs. This may result in a system using older technology. You can avoid this in two ways.

Insist that they add a section to the specification allowing the use of newer technology or products and that the bidder is free to submit a different design if it will result in a overall lower price. A sample section would go like this : *"Nothing in this specification will preclude the use of newer products or materials or a different system design if it results in a substantially improved system and / or reduced overall cost."*

Secondly, you should ask the bidders if the specification was good and up to date. This is a good check and balance of the expertise of your consultant.

Finding a security vendor

As in many things in life, finding a good security contractor can be as easy as asking a friend or associate. We always recommend gathering such suggestions as a starting point. We say starting point because unless your associate's needs are exactly the same as yours, you will likely need someone different.

The American Society of Industrial Security (ASIS) is a professional organization devoted to both electronic and physical security. Their membership rolls are another good starting place. If you are a member of other professional organizations such as BOMA (Building Owners and Managers Association), ask your colleagues for suggestions.

Chances are that local architects, building contractors, even city officials (planning, inspection or in some places the police department) will be familiar with or have security vendors they work with and trust. People are usually quite open to sharing good contractors they've worked with- and which to avoid.

Electronic security equipment manufacturers are also a good source for security dealers and installers. If you happen to already know which system you want, you can contact that manufacturer direct and ask them to come in to discuss your location. You can also request they bring in three dealer / installers / integrators to bid on the project. Of course, if you're just doing a small residential system you won't be able to take advantage of this.

Once you've compiled a list of possible candidates, check them out with your state government. Almost all states require one or more special licenses for security contractors. Often you can simply go on line to the state website and check for license status and any complaints filed against that contractor or company. Once you've narrowed your list and checked for proper licenses and complaints, it's time to start interviewing potential vendors. It's probably going to be too intensive a task to wade through more than three proposals so weed your list down to that number.

What to look for in a security contractor

References, references, references! Just because someone recommended a security vendor, it doesn't mean they can perform on your particular situation. Get references from satisfied customers in your area with similar sized projects- and call them.

Manufacturer's certifications are also important. The security contractor should have at least one person on their staff who went to training and was certified on the product. Ask for copies of the certifications and check the date- it should be within the past year or two at the most.

Underwriter's Laboratories (UL) listings are a very good indication of a company's experience and proficiency; but only in fire and intrusion. UL listings carry less weight when dealing with security integrators- but if they have a UL listing then that should put them at top of your list.

Designing the right security system

Of course, you're not going to be designing the security system but you will be essentially guiding it along- since you're paying for it. The "right" security system will be neither too much nor too little but just enough to provide you with a security solution. Easy to write but hard to accomplish? Not necessarily if you stay the course. You must be prepared to state clear and concise goals and objectives and stick with them, within reason.

We have seen many systems start at point A and then go radically off course somewhere down the line costing way too much and not accomplishing the initial goals. This usually occurs, unfortunately, because of you- the customer. Just like in many construction projects, if the owner makes constant, and many time conflicting changes- don't wonder why the project went way over budget.

While it is certainly true that during installation is the time to get what you want rather than after it is complete; you really should have known exactly what you wanted *before* the installation started. Electronic security is very complex and systems frequently depend on each other's interaction to perform. If you change one piece of equipment mid-stream, you often create a domino effect rendering other systems ineffective or requiring expensive changes in downstream equipment. Similar to pulling the bottom card out of a house of cards- the whole thing collapses.

It is very important to have a plan and stick with it. Once you settle on the final solution do not allow or entertain any changes and you will end up with a successful installation and solution.

Putting together a security specification

Unless you employ a consultant, you are probably not going to publish a detailed security specification, although most manufacturers will provide sample ones –usually available on their web sites. Detailed specifications, believe it or not, tend to limit contractors and often cause unnecessary extra expense. The best approach at this initial stage is to put the workload on your potential security contractors.

Many detailed security specifications are available for free download from the manufacturers. If you are familiar with the product you want, go to their website and chances are a written spec will be available. This is sometimes called A&E spec. We have included a sample one from an intrusion alarm manufacturer at the end of this guide.

It may be best left to the professionals, however. Most security dealers and contractors will be happy to put together a spec for you as long as they have a reasonable chance of getting the job. They may suggest a certain fee for doing the spec and then be will to credit that amount back if they get the contract.

You should create a worksheet or document outlining your initial needs. For example, if you're in the market for an intrusion and video system; simply write down the areas you want to cover.

Intrusion System						
Areas	Doors	Windows	Skylights	Overhead Dr	Motion	Keypad
Main Lobby	1	1			1	1
Employee Entrance	1				1	1
Accounting Office	1	2			1	
Warehouse	3		6	5		
Computer Room	1					
CCTV						
Area	Viewing					
Main Lobby	Entry					
Employee Entrance	Entry					
Warehouse	Entry					
Warehouse	Dock					
Warehouse	Cage					
Computer Room	Entry					

A sheet like this will help you organize your needs and thoughts and provide a starting point for the security vendors proposal process. Plan on giving this sheet to your three bidders.

Arrange for a job walk with each of the potential bidders.

There is divided opinion of whether all three should walk at the same time or separately. While you can save time by doing it once, we have found security sales people hesitant to speak in front of competitors and consequently fail to bring up important items or concerns for fear of tipping off the others. It's best to conduct the walk three times, you'll then be amazed at the different responses you get. Explain to each sales representative that you are open to their ideas, concerns and suggestions.

Be sure to clearly specify what you expect them to provide and what you may be willing to furnish. For example, an access system will likely require a PC. You can buy a Dell to the access control manufacturer's specifications at a much lower cost than the contractor- who will purchase the same computer but mark it up.

Each company should ask numerous questions and take notes. If they don't, it's cause for concern. Each company must then respond with a detailed written proposal. Always require a set deadline date for the proposals. It's best to not allow them to drop them off in person because you should have the time to thoroughly read over each one in private and decide which one comes closest to what you had in mind.

Once you've had a chance to look them over, invite each company back to go over the proposal in person. Of course, if one proposal is just a rehash of what you gave them and doesn't offer any new ideas or suggestions, it's probably best just to eliminate that company right then and concentrate on the remaining ones.

Be careful with items that may not be included by the security contractor. Some companies will try and require you to provide things like 110 VAC power at specific locations, roof penetrations, painting & patching, and even electric locks. Leaving these out of a bid can have a major impact, it looks cheap, until you realize you have to pay someone else to do it at very high cost. You should require the bidders to provide a complete turnkey system with all costs. Then you can back out items you might want to take care of later to save money.

It will often be pretty obvious which should be the successful contractor. One company will usually immediately stand out as having the most complete solution or the best suggestions. It will also almost never be the lowest priced proposal!

Negotiating the final price

Any sales driven organization will go in with their highest price unless they know they have competition. Since you should have three proposals, you can cross check prices with one another and arrive at a pretty good average cost for each component of the system. If one company seems way out of line they ask them about it.

Remember that some security equipment varies wildly in price- and quality. A Panasonic security camera is going to be considerably more expensive than some no name brand from China. Take this into consideration when weighing the total cost. We do not advise cutting costs by buying no name, potentially inferior equipment; it's just not worth it in terms of your security and future service and reliability. A security system is worthless if it doesn't work!

Most of the equipment will not vary that much except in the case of expensive items like Digital Video Recorders, computers, and access control software. Such software is usually priced in quantities of readers, for instance 8 readers, 16 readers, etc. If one company quotes software licenses for 8 readers and the other 16 readers, it will be a significant difference.

The best place to reduce the final price is in the security dealer's markup and other items you can provide. Most security contractors will attempt to get around a 35% margin. You should easily be able to get a 5% reduction on the total system just by asking.

Providing items, services, or labor from your organization will also help reduce the price. We mentioned electric power. If you have an electrician or work with one, chances are you can get this work done cheaper. The same goes for painting and patching. Unless you have a very skilled locksmith, familiar with electric locking hardware, stay away from locks. We recommend the security contractor handles this. Don't accept inferior locks either. All locking hardware should be brand names like Schlage or Von Duprin.

Once you settle on the contractor and the final price, expect them to request a deposit. This is not unusual. The amount varies between 10% and 25%. Giving the security contractor a deposit check does tend to guarantee a commitment on their part to schedule a timely installation so we have no problem with it. Use you own judgment. The installation should start within 6 weeks at the very outside. Don't accept a longer time than that and 4 weeks is more typical.

Lease or Buy

If you're contracting for a straight out intrusion or fire alarm, the security company will almost always lead with a lease type arrangement. Usually you will pay for the installation labor up front and the equipment cost and monitoring will be included in the monthly fee. The contract term is generally five years and while you won't own the equipment, all service & maintenance is included. These can be good deals but if you find the service or monitoring not up to par you're still locked in for the five years and even then you won't own the system.

Most companies will allow you to purchase the entire system and contract for the monitoring separately. Service will also be extra. If you're contracting for a fire alarm, most jurisdictions require some form of maintenance contract in place before they will approve the system.

The Contract

The type and number of contracts will vary depending on the types of systems. There is the lease as discussed above, and also the purchase (also known as outright sale), monitoring, and service contracts. Security companies structure their contracts to protect themselves from liability since security systems are high risk. Most will limit "Liquidated Damages" to $250 maximum. This has been upheld in many courts throughout the United States. Alarm companies take the position they are not insurance companies and this is a realistic approach. However, most companies will negotiate that $250 limit so have your attorney look at the contracts carefully.

Warranty

On a lease system, since you are generally covered 100% for service as long as the lease is in effect, warranty is not such a big issue; on purchased systems however, it is very important. Traditionally security integrators offered one year parts and labor as standard. There has been a recent trend to lower that to 90 days. This is definitely a negotiating point.

Read the contract carefully for the warranty terms, if it's less than one year ask for a full year but don't agree to pay more. Some companies will simply tack on more money to cover the longer period so don't agree to that. Most reputable companies will agree to one full year without much haggling. The warranty should commence when the system receives final approval from you or your consultant.

Service

If you don't lease the system, you will be faced with the decision as to whether to buy a service contract. If you are buying a fire alarm or monitoring system, you need the service contract; either due to code requirements or at the least because annual inspections are required.

On all other security systems there are different considerations. If your system is installed in a relatively benign environment and won't suffer excessive wear & tear than let's examine only the devices which are most likely to fail. Those would be DVRs and electric locks. It is probably not worth the cost of a service contract on either. DVR technology is rapidly changing so you may just want to change it out for a new model or technology when it fails. Locks are expensive to install but reasonably cheap to repair. Most other electronic security device fail only rarely. Some will last virtually forever so we do not recommend service contracts unless you like the feeling of extra protection.

Installation

While waiting for the installation to start you should complete any tasks or furnish equipment you agreed to provide. Get everything done now so that the installation crew has no excuses why they can't complete the project in a timely manner. Many installations go awry when crews are delayed. If they can't work on your job, they'll leave and go to a different one and it may take time to get them back.

Don't be alarmed if the people that show up to install your system are not from the security vendor. It is common practice to use independent sub-contractors. This is usually a very good thing because contractors that have been around for a while often have much more experience then even the security company's own employees. The sub-contractors have also agreed to install your system for a fixed price so time is money to them. They are committed and have enormous incentive to finish your system in a timely manner.

You do need to keep an eye on them however. You should require them to check in and out every day with you and let you know if they are not going to be on site the next day. Once in a while it is unavoidable for sub-contractors to not show up. They may need to finish some minor item on another job or attend an inspection. This should not happen more than once or twice at the most and never for more than a day or two. Not seeing the sub-contractors more than this is major cause for concern.

Some sub-contractors will take on more work than they can handle so they just travel around and around to each job only spending a few hours on each. Call the security company and complain.

Do not be concerned if you don't see much progress right away. A good installer may take up to a week (for a large system) to investigate, examine, and map out the areas where he will be working. They will take time to plan and organize the equipment and wire.

The proper sequence of installation should be: wiring, main control installation, powering up and testing the controls, programming, and then connecting field devices one at a time and testing each as they go. The worst thing an installer can do is to install the entire system with all the equipment at once and then powering it up and trying to make it work. A large system will always have some problems. If the technician is overwhelmed with problems it makes troubleshooting so much more difficult and time consuming. By connecting and testing devices one at a time, any problems can be addressed immediately and easily.

Workmanship

The system and all it's components should like nice and neat. All panels and main equipment should be mounted on a sheet of fire resistant plywood. Do not allow them to be mounted directly to drywall, concrete or plaster. Always insist on a plywood sheet. Provide it yourself if necessary. In most jurisdictions, it must have some fire resistant or approval stamp clearly visible so never paint it!

All panels and devices should be straight and level. Conduits and raceways should be straight. Wiring and cables must be properly secured both below and above the ceiling. Cabling must never be laid across or touching ceiling tiles, it must be secured in existing or new hangars.

The installation crew should clean up after themselves at the end of each day. They should have their own vacuum and use it!. There should be no obstructions in hallways or common areas such as boxes or wires hanging down at the end of the day. Professional installers do not have to be told these things and this is a good indication of their experience.

Testing of the finished system

This is the number one area where installers- and especially sub-contractors, fail. They will frequently leave the system as completed, only for you to discover numerous items not functioning. It takes two people minimum to properly test a system- one at the control, keypad, or computer; and one walking around testing the field devices.

Insist on a thorough point by point test in your presence and offer to help. This is where your equipment list comes in, you can check off each device as you go. You will also learn much about the system in the course of testing it. We have seen so many instances where the customer was too busy on completion day and just signs it off instead of actively participating in the testing.

Test each device for functionality. For example, all doors and motion detectors should be tested when the system is armed to make sure the alarm trips. When the system is disarmed, have the installer disconnect one wire from a motion detector and make sure the keypad displays some trouble indication.

On access systems, test each door for good card reads and that the door unlocks and relocks without sticking. Opening a door without using a card should generate an alarm. Holding the door open past the programmed time should generate an alarm. Judge the door unlock for each door and decide whether it is too long or too short. Make sure all events and alarms show up at the computer.

On CCTV video systems, check that the view is the one you expect. The picture should be sharp and clear and the lighting should be even. There should be no fuzziness, tearing or distortion. Turn lights on and off and make sure the picture looks good. A very common problem on outdoor cameras is the picture at night. As the lens opens wider to bring more light into the camera, the focus can go blurred. Always check the picture at night (you can play back the recorded video the next day) as soon as possible and call for service if the pictures are blurry. Generally, if the cameras are focused correctly during the install they will be okay at night but check them carefully.

You don't have to worry so much about fire alarms. The local fire inspector should be testing that thoroughly.

Service after the sale

Unfortunately, many security firms fall down when it comes to service. It is widely known in the industry that many contractors do not service their customers- they are mainly in it for the initial installation. When you're evaluating bids take this into consideration and always ask references about their service experience after the sale.

Service departments are expensive to run and rarely pay for themselves so even when a company does provide service it is not always the best. Most service departments will consist of both newer and more experienced technicians.

Frequently security companies will send out the newer techs first because the experienced one is busy doing the difficult calls. Although companies track what is known as "call backs" – having to go back a second or third time to fix a problem- it is still very common. You can fully expect not to have a problem fixed the first time unless it is very simple.

We will give you a tip that in virtually every company there is at least one guru who can fix your system. This person is protected and hard to communicate with- quite naturally because he is busy. He may be a manager, or engineer, or just a senior technician but if you persist and ask for them, you will eventually get to them and have your problem solved.

Liability concerns

Liability can be one of the most complex and Byzantine subjects imaginable. This section is designed to help you avoid liability with simple suggestions; but always consult an attorney with any questions. Legal actions resulting in damages are most likely going to occur when you own or manage a facility where the general public has access; although your own employees are certainly cause for concern. Liability usually results if it can be shown that you did not take sufficient action to prevent physical harm to someone.

Some examples of actual cases may be in order. We were involved with a large software company that was building a new headquarters campus consisting of four buildings. Since the occupancy initially was B (Business) nothing special was required by the fire code except sprinkler monitoring because each building contained more than 100 sprinkler heads.

During the final design stages, it was decided to add a large meeting room sufficient for employees from all four building to attend. This created an occupancy load for that room only above 300 people and made it an A (assembly) occupancy. This in turn mandated a fire life safety evacuation system (horns and strobes) for that area. Typically in most jurisdictions, this would have required the whole building containing the A occupancy to comply and install a full fire evacuation system throughout. The fire department in this case negotiated with the architect and decided that the system only needed to be in that one room.

The security contractor was asked to provide such a system for the meeting room only but objected due to potential liability on their part. The reasoning was solid- what if a fire broke out in another part of the building and occupants were not warned and someone was injured or killed? It could be argued in court that the company chose to protect some people in the meeting room but not other employees due to cost considerations. What do you think a jury would decide?

The software company requested a legal opinion from their lawyers, who agreed with the security contractor. Install the fire evacuation system in the entire building. This was done and later when all four buildings were occupied, an employee safety committee recommended that the fire evacuation system be extended to all four buildings. Since the situation was now a matter of record, the company agreed and all four buildings have fire evacuation systems that actually exceed fire codes.

This same logic can be applied to all types of electronic security. Suppose you had cameras installed to watch an outside executive parking area but not the employee parking. An employee is then assaulted on the way to their car some night. Can you imagine their attorney arguing in court- "The company installed cameras for the executives but was too cheap to do the same for the employees".

Apply all security systems evenly to all areas. Be sensitive to employee and visitor concerns. Never install cameras in any areas that could be considered an invasion of privacy such as restrooms. Lunch rooms and gyms are ideal areas to place video cameras to help avoid damage to vending machines and other liability from misuse of exercise equipment but always get signed releases from all employees using those areas that they understand the video is there for their protection.

Employee Violence

Internal violence can take many forms- disgruntled employees, past & present; domestic partners of employees; and even customers. The past ten years has seen a rise in such violence and great fear among managers. As in many things in life, prevention is always better than having to deal with such a serious problem.

The best way to prevent employee violence is to limit the ability of persons to commit such violent acts on your property. A secure, access controlled facility will prevent most acts by outsiders or recently terminated employees. Rigidly controlling who has access cards- and deactivated cards immediately upon termination, goes a long way to making it very difficult for people wishing to commit violent acts from having such opportunities.

If possible, lock off all exterior doors and require access cards 24 hours a day. If your company or location deals with visitors and / or the general public then more complex designs must be considered. We suggest that visitors and the public be directed to one lobby entrance only. This area must then be segregated form the rest of the facility by controlled access. The area should preferably be controlled by security personnel but if that's not a possibility then consider have the receptionist situated in her own secure area. A glass partition or an ornamental metal barrier will protect the receptionist from being used as a hostage.

Always equip the receptionist area and any other entry point with panic buttons. If you have on site security then these panic signals can report there. If not, they should be transmitted to the central monitoring station for police dispatch.

If you have visitor control software then ex-employees should be flagged by their picture to prevent entry. We do not recommend allowing ex-employees back on site for any reason. Conduct any necessary business with them outside in the secured lobby. If you have high turnover, then set up a small meeting room in the lobby for such purposes. Allowing ex-employees into secured areas is a huge risk, even if you think they're fine.

Encourage employees to report domestic abuse and obtain photos of any such partners so you can post theses at the lobby or enter them into your access control system for flagging. Both for liability reasons and to prevent violence, you should never allow visits by domestics partners or spouses. Again, use the lobby meeting room for special visits if necessary.

If your particular facility or business has a problem or history with employee violence then by all means install a metal detector. These are about the size of a phone booth and the cost has come down considerably over the years to where it is now a reasonable investment. Installation is simple and the alarm can be directed anywhere.

Metal detectors are designed to be manned of course, but if used in conjunction with a **man trap**. Think of two doors- one leading to the exterior and one leading to the interior with the metal detector in between. A person walks through the outer door and if no metal is detected, the inner door unlocks (while the outer door locks –preventing another person from entering until the first is clear). If the detector does sense metal, the alarm output signals security while the inner door remains locked- preventing the person from entering until checked out. This may seem extravagant, but if you operate a high risk facility it could save your business and immense liability.

Of course being proactive is the first line of defense against employee violence. As we said, encourage employees to talk about problems- theirs and others. While this may at first glance seem a little like encouraging gossip, having employees open up will often not only give you a sense of morale but often will provide early warning signs of potential trouble.

If one of your employees is involved in a domestic dispute or messy divorce, these

problems will undoubtedly spill over into the workplace. If it appears the situation is approaching violence, it is time to alert receptionists and security to watch for the spouse or partner and bar entry.

Employees with other personal problems, financial problems and high stress levels are also candidates for closer scrutiny. While you may detest or hesitate to get involved in another's personal business, it is your livelihood- and many others no doubt. Sometimes just lending a sympathetic ear can go a long way to alleviating someone's stress about a situation. If nothing else, it will help you get a handle on how bad the situation is and whether you should be concerned.

Some jobs will never be made stress free, less frustrating, or less boring. If possible try to create an atmosphere where at least employees get frequent breaks and are able to get outside and relax.

Dealing with the general public can often be very stressful and this calls for employees with even or upbeat attitudes. It is a recipe for disaster to put people in the wrong situations. You will find matching the right employees to the right jobs and having a general environment of casualness and caring will go a long way to preventing employee violence while actually increasing productivity.

Bomb Threats

Bomb threats can be one of the most frustrating issues property managers face. We have seen situations where bomb threats were phoned in daily at almost the exact same time every day to the same building. Bomb threats have almost completely replaced false fire alarms- where people used to pull fire alarm boxes.

Bomb threats are almost always the work of employees, ex-employees, or more rarely- dissatisfied customers. Employees in tedious, low to mid range paying jobs want a break. You will rarely get a bomb threat in bad weather- unless it's an ex-employee! So the circumstances surrounding the bomb threats are a very good indicator of where they are originating.

So what do you do about bomb threats? If this is the first one you ever received and you are not entirely confident of your security, then it is probably prudent to go ahead and evacuate the building. The police should be notified and they will probably in turn notify the fire department.

Plan on being outside several hours while a thorough search is conducted. The person phoning in the threat is counting on this and wants to go home so many bomb threats will occur in the afternoon. You will probably only want to evacuate your building once since it is so disruptive. Here are some guidelines for what to do if you experience multiple or repeated threats.

Document- instruct your receptionist – and all tenant receptionists to write down any bomb threats! The log should include the exact time the call was received, male or female caller, any specific details such as: was a certain tenant mentioned? How did they refer to your building (name or address)?

Video Cameras and recorder- it is vital to place cameras at the entrances to your building. This accomplishes two important things: One, you'll always know or be able to review who actually came and went. This will be invaluable if a bomb is actually ever found. You will also have a high level of confidence that no one actually planted a bomb is you never see anyone suspicious.

Two, you'll be able to identify specific persons leaving or re-entering before and after repeated bomb threats. Most pranksters will know better than to use an internal phone so they will likely go out to a pay phone if they're going to do this over and over. By cross checking the time of the bomb threat with who came and went right before and after you should be able to pinpoint suspects.

Restrooms – it's always a good idea to keep these locked at all times- as well as storerooms, janitor closets, phone rooms, electrical rooms, etc. If unmanned areas are not accessible it's much more difficult to actually plant a bomb.

Meetings – meet with your tenant managers and discuss how they feel about bomb threats. Explain the facts and invite participation. Chances are one of them will be invaluable at discovering the source of the bomb threats (since it's almost certainly one of their employees or someone they let go.)

Patterns – If the bomb threats occur in the afternoon, during good weather, it's almost certainly a present employee. They want a break or want to go home. If the threat occurs during bad weather and/or at odd times, it's very likely it's an ex-employee who wants to make it miserable for their ex-employer!

HIPAA & Sarbanes-Oxley

HIPAA (The Health Insurance Portability and Accountability Act of 1996) was designed to regulate health insurance but had the additional impact of ensuring medical records privacy. This can have wide ranging effects on information security and physical access to records and file rooms, as well as electronic access to patient records.

Most regulators and medical organizations have interpreted HIPAA to require safeguards to insure only authorized persons view patient records and to maintain a full audit trail of such access to patient medical records. HIPAA affects every type of medical facility which maintains records from a one man medical office to hospitals and includes all other entities which access patient records such as insurance companies and underwriters.

The best way to comply with HIPAA is to control access to patient medical records both electronically and physically through card access systems. By installing card readers on all file rooms, you automatically limit, control, and document access to records.

Computer terminals that can be used to access medical records need to be secured in such a manner as to be able to prove and document the person accessing the information is authorized. Some regulators have questioned passwords and even access cards as not strictly proving a person's identity because passwords and cards can be exchanged.

We see a distinct necessity to use biometric type readers to access medical records. At the very least, such systems provide unequivocal proof of who actually accessed medical records. Basically, you can't go wrong in using such systems. While more traditional types of readers and passwords may meet the intent of HIPAA, we can't guarantee they will pass muster during an audit.

Sarbanes-Oxley created a very similar situation to HIPAA but in the financial sector. There is a real concern in Congress to insure the reliability of financial records after the scandals of Enron, Tyco, and other large corporations where duplicate books, fraudulent reports and shredding of documents were the norm. Auditors are now demanding detailed records of who in the organization has or had access to financial records.

While providing such reports is possible to do manually, it can be extremely time consuming; and if it later turns out the report was inaccurate, the person generating the report can be criminally liable. By installing a card access system on record rooms, you can usually satisfy the toughest auditors by providing a report of access system activity on the critical doors.

Card access systems which help you comply with either HIPAA or Sarbanes-Oxley can be part of larger building wide systems resulting in very cost effective solutions. The additional cost of installing readers or biometrics on record rooms is very small when added to a new or exiting system covering the rest of the building or facility.

The Last Line of Defense

While we previously spoke of employee theft- which is a real concern- the truth is your employees are often the last line of defense against loss. Long time employees have inside knowledge of your business which is invaluable at preventing loss. Loyal workers are loath to see others commit vandalism, abuse company property, or steal. But frequently these employees will not come forward and "rat" on fellow workers.

It is entirely up to the management to foster an environment in which loyal employees can report such acts without fear of reprisal or ridicule from their co-workers. Often just letting people know you will hold information in trust and confidence will be enough.

Another area where employees can be of huge benefit is properly utilizing their eyes and ears; something that unfortunately is almost never done properly. By this we mean that employees must be trained to recognize suspicious activity on the company's property, challenge strangers and report incidents immediately. Employees will respond to such needs in varying degrees so each individual personality must be taken into consideration. However, often the training itself will be enough to instill confidence to act when needed.

Especially important is just being aware of what is going on around them and challenging strangers wandering around the premises. You may find this concept too simple to warrant further consideration but we have continually observed actual events where employees not only did not challenge strangers but actually assisted them unknowingly in stealing.

A company was experiencing thefts of laptop computers in a high rise office building in Westwood, California so cameras were installed throughout the floor. Within a week more laptops turned up missing. Upon reviewing the video recordings, we observed total strangers dressed in business attire simply walk through the tenant space until they observed an unattended laptop. They would them calmly pick it up and walk out the door. Not one single employee asked who the person was or what they were doing there.

In another case, a well dressed man in a business suit walked into a company and went into the unsecured computer room. He then proceeded to disconnect and remove the company's servers! After placing two large servers in a roll around luggage case, he simply walked out the door. The employees, in the meantime, were frantically wondering why they computers were down! This incident was also captured on video- and again no one challenged the man at all.

Professional criminals and even some hackers take advantage of employee "helpfulness" and respect for authority by posing as repairmen or inspectors and requesting entry into secure areas.

There are documented cases where thieves posing as fire inspectors flashed phony badges and demanded entry to a data center. Employees failed to question them or verify their IDs. The thieves then planted a Trojan horse virus on the company's server so they could access information at will from a remote location.

While employees should be helpful and courteous it is imperative that all visitors be thoroughly checked out before admitting them to any sensitive area. Further, strangers and visitors should never be left alone to wander unattended around company property no matter how harmless or important they appear.

How can you prevent such incidents? *Training, training, training.*

IF IT'S PAPER, SHRED IT

Thieves & hackers regularly dives into Dumpsters. Even a Post-it note with a customer's name and phone number provides enough to begin a scam. Employee names, positions and work schedules are invaluable to con artists.

ALWAYS ESCORT STRANGERS

Never let pairs split up, and never, ever leave them alone--no matter what the reason. Thieves have even stooped to faking illness, and then spending as long as it takes in a bathroom until the most vigilant escort gives up.

VERIFY IDS

Take the time to ensure that a stranger is whom he claims to be, even at the risk of giving insult. Check the name on a badge against a driver's license, and then call the purported employer --to make sure the person is legit. This includes Fire Department personnel, Police, repairmen, pest control, fire extinguisher servicemen, Electric Company, Gas Company, and especially the telephone company.

Just because you called for service (or have regularly scheduled service) doesn't mean the person that shows up is legit either. Thieves and con artists will often know service schedules or overhear requests for service and arrive <u>before</u> the *real* service person.

DOUBLE-CHECK E-MAIL REQUESTS

Thieves will set up a fake e-mail address and credit-union website, then send out e-mails claiming to be from the credit union's IT manager, asking employees to "test" the new website by entering their own account and password information. They often give thieves all they need to empty out those accounts.

Risk Assessment

The Risk Assessment or security survey is simply a way of analyzing your unique situation to help determine an overall solution. Such assessments are valuable in gathering information and not only helping you see problem areas but providing information to prospective bidders should you decide you need a security system.

The risk assessment is a guide to understanding your specific needs and will assist in completing a complete security survey of your location.

LOCATION

A) Neighborhood   ___ Good   _____ Average   _____ High Crime

B) Location   ___Isolated   ____ Other Businesses____Residential

C) Proximity to freeways, major roads ____Yes   ___ No

D) Have you experienced vandalism? _____ Yes   ___ No

Comments_____

E) Have you had any burglaries or break ins?   ____Yes   ___ No

Comments_____

F) Police Response   ___City ___ County ____Good   _____ Poor / Slow

G) Fire Response   ___City ___ County _____ Good   ____ Slow

H) Fire Codes Special Requirements?   _____ Notes

I) Other facilities, locations, branches?   ___ No ___ Yes _____

PARKING

A) Do you have parking?   ___ Yes   ___ No

B) Location   ___ Surface lot___ Underground   ___ Remote

C) Types   ___ Employee ___ Visitor   ___ Executive

D) Is the parking controlled by gates or guards?   ___ Yes   ___ No

      Specifics: _____ # of Gates   _____ # of Guards

E) Is the parking a revenue source?   ___ Yes   ___ No

F) Problems you have encountered:

      ___ Vandalism ___ Break ins   ___ Auto theft ___ Accidents

G) Are company vehicles parked on premises? _____No   ___ Yes   ____Overnight?

H) Are other trucks parked overnight?   ___ No   ___Yes___Loaded

I) Are company vehicles and/or trucks logged in & out?   ___Yes___No

EXTERIOR

A) Do you have a trash compactor or dumpsters?   ___ Yes   ___ No

B) Are doors left unlocked during the day?   ___ No   ___ Yes
        _____Specify

C) Is the roof accessible   ?___ No   ___ Yes ___ Ladders ___ Stockpiles ___ Skylights

STRUCTURAL

A) Description _____ Sq Ft   ____ # of floors

B) Construction ___ Concrete   ___ Steel   ___ Wood Frame   ___ Glass

C) Fire Protection ____ Sprinklers (___ # of risers) ___ OS&Y ___ PIV___ Pump house

D) Fire Detection   ____ Flow Monitoring___ Smoke   ___ Heat   ___ Evacuation

E) Fire Exits   ___ How many   ___ Blind spots   ___ Alarmed

F) High Rack storage? ___ Yes   ___ No

G) Hazardous storage / materials?   ___ Yes   ___ No

EMPLOYEES

A) Number of employees ____   ___ Temp ?   ___Visitors? ___ Contractors?

B) Union   ___ Yes   ___ No

C) Shifts   _____ Specify

D) Weekends ___ Yes ___ No

E) Turnover   ___ Low   ___ High   _____ Department?

F) Have you had workman's comp claims or on the job injuries? ___No   ___Yes

G) Do you have employees who smoke? ___No ___Yes   _____Where?

H) Theft / Shrinkage? ___ No   ___ Yes

I) Theft by employees?___ No   ___ Yes

OPERATION

A) Do you get visitors? ___No ___Yes ____Approx how many?

B) Do you receive vendors? ___No ___Yes ____Approx how many?

C) Do visitors and vendors use the same entrance? ___No ___Yes

D) Are visitors and vendors controlled or logged in & out? ___No ___Yes

E) If so, how? _____

G) Do you use, employ or have outside contractors? ___No ___Yes

H) If so, are they controlled? ___No ___Yes _____How?

I) Are any of the above permitted after normal business hours? ___No ___Yes

J) Are there janitors? ___No ___Yes

K) Are they in house or contracted? ___Employee ___Contract

L) Do they have keys? ___No ___Yes

M) Do you need or want to keep track of their hours? ___No ___Yes

N) Do the janitors have regular, set working hours? ___No ___Yes

O) Are executives in a specific area? ___No ___Yes _____Where

P) Do you or is there a need to restrict access to executive areas? ___No ___Yes

SPECIAL CIRCUMSTANCES

A) Is your organization self insured? ___Yes ___No _____Company?

B) Do you do any classified work? ___No ___Yes

C) Do you perform any work of a confidential nature? ___No ___Yes

D) If either B or C is Yes, where do you store the data or product?_____

E) Do you operate under any government regulations? ___No ___Yes

If so, explain_____

E) Do you do research & Development on site? ___No ___Yes

F) Are any laboratories located on site? ___No ___Yes

G) Are there clean rooms? ___No ___Yes_____ Level?

H) Has any test equipment gone missing or been stolen? ___No ___Yes

I) Are there storage areas for sensitive, critical, or valuable items? ___No ___Yes

If yes, explain _____

J) Do you feel you are in ADA Compliance?   ___Yes   ___No

K) Do you regularly check fire exits for blockage and function? ___Yes   ___No

MATERIALS & PRODUCTS

A) Are there documented procedures for receiving and shipping?   ___No ___Yes

B) Are there special hours for receiving?   ___No   ___Yes   _____ Note

C) Are deliveries supervised and documented?___No   ___Yes _____How?

D) Are your materials or products valuable?   ___No   ___Yes

_____Explain

E) Are your products or services controversial?   ___No   ___Yes

_____to whom?

F) Do you have products not yet released to the public?   ___No   ___Yes

DIGITAL VIDEO BANDWIDTH CALCULATOR

4 CIF Image Size 720 X 256 18Kb (18,000 bits)		
Frames	6 FPS	15 FPS
Cameras	Mb/sec	Mb/sec
1	0.824	2.06
2	1.648	4.12
3	2.472	6.18
4	3.296	8.24
5	4.12	10.3
6	4.944	12.36
7	5.768	14.42
8	6.592	16.48
9	7.416	18.54
10	8.24	20.6
11	9.064	22.66
12	9.888	24.72
13	10.712	26.78
14	11.536	28.84
15	12.36	30.9
16	13.184	32.96

Fast Corporate LAN = 100 Mbps
Standard Corp LAN = 10 Mbps
T-1 (Full)   = 1.544 Mbps

4CIF = 704 X 576
2CIF = 352 X 288
1CIF = 176 X 144

Real time = 20 Frames per second (FPS)
All frames rates must be divided by number of cameras
6 FPS / 6 cameras = 1 frame per second

AHJ (Authority Having Jurisdiction)

The person or entity having final approval over a required system. This is usually the local fire inspector but can also be a state or federal fire or building inspector or even a representative of an insurance company.

Annunciator

A display of fire or intrusion points. This display can be as simple as a light representing each zone or point or as complex as a graphic map or even a computer display. The display often also includes controls for bypassing or arming each zone.

Anti-passback

A means of controlling card access entry doors or gates so that a cardholder can not use his card repeatedly to let in others. This is common at parking gates to prevent people from allowing free parking to friends. It is a software setting that specifies once a card is used it cannot be used again on the same entry until it is used on the exit.

Areas

A virtual grouping of zones or detection devices that allows such groups to be armed or disarmed together. Examples would be all the devices in the "Office area" and all the devices in the "Warehouse".

Arming

The act of turning on a security system so that any device detecting intrusion would cause an audible alarm and transmit a signal to the central monitoring station. Disarming would be the opposite.

Beams

A pair of devices, consisting of a transmitter and receiver, used for intrusion detection. The transmitter sends an invisible infrared beam to the receiver. As long as the beam is present, the system is normal. If the beam is interrupted – as if by an intruder passing between them, an alarm is generated. These beams can be effective to distances as long as 1000 feet.

Biometrics

A method of identifying a person through some unique human characteristic such as fingerprint, hand geometry or retinal pattern.

Call list

A list of persons to be notified by the alarm company if a fire or burglar alarm is received from their premises. Also it usually is a list of persons authorized to arm and disarm an intrusion system.

Card

An electronic device, resembling a credit card, with a unique number to identify a person wishing to gain entry into an area with a access control system.

Card Access

A system used to control access to an area through the use of electric locks and readers. People authorized to gain entry would be required to carry and use a card or some form of biometric identifier.

Cardholder

A person who is authorized to carry and use an electronic key card.

CCTV (closed circuit television)

A system consisting of cameras, monitors, and recorders used for security surveillance.

Central Station

An independent company which monitors intrusion and fire alarms. Alarms come in from many areas and customers and are decoded and then human "operators" take appropriate action such as notifying police and / or the customers.

Contact

A set of devices consisting of a magnet and sealed reed switch used for sensing door opening. The magnet is mounted on the door and the switch on the door frame. As long as the magnet is in close proximity to the switch (door closed) the alarm is normal. When the door opens, the magnet moves away from the switch causing an open circuit and an alarm if it is armed.

Control panel

The "brains' of an intrusion or fire alarm system. All the detection devices, keypad controls, and power are connected to the control panel.

Dedicated phone line

A separate phone line to be used by the intrusion or fire alarm system only. Fire alarms require two voice lines (only one must be dedicated) and intrusion systems require one line. Many alarm companies insist on dedicated lines to insure proper uninterrupted operation.

Door Controller

The "brains" of an access control system. Locks, readers and other devices are connected to the controllers which then makes decisions about who can gain entry based on downloading of information by the access control server and software.

Door Forced

An alarm generated by an access control system if a door connected to the system is opened without using an authorized card.

Door Help Open

An alarm generated by an access control system if a door connected to the system is left or held open past a programmed door open time period.

Door Unlock Time

The programmable amount of time a door remains unlocked after an authorized card is read and the user enters.

(DPD) Double Pedestrian Door

An abbreviation for a double door

(DVR) Digital Video Recorder

A computer based CCTV recorder. DVRs are usually purpose built for the specific purpose of recording video with special video capture boards to convert the analog video to digital. DVRs (unless they are Linux based) can have the same problems as PCs- virus and spy ware infections, along with crashes.

Duress Code

A special PIN sequence or code word used by an alarm customer to signal the central station that they are being forced to disarm their alarm system under duress.

EAS (Electronic Article Surveillance)

A system comprised of electronic tags and sensors designed to detect and deter shoplifting. The tags or labels are affixed to merchandise and are scanned by sensors at the store exits. If the tag has not been deactivated at the checkout, a local alarm sounds.

Elevator Recall

Elevator codes require that elevators be sent back to the first or ground floor in the event of a fire to prevent occupants from using them. This is usually accomplished through smoke detectors installed on each floor in the elevator lobby.

Entry / Exit Delay

This is a programmable time period to allow occupants to leave or entry without setting off the intrusion alarm. Once you arm the system, you usually have from 30 seconds to 2 minutes to leave. During this period detection devices are ignored. The same applies when the alarm is armed- you open a door and the time period starts, ignoring detection devices for the time period until you disarm the system.

(EOL) End of Line Supervision

This is an electrical means of verifying the fire or intrusion circuits are functional and intact. By sending a small voltage through the system wiring at all times, the control panel monitors the wiring integrity. If any wire becomes open or shorted (such as from a cut or attempt to bypass it) the panel displays a trouble message which is also usually transmitted to the central monitoring station.

Equipment Cost

The selling price of the hardware of your system. This amount is usually shown separately from the labor cost to install it.
It is often used to calculate the monthly lease on a fire or burglar alarm system.

Exception Reporting

Software packages that analyze POS data to look for suspicious transactions to reduce shrink and losses in retail.

Fire Alarm

A system to detect fires. These days, the term "alarm" is generally used to mean a system that provides audible warning to occupants that a fire is in progress.

Fire Monitoring

A system used to transmit a signal that a fire is in progress. Technically speaking, a fire monitoring system is connected to a fire alarm. The fire alarm warns the occupants and the fire monitoring transmits the signal to a central station that then notifies the fire department to respond. Also see Waterflow monitoring.

Fire sprinkler

A mechanical system of plumbing that used water to extinguish a fire. The idea is that the sprinkler head will deluge a fire before it grows. If the fire does spread, more sprinkler heads will discharge water in the vicinity of the fire. Unless there is an explosion over a wide area, sprinklers are usually quite effective at extinguishing fires very quickly.

Fire Suppression

A means of actually putting the fire out as opposed to simply detecting a fire. Fire sprinklers are a suppression device. Also included are systems which discharge inert gas (such as the old Halon) and chemicals. These are designed to smother a fire (robbing it of oxygen). These are most often used in computer rooms to prevent expensive water damage and in kitchen hoods to quickly extinguish grease fires.

Fobs

A form of electric key. These function exactly like access control cards except in a small form factor similar to a key. These are designed to be worn on a key chain for convenience.

(GBD) Glass Break Detectors

A device for detecting breaking glass. Although these are usually audio based (listening for the sound of breaking glass), they can also be vibration or shock sensors that detect the impact of breaking the glass. The audio type are sometimes combined with infrared detectors in an attempt to alleviate false alarms.

(HUB) Hold Up Button

A button similar to a door bell used to signal a holdup or panic situation. Newer types use two buttons which must be pressed simultaneously to prevent false alarms or accidental activations.

Intrusion

A term used to describe a system to detect break-ins by burglars.

Keypad

A term used to describe the part of an intrusion system used to arm and disarm it. This is usually in the form of a keypad with a alpha numeric display. The keypad portion is used to enter the user's PIN (Personal Identification Number) or combination.

Late to Close

A term used by monitoring companies or central station to indicate a customer's alarm was scheduled to be armed by a specific time and that time has passed with the alarm still off.

Line Security

A method of insuring the transmission line between an intrusion system control panel and the central station is secure and intact. This is often accomplished by sending a continuous encoded signal between the two.

Logical Access

A system used to control log on and access to computer systems and networks.

Mag (Magnetic) locks

Locks which are electro magnetic and actually "hold" the door closed until power is removed. When power is applied to the mag lock, the magnet is energized and the door is held closed "locking" the door. These locks can have 2000 lbs or more of holding strength.

Mantrap

A series of interlocking doors to prevent more than one person from entering an area at a time. The doors are generally close together creating only space for one person between them. Typically the outer door is unlocked and the inner door is locked. When a person enters, the outer door is then locked and the inner door is unlocked. Often used in jewelry stores to keep gangs of thieves from getting in.

Money Clip

A special hold up device that fits in the money drawer of a cash register. A twenty dollar bill is inserted in the clip and the clip is placed at the bottom of the $20 slot. Other twenty dollar bills are then placed on top. If the cashier is held up, all they have to do is grab all the twenties- also removing the twenty in the money clip. When this twenty is removed the clip then completes a circuit to the control panel and a silent alarm is transmitted to the central station.

Monitoring

This is the process of receiving alarm and trouble signals by a central station. The central station receives alarms from various customers and location and takes appropriate action such as notifying police or fire departments.

Motion Detector

A device for detecting movement by intruders. These are used to back up door contacts and window protection.

Nesting

A software configuration in which one anti-passback level is inside another for the purpose of limiting parking in a garage or lot to higher paid or more desirable spots. For example, let's say a parking garage has an access control system at the main entrances. Once inside the garage there is another set of gates or barriers to get into spaces next to the elevators. This would be the nested area and usually has higher monthly rates or is limited to a certain tenant.

(PEC) Photo Electric Cell

A term left over from earlier times when beams actually used photoelectric cells which were sensitive to visible light. These days such device uses invisible infrared beams but are commonly still referred to as PECs. See **Beams**.

PIN

Personal Identification Number- a fancy way of saying "combination". This is usually a unique number sequence you enter into the alarm keypad for arming and disarming the system.

(PIR) Passive Infrared detector

This is the most commonly used device for detecting motion. The device consists of a highly sensitive temperature sensor using mirrors and optics to divide the area into zones. The PIR can detect a very minute temperature variation and if it "sees" this temperature difference across two or more zones, the PIR assumes someone is moving through the detection pattern and it triggers an alarm condition to the control panel.

POS (Point of Sale)

The computer system that tracks register transactions in retail. These systems can be interfaced with Exception reporting software and video from the store's cameras to develop Loss Prevention systems to reduce shrink.

(Prox) Proximity

Usually refers to a card reader which does not require any insertion or swiping (sliding a card through) to read the card. The prox card only needs to be brought within a few inches of the reader to recognize it.

PTZ (Pan / Tilt / Zoom)

Cameras which are movable via remote controls. These days such cameras are usually mounted in domes and can be located either indoors or outdoors. Cameras can be rotated (panned), moved up and down (tilt) or zoomed in and out. Current models have very powerful zoom (or telephoto) lenses and function in very low light.

Public View

A camera and video monitor installed at entrances. The camera image is displayed on the monitor and shows people entering an area. It is used to deter shoplifting, theft and vandalism.

(ROR) Rate of Rise

A type of heat detector which is designed to alarm when the temperature rises too fast from a base point. For instance, if the ambient temperature suddenly increases more than 15 degrees per minute the detector triggers an alarm.

Remote viewing

A configuration allowing you to view your security cameras from another (or any) remote location. This is usually a function of the DVR (Digital Video Recorder). The cameras are connected to and recorded by the DVR. The DVR has a network connection to the Internet. You can then connect to the DVR from anywhere and view the cameras connected to that DVR.

(REX) Request to Exit

A device connected to an access control system which recognizes someone is leaving the secured area so the access system can unlock the door and bypass door position sensors so no alarm is generated. This is usually a specialized PIR but can also be a pushbutton.

RFID (Radio Frequency Identification Device)

A tag with a tiny radio transmitter with a unique ID number designed to be embedded or attached to products so electronic scanners can read the tags. These are mostly used for tracking goods but could be applied to many other items- including humans.

Security Integrator

A security company which specializes in installing multiple types of security systems, such as intrusion, card access, and video; to provide an integrated security solution.

Smart Card

An intelligent device, similar to a credit card, which has a microprocessor and memory chip built into the card. A smart card can be used for many purposes such as security, parking control, transportation and vending. For example, the smart card can be loaded with funds via a wrirtor and then used for train fare. Each time the card is used, the fare is deducted. Different applications can reside on different sectors of the same smart card.

Smart Card Readers

A special type of card reader that is designed to read (and sometimes write) smart cards. Previously such readers could only read smart cards but now there are readers that can read traditional prox cards as well as smart cards. These are good solutions for facilites wishing to switch over from prox to smart cards slowly.

Smoke Beams

This device is very similar to beams used for intrusion in that they consist of an infrared transmitter and receiver aimed at each other but are calibrated to a very high sensitivity. If just 3 to 5% of the infrared beam is blocked by smoke, the beam triggers an alarm. These beams are very effective in covering large areas such as churches and atriums.

Smoke detector

A device consisting of a small chamber with a photoelectric cell inside. If smoke enters the chamber, the photocell becomes slightly obscured and it's voltage output drops a tiny amount. When this drop equals the detector's sensitivity rating, an alarm is generated to the control panel or locally if it is a stand alone detector with a built in horn.

Shrink

The difference between inventory and sales that represents an overall loss to a retail establishment. Most businesses experience 4-5% shrink caused by waste, employee theft, and shoplifting. The shrink loss is generally right off the bottom line of net profit.

(SPD) Single Pedestrian Door

An abbreviation often used by burglar alarm companies in zone designations.

Tail Gating

An access control term used to describe a person following a cardholder through a door after that cardholder used their card to gain access. If the door unlock time is too long or the system is not properly configured, a legitimate cardholder uses their card and then a unwanted person follows them in by simply pulling the door open behind them.

Turnstile

A means of controlling access to an area. Although turnstiles can be mechanical, in the access control world they are usually optical based. A beam is sent between two pedestals and if the person uses their card, the beam is bypassed. If the person walks through and breaks the beam without using a card, an alarm is generated. These optical turnstiles are generally used to control and log access to a lobby of commercial buildings.

(UL) Underwriter's Laboratories

UL also regulates, lists, and inspects fire and burglar alarm systems and companies. UL was formed by the insurance industry to develop standards for electrical devices and eventually also took on the task of developing standards for fire, burglary and recently access control devices. UL regulates equipment and installations separately. To have a complete UL rated system, the company must be listed to do the installation and use UL listed devices. The monitoring company, as well as the serving company, can also be UL listed. While this is often the same company, it is not strictly necessary. UL conducts regular inspections of all listed companies so choosing a UL listed security or fire company is an excellent sign of a reputable dealer.

Valve Tamper

A detection device used to determine whether a sprinkler valve is open or closed. This is part of the fire monitoring system. Valves need to be open at all times in order to be able to extinguish a fire. The only time a valve should be closed is during service or when a sprinkler head needs to be replaced (after a fire).

(VMD) Video Motion Detection

A software program usually built into or provided by the DVR. Each camera view is broken up into pixels and you can then turn on areas so that if these groups of pixels change an alarm or event is generated. A good example would be a door. A grid is set up consisting of the door pixels, as long as this image does not change, no alarm is generated- and often no recording takes place because nothing has changed. If the pixels changes, an alarm or event is generated and the changed imaged is recorded for a period of time.

Water Flow

A fire monitoring device designed to detect the flow of water through a fire sprinkler system. Normally fire sprinklers are static- the pipes are full of water but it doesn't move or flow. If a sprinkler head discharges, then water must begin to flow through the system, the water flow switch detects this and generates an alarm condition to the fire control panel.

Waterflow monitoring

A water flow monitoring system consists of water flow switches and valve tampers as described above. Waterflow or fire sprinkler monitoring systems are required whenever there are more than 100 sprinkler heads in a building.

Zone

A designation used in fire and intrusion alarms generally meant to describe one detection device. In early times when communications were poor and microprocessors didn't exist, it was common to connect many detection devices to one zone. These days, it is always preferred to connect only one detection device per zone.

About the author

Ed Morawski has been involved with electronics since his teens. After joining the U.S. Air Force in 1966 he was trained as an Aircraft Instrument Technician and spent the next eight years working on every aircraft in the inventory on bases from Langley AFB, VA. to Vietnam and finally at Edwards AFB, CA.

After receiving an Honorable Discharge he began working as a technician for American Alarm Company in Cincinnati, OH. He become manager of the central station and worked there for ten years until the company was acquired by Honeywell Alarm.

Mr. Morawski moved to Los Angeles in 1983 and became Technical Support Manager for API, the largest security company in California. Over the next 13 years he held various positions such as Applications Manager, Director of Engineering and Sales Support Manager. API was acquired by ADT in 1996 and Mr. Morawski became Regional Installation Manager and later Western Region Manager for the Engineered Systems Division.

In 1998 Mr. Morawski helped start UPS Security, which was primarily involved in remote management of security systems for the Irvine Company and 300 other large customers. He helped developed several unique services and systems for customers such as Memorial Care Hospitals and the City Of San Diego.

Mr. Morawski moved to Brassfield Communications in 2006 where he is the Director of Engineering overseeing security system design for many other large customers such as Amgen and Kaiser Healthcare.

Mr. Morawski also started Hi-Tech-Consulting (www.hi-tech-consulting.com) in 2005 to assist small business customers in getting electronic security systems utilizing the very latest technology and thinking.